The Architecture of South-East Asia through
Travellers' F

G000160714

The Architecture of South-East Asia through Travellers' Eyes

ROXANA WATERSON

With a Foreword by
VICTOR T. KING

KUALA LUMPUR
OXFORD UNIVERSITY PRESS
OXFORD SINGAPORE NEW YORK
1998

Oxford University Press

Oxford New York
Athens Auckland Bangkok Bombay
Calcutta Cape Town Dar es Salaam Delhi
Florence Hong Kong Istanbul Karachi
Madras Madrid Melbourne Mexico City
Nairobi Paris Shah Alam Singapore
Taipei Tokyo Toronto

and associated companies in
Berlin Ibadan

Oxford is a trade mark of Oxford University Press

Published in the United States
by Oxford University Press, New York

British Library Cataloguing in Publication Data
Data available

Library of Congress Cataloging-in-Publication Data
The architecture of South-East Asia through travellers' eyes/
[compiled by] Roxana Waterson; with a foreword by Victor T. King.
p. cm. — (Oxford in Asia paperbacks)
Includes bibliographical references.
ISBN 983 56 0033 3
1. Architecture—Asia, Southeastern.   I. Waterson, Roxana.
II. Series.
NA1511.A73   1998
720'.959—dc21
97-17080
CIP

Typeset by Indah Photosetting Centre Sdn. Bhd.,
Printed by KHL Printing Co. Pte. Ltd., Singapore
Published by Penerbit Fajar Bakti Sdn. Bhd. (008974-T),
under licence from Oxford University Press,
4 Jalan Pemaju U1/15, Seksyen U1, 40150 Shah Alam,
Selangor Darul Ehsan, Malaysia

Foreword

VICTOR T. KING

THERE is no one better qualified than Dr Roxana Waterson to compile an anthology of the architecture of South-East Asia. The author of *The Living House*, the widely read and quoted anthropological study of the region's vernacular architecture, now in its third impression in paperback (1997), she brings to this present book an indispensible knowledge and sensitivity. She has managed to assemble a truly remarkable range of extracts to demonstrate the diversity of South-East Asian built forms, from the impressive stone and brick temple complexes of bygone Hindu–Buddhist kingdoms and empires to the modest peasant houses of timber, thatch, and bamboo of remote Malay and Indonesian villages. She also includes sections on indigenous imperial palaces, colonial residences, and a variety of native and European townscapes. As far as the literature allows, she has covered nearly all the major regions of South-East Asia, from Burma to the Philippines, from Thailand to Indonesia, and the main cultures and religions.

As Dr Waterson has said, she has tried to select materials which describe South-East Asian architectural styles in as vivid, lively, and arresting way as possible, to capture 'atmosphere and romance'. She therefore chooses Pierre Loti's description of the ruins of Khmerian Angkor for example, rather than the dry and sober narrative of Henri Mouhot, who was credited with 'rediscovering' and recording the details of Angkor for a European audience. Indeed, Mouhot recognized his own inability both in word and picture to do justice to these spectacular reminders of a lost civilization. In the French edition of his book *Voyages dans les royaumes de*

Siam, de Cambodge, de Laos et autres parties centrales de l'Indo-Chine, published in 1868, he laments, 'Ah, if only I were gifted with the pen of someone like Chateaubriand or Lamartine, or the brush of Claude Lorrain, to be able to convey to the lovers of art how grandiose and beautiful are these incomparable ruins, the only remains of a people which no longer exists.' One temple, he suggests, is 'a rival to that of Solomon, and erected by some ancient Michael Angelo'. Needless to say, Dr Waterson's anthology provides us with a feast of descriptions of what remains of the ancient Cambodian capital. But a sense of grandeur and beauty is also conveyed in various extracts which describe the wonders of such sites as Pagan, Ayutthaya, and Hue, the centres of other once powerful indigenous states of mainland South-East Asia.

Not only do these ancient buildings embody the history and spirit of communities, and remain as an everlasting reminder of their identity and social and cultural life, but the smaller scale vernacular architecture of the tribal and peasant societies, though constructed of much less durable materials, also contains the 'soul' or spirit of a people. In her previous book *The Living House*, Dr Waterson demonstrates that houses are cultural constructions; they provide both residential and social space, and express cultural symbols, ideals, values, and principles. They contain messages about social and political relations; they embody symbolic meanings and are intimately interrelated with forms of family organization. In short, houses both reflect and structure human social and symbolic forms. However, they are one among many ways of expressing values and relations; these latter can also be encoded in such things as monuments, temples, mausolea, palaces, gardens, fields, and the arrangement of village and urban communities. Dr Waterson's anthology conveys not only the aesthetic qualities and practical functions of houses and other buildings and living spaces as seen through the eyes of early writers on South-East Asia, but also something of their social, symbolic, and religious meanings as well.

An important point to note in this anthology, mainly determined by the need to use older English language materials not covered by copyright, is that most descriptions have been provided by foreign, usually Western, observers. The major part of the collection comprises the work of British, French, Dutch, and American commentators, though here and there solitary German, Mexican, Norwegian, and Chinese writers also make an appearance. These are not then the descriptions, interpretations, and impressions of natives of their own architecture. Thus, as Dr Waterson reminds us, one has to beware the prejudices and cultural preoccupations of those who were usually members or representatives of the colonial élites. Sometimes one gets hints of the differences between Western perceptions of local buildings, and what we know from subsequent ethnological studies :o be native views of architecture and spatial arrangements. Nevertheless, the anthology has brought together the writings of a relatively broad range of sympathetic and sensitive outside observers, both men and women, from different walks of life. There are, of course, passages written by European colonial administrators and military personnel, but we also have extracts provided by travellers from the worlds of science, art, photography, business, and journalism.

For those of us who know South-East Asia well, many of the extracts will strike a chord. I do not think one can help but be moved by some of the descriptions of the enduring splendour of the great temple complexes of Burma, Cambodia, Thailand, and Java. Yet even the houses of the hill and hinterland populations of the Malay–Indonesian archipelago, of smaller scale and much less durable, have a grandeur about them. Based on her field research among the Toraja of Sulawesi, Dr Waterson has described in great detail elsewhere their strikingly beautiful origin-houses, and though perhaps less decoratively impressive, the Dayak long-houses of the stratified societies of central Borneo cannot fail to excite admiration in the visitor at their scale and height. Certainly the image of the great Embaloh longhouse of

Sungei Ulu' in the remote hinterland of Indonesian Borneo when I first caught sight of it in 1973 will stay with me forever. As I rounded a bend in the river it seemed that the house filled the whole valley. What increased this sense of human domination over nature was that downstream of the house one passed through a landscape almost devoid of signs of human habitation. Then one was confronted suddenly by an enormous timber-framed structure which stretched almost as far as the eye could see along the river bank. It appeared like some gigantic fortification. Its ironwood support posts lifted the house floor some four metres above the ground, and the roof-ridge which overwhelmed the sky-line towered about ten metres above the river. Although it had been built in the early 1940s, in its solidity and sheer size, it seemed that the great house had stood on that same spot for centuries. It was home to well over three hundred people, and the concentration of human activity, sound, and movement combined with the cacophony of animal noises was quite overpowering. At the entrance to the house and on the opposite bank at the village charnel house, numerous large red and white flags were flying and, above the roof of the house, smoke from kitchen fires hovered so that the trees beyond were obscured in a dull greyish haze. This house was indeed 'living' and vital, but because it so monopolized my field of vision I was overcome with a feeling of claustrophobia and helplessness. In reading various of the descriptions in Dr Waterson's anthology I found myself reflecting on my experience of South-East Asian architecture and remembering the feeling of awe and wonder when I first set eyes on some of the 'great houses' of the tribal populations of the archipelago.

A final impression which has stayed with me in reading passages from this anthology is one of change and transformation. The built forms of South-East Asia have been subject to continuous processes of replacement, adaptation, and renewal. The religious buildings of the former great kingdoms of the region have suffered from decay and abandonment, though governments and international organizations are attempting to preserve and restore this tangible evidence of their long cultural heritage. Domestic and other village structures of wood and bamboo are constantly subjected to the forces of nature and have to be replaced, modified, or repaired. Vernacular architectural styles have been influenced by other cultures, from India, China, the Middle East, and the West. Dr Waterson also gives us many examples of earlier urban landscapes, which have been dramatically transformed as a result of recent economic growth and the increase in urban populations. The urban sprawls of Jakarta, Bangkok, and Manila are cases in point, and the appearance of the city centres of Kuala Lumpur and Singapore has been altered radically during the past two decades.

Despite all these changes, South-East Asian vernacular architecture has survived, and in both towns and rural areas one finds many examples of the imaginative combination of indigenous and modern forms. In her careful selection of some of the best descriptions of local architecture, Dr Waterson's anthology serves to remind us of the diversity and beauty of these forms and the fact that South-Eastern cultures and their material expression in domestic, public, and religious buildings are indeed living and vital traditions.

Acknowledgements

THE source of every passage is given at the end of the passage and the captions to the illustrations contain similar information.

The compiler and the publisher gratefully acknowledge the permission given by the following copyright holders to reproduce the passage identified by the number in brackets in the anthology:

The Estate of Malcolm MacDonald and Jonathan Cape (2)
David Higham Associates (24)
Alfred A. Knopf (Copyright 1936, 1937; Inc. and renewed 1964, 1965 by Rosa Covarrubias, reprinted by permission of the publisher) (25, 46, and line drawing, 'A Granary')
Graham Brash (28)
T. C. Skeat (38, 39)
Times Editions (51)
E. J. Brill (31)

If there are any other passages in respect of which copyright has not expired, the compiler and the publisher trust that the copyright holders will accept their assurance that every reasonable effort has been made, but without success, to establish the copyright position and to contact its holders, and accept their apologies.

Contents

Introduction

ROXANA WATERSON

SOUTH-EAST ASIA is a region unrivalled in the richness and
diversity of its cultures, a diversity evidenced most remarkably in its many distinctive styles of architecture. It is not surprising, therefore, that architecture should have made a
strong impression on travellers from other parts of the world,
who, within their often vivid accounts of their adventures,
have left us records of their reactions to the genius of South-
East Asian builders. This volume draws together some of the
very best of these writings, with the aim of conveying to the
reader as much as possible of the diversity of styles and types
of building, from the magnificence of stone temples
or mysterious palaces to the ingenuity of the more humble
vernacular styles of domestic architecture. Other passages
describe the character of settlements, from tiny mountain
hamlets to the booming commercial cities that developed in
colonial times. Each of these buildings and settlements had
their distinctive lifestyle, too, and some accounts, while
sketchy about architectural details, have left us particularly
evocative impressions of the inhabitants' mode of life. Those
authors who wrote in real detail about architecture are relatively few; but many others managed superbly to convey the
feeling of what it was like to be in a place—to explore the
lost temples of Angkor, to inhale the aroma of an east coast
Malaysian fishing village, or to spend the night in a Borneo
head house. This is the essence of travel literature, and what
makes it such an enjoyable genre. I hope, therefore, that
the contents of this volume may give as much pleasure to
the armchair traveller, who has never visited the places

mentioned here, as to those who have, who will find these descriptions resonating with their own personal memories.

Most South-East Asian vernacular architectures are of timber, and unlikely to last above two hundred years at the most; yet the house is a crucial focus of organization in South-East Asian societies. In some of them, it is common for houses to be repeatedly renewed on the same site, as a powerful embodiment of the history and continuity of a kinship grouping. Use of giant tropical hardwoods has enabled some houses to reach very impressive sizes, like the longhouses of Borneo (some of which are capable of housing an entire village), the 'great houses' of the Minangkabau of West Sumatra (one of which is here described by Sir Stamford Raffles), or the towering chiefs' houses of South Nias on their ironwood pillars. In other cases, the structure of the house may be slight, and yet its symbolic load great, for it may be at once an embodiment of ideas about the cosmos and a reflection of the human body. The house is thought of typically as having a vitality of its own, one which interacts with the life-force of the inhabitants and which may influence them for good or ill.

Construction in more durable materials of stone and brick is not lacking in South-East Asia, but it has generally been reserved for religious buildings. These in turn have often served to express the glory of centralized kingdoms. Rulers sometimes deliberately prevented their subjects from building in stone, as a means of maintaining control over them; wherever they permitted the Dutch, British, or Portuguese to build forts, they subsequently found it impossible to dislodge them. But tremendous resources have at times been invested in religious architecture. If we look at the history of state formation in both mainland and island South-East Asia—from the Buddhist empire of Srivijaya in Sumatra (seventh–tenth centuries), to the Sailendra dynasty who constructed Borobudur in the eighth–ninth centuries, from the Khmer empires of Cambodia (ninth–thirteenth centuries) to the glories of Hindu Majapahit in eastern Java (thirteenth–fifteenth centuries), or the Islamic maritime states of Aceh and Demak of the sixteenth century—we find that all these states have used religion as an ideological device to inspire and impress subject populations. But as empires rose to greatness and passed away, their architectural legacies were left to crumble, and engulfed by jungle, were sometimes all but forgotten by later inhabitants. The Javanese appear to have lost all interest in the 'mountain' of Borobudur, until Raffles, acting on information given him by a local person, sent a team to dig it out of the jungle; while the Khmers had developed a legend that Angkor had been the work of angels. The tales of the 'rediscovery' of these great masterpieces during the nineteenth century still make for thrilling reading today.

From the sixteenth century onward, but particularly from the nineteenth, European travellers arrived in South-East Asia in increasing numbers. Whether they came as colonialists, traders, missionaries, or just for the sheer love of adventure—of which they found plenty—they wrote with great enthusiasm, and varying degrees of insight, about their experiences. Among them were many magnificent eccentrics, which has made the researching of them as amusing as it is interesting. There were undoubtedly some remarkable and gifted individuals, whose stories reveal both toughness and sensitivity. Those who stayed long in South-East Asia often paid a high price, in terms of their health and the loss of those dear to them from fevers in an age when life expectancy was short and the understanding of tropical diseases was very undeveloped. In introducing their writings I have tried to convey something of the more unusual characters. There is great unevenness among the authors in the degree of attention they chose to pay to architecture—some scarcely notice it, or satisfy themselves with mentions of native 'huts'; others show great curiosity and powers of observation. What they saw called forth a wide range of reactions, too, from the ecstatic to the hostile and dismissive—though misunderstandings and negative judgements may be just as revealing of the author's own preconceptions as their enthusiasms are.

Our anthology opens with some accounts of the great ruined sites, which remain as magical and beautiful to the visitor of today as they were then. Ruins, as one might expect, called forth strong romantic responses from Europeans. When Pierre Loti manages to get stuck in a bat-infested turret at the top of Angkor Wat in the middle of a thunderstorm, one almost suspects he must be doing it on purpose. V. C. Scott O'Connor revels in the reflections aroused by the poignant contrast between the sight of the dusty, deserted cart track winding through the plain of Pagan, and the thought of its vanished splendours of six hundred years before. Behind his more erudite depictions of Pagan, one senses a deep and genuine affection. Moving on to towns, cities and palaces, one finds great variety even within one category. Over time, accounts have gained in historical interest, as the locales they describe have irrevocably altered. In searching for descriptions of cities, I have selected from different periods, so that the reader may gain an impression of what some by now great metropoles were like in their early days. Alfred Russell Wallace's description of Makassar [Ujung Pandang] when it was still a town of one street, as being 'prettier and cleaner than any I had yet seen in the East', may come as a revelation to the traveller arriving in the sprawling mess of today's vastly expanded city of 900,000 people. We may feel a similar shock at John Cameron's description of Singapore's Orchard Road in the 1860s, when it really was a quiet haven lined with fruit trees, or Frank Vincent's of Saigon at this date as a collection of bamboo huts dominated by the newly built French Government House. Among palaces, too, there is great variety. Some early reports of diplomatic missions capture vividly the exotic pomp of royal audiences in places like Ayutthaya and Hue; other descriptions reveal the decidedly less luxurious accommodations of lesser monarchs in parts of island South-East Asia, where palaces were basically enlarged versions of ordinary timber houses.

In the selection of villages and domestic architecture, the

embarrassment of choice becomes even more acute, and inevitably some distinctive and fascinating architectures are not featured here. Sometimes it has been hard to find satisfactory passages of sufficient detail from within the time period chosen, that is to say up until the 1940s; really full descriptions have often had to await the work of later ethnographers. Naturally, all of the authors, even the most progressive of their day, shared certain assumptions and prejudices of the time, which tend to find expression in their writings. Attitudes of condescension became particularly automatic in the nineteenth century, introducing a sense of distance from the subjects of investigation even where an author found much to admire. I am struck by the number of adventurous women travellers who were sometimes less ready to make stereotypical judgements than the men. Not infrequently, travellers were also quick to write sarcastically of the perceived shortcomings of colonists of nationalities other than their own, though in rare instances the reverse is true. On the whole, I have aimed to omit offensive comments, whatever they may be considered to reveal about their authors. But it is clear that in some cases, racism obstructed a person's ability to observe the architecture properly, in which case they have found no place here. Ignorance allied with sensationalism sometimes results in sheer absurdity. What is one to make, for example, of a French writer on Borneo who, as late as 1897, assures his readers: 'In the mountains are to be found indigenous races, completely barbarous, about whom we possess only the vaguest information, who are hardly superior to the lord of these forests, the gorilla [sic]'?[1] By contrast, those whose work or explorations really brought them into close contact with indigenous peoples reached a radically different appreciation of their humanity, rationality,

[1]Emile Delmas, *Java, Ceylan, les Indes. Excursions dans l'Equateur et la Zone Torride*, 1897, cited in Franck Michel, *En Route pour l'Asie: Le Rêve oriental chez les Colonisateurs, les Aventuriers et les Touristes Occidentaux* [Travelling to Asia: Orientalism among Western Colonialists, Adventurers and Tourists], Strasbourg: Editions Histoire et Anthropologie, 1995, p. 32.

and ability—as well as the appropriateness of their architectural designs for living. Their writings contributed enormously to a wider knowledge of the cultures they encountered.

The greatest challenge in assembling this anthology has been to assure reasonable coverage, not only of both mainland and island South-East Asia in all their cultural variety, but of the many different types of architecture which travellers found worthy of attention. The range is vast, and yet it has been difficult to ensure that all the best descriptions have been unearthed; I still cannot be sure that they have. Many interesting materials have had to be excluded for reasons of space. For instance, Charles Hose's marvellously readable account of 'Life in a Longhouse' does not feature here, only because it has already appeared in a companion volume in this series (John Gullick, *Adventures and Encounters*, Kuala Lumpur: Oxford University Press, 1995); instead I have taken his equally interesting and unusually detailed description of how a longhouse is constructed. In some cases I have opted for atmosphere and romance over technical detail (though the latter itself is something of a rarity). Hence, I select Pierre Loti's over Henri Mouhot's account of Angkor Wat. Although Mouhot's account is of historically greater interest, its dry and factual descriptions do not convey the feeling of being there as vividly as Loti's lyrical prose, even though in other respects Loti may appear as a much more superficial person. Some fine pieces, such as Tom Harrisson's evocative, sympathetic portraits of Malay villages in Sarawak, were omitted because they belong to a slightly later period than that chosen for this volume.

For much of the information available about individual authors, I am indebted to their biographers who have edited the invaluable reprints of early travel writings already produced by Oxford University Press. My special thanks go to John Gullick, whose *Malay Society in the Nineteenth Century* (Singapore: Oxford University Press, 1987) is such a mine of information, and who generously responded at length to my various queries. About some individuals it has not been possible to unearth much biographical detail at all. Every effort has been made to trace and clear copyright of the materials reproduced here, though in some cases this has been difficult.

By and large, the original spellings have been retained in all the passages though modern spellings have been added in brackets for some place-names. I have translated Passages 18 and 50 from the original French. I hope that readers will find as much enjoyment as I have in sharing the adventures of these remarkable travellers, and looking at South-East Asian architecture through their eyes.

Ruins

1

Exploring the Ruins of Angkor

PIERRE LOTI

There could be no better place to begin this anthology than with the ruins of vanished empires, for among them are to be found some of the world's great architectural wonders. And no one exemplifies better than Pierre Loti the European romantic response to ruins in exotic places. Although Henri Mouhot (who travelled through Siam, Cambodia, and Laos in 1858–61) must take credit as the one who 'rediscovered' the lost kingdoms of Angkor for a European audience, his restrained and factual account of his finds does not summon the extraordinary atmosphere of Angkor in quite the way that Loti's more impressionistic one does.

Loti (1850–1923) is one of the most prominent figures in French colonial literature, who enjoyed enormous popularity during his lifetime and whose images of the exotic arguably had a lasting influence on how the French public viewed the imperialist adventures of the 1880s and 90s. As a naval officer he travelled exceedingly widely, and was a member of the expeditionary force sent to impose a French protectorate on Annam (central Vietnam) in 1883. But he never stayed long in any one place, and his impressions of each, it must be said, remained superficial. He published nearly forty volumes of prose, half of them travel sketches; he also wrote several by now unreadable novels. Curiously, he has been given a reputation in France of having been a staunch opponent of colonialism and a man who showed a deep and sympathetic understanding of native peoples, but unfortunately this impression does not hold up under examination. Certain inconsistencies in his attitude can be traced to personal experiences and obsessions. As a child, he was captivated by dreams of adventure in far-away lands, but when his elder brother Gustave, a naval surgeon, died of an illness contracted in Indo-China in 1865, the whole family was traumatized. This event, and Loti's own fear of death, seem to inform many of his judgements about what he saw as the waste of French soldiers' lives in Indo-China. Still, he had no objection himself to participating in military adventures, in fact he seems to have found them alluring and sometimes exaggerated his part in them. Ever the sensualist, Loti was a person of limited intellect whose contact with the peoples he visited never went beyond the formation of fleeting relationships with native mistresses, a theme which provided the sole plot of his novels. His absurdly racist comments on the inhabitants of Africa and the Far East must strike the reader of today as an embarrassment. On the subject of ruins, however, he is less offensive, and the intense lyricism which typifies the best of his writing is used to great effect here, as he conveys the moods of Angkor Wat in ever-changing weather conditions.

Friday, 20th November 1901.

I AM awakened at dawn by the matinal crescendo of the psalmodies. There has been such an excess of humidity during the night, so heavy a dew, that in spite of the thatched roof everything around me and on me is soaked, as after a shower.

In the comparative freshness of the early morning, I climb again the first steps of the temple, between the worn balustrades, defaced by the rains of centuries. And, mindful of the guardian bats, I enter with an excess of caution, making no more noise than a cat. My enemies of last night are all asleep above, hanging, head downwards, by their claws to the stones of the ceiling, and simulating at this hour myriads of little bags of dark-coloured velvet. I have entered now, and none of them has so much as moved. I recognise the gallery, with its resonance as of a cave, which is decorated, as far as eye can see, with the endless bas-relief of battles. And now that I see it in its entirety, diminishing before me in unbroken perspective, it seems even more infinitely long than before. A green half light has replaced all at once the clear daylight that

Mouhot's drawing of Angkor Wat as he saw it in 1860. From Henri Mouhot, *Travels in the Central Parts of Siam, Cambodia and Laos during the years 1858–60*, London: John Murray, 1864.

was broadening outside. There is a smell of dampness, such as one meets in subterranean places, but it is dominated here by the fusty musk-scented odour of the excrement of the bats, which is deposited in a layer upon the ground as if a rain of brown grains fell constantly from the vault.

To illumine the unfolding of the bas-relief, which covers all the interior wall of the gallery, windows at intervals open on to the surrounding park, and admit an attenuated light, made green by the foliage and palms. Very sumptuous windows, too, framed with carvings so delicate that one might think lace had been overlaid on the stone. They have annulated bars, which look like little columns of wood, elaborately turned by lathe, but are, in fact, of sandstone, like the rest of the walls.

This bas-relief, which stretches its medley of personages for more than a thousand yards, on the four sides of the temple, is inspired by one of the most ancient epics conceived by the men of Asia—the Ramayana....

The churning of the ocean alone fills a panel more than fifty yards long. Then come the battles of the gods and demons, and those of the monkeys against the evil spirits of the Isle of Ceylon, who had ravished the beautiful Sita, the spouse of Rama.

All these pictures, which formerly were painted and gilded, have taken on, under the oozings of the eternal dampness, a mournful blackish colour, varied in places by glistenings of actual wetness. And, moreover, the bas-relief, which measures some sixteen feet in height, is worn, as high as a man can reach, by the secular friction of fingers—for in the times of pilgrimage the whole multitude makes it a duty to touch it. Here and there, in the parts illumined by the beautiful windows with their wreathed bars, one can still see traces of colouring on the robes and faces; and sometimes in the tiaras of the Apsaras, a little gold, spared by time, continues to shine. As I advance I do not cease to watch the velvet guardians above; the flagstones give out a hollow sound, and when my footsteps make too great a noise, some pairs of hairless wings are unfolded; a bat stretches itself, wakes another one, and a general stirring ensues. Then I stand quite still, as if turned to stone, until all are asleep again.

What is difficult to understand is that the wall with its multitude of figures seems to be in a single piece over a length of some hundreds of yards; it needs a close scrutiny to detect the joints of the enormous stones which have been placed together in line without the help of any cement, and adjusted with the same rigorous precision as in the monuments of Egyptian antiquity.

In the middle of each side of the quadrilateral, a portico opens from this outer gallery and gives access to the central court, where rises the pagoda properly so-called, the prodigious mass of sculptured stone scaling the blue sky. Into that I hesitate to penetrate, intimidated, perhaps, or wearied in advance by such an entanglement of stairways, terraces, and towers, by such a complication of lines, by the unspeakable grimness which characterises the silent whole. Rather than enter, I continue to loiter, following the bas-relief of the outer wall.

In the gallery on the fourth side I encounter two young monks—clothed in lemon-yellow robes beneath orange yellow draperies. What are they doing here with a wheel-barrow, a shovel, and a broom? Nothing more nor less than gathering the dung of the bats to manure some little monachal garden. I wonder how many thousands of millions of insects, eaten in the air, are represented by these heaps of brown grains in their barrow, which are on the way now to fertilise flowers, which will nourish other insects, which will be eaten by other bats!

But they are making too much noise, these young monks—although in truth they make scarcely any—for, above, the velvety sleepers are awakening.

To avoid their hairless wings, I rush hastily through one of the porticoes into the central courtyard. And thus, after having lingered for a long time around the wooded chaos of the sanctuaries, I enter at last with precipitation, in an impulse of flight.

It is at a moment when the light all at once becomes over-cast, as if the sun were passing through some great eclipse. Above the masses of terraces, of porticoes and stairways, entangled with prodigal verdure, the clouds have suddenly spread a canopy of darkness; a diluvial rain is about to pour upon the ruins. And all the beasts which dwell there under the trees and in the breaches of the walls become silent, attentive to that which is about to fall.

This temple is one of the places in the world where men have heaped together the greatest mass of stones, where they have accumulated the greatest wealth of sculptures, of orna-ments, of foliage, of flowers, and of faces. It is not simple as are the lines of Thebes and Baalbeck. Its complexity is as be-wildering even as its enormity. Monsters guard all the flights of steps, all the entrances; the divine Apsaras, in indefinitely repeated groups, are revealed everywhere amongst the over-hanging creepers. And, at a first view, nothing stands out; there seem only disorder and confusion in this hill of carved stones, on the summit of which the great towers have sprouted.

But, on the contrary, when one examines it a little, a per-fect symmetry is manifest from top to base. The hill of sculp-tured stones forms a square pyramid of three stages, the base of which measures more than a thousand yards in circumfer-ence; and it is on the third and highest of these stages that we shall find, no doubt, that which is pre-eminently the holy place. We have to climb, therefore—I was prepared for it—to climb by steep and uneven steps, between the smiling Apsaras, the crouching lions, the holy serpents spreading like a fan their seven heads, and the languid verdure, which at this moment is motionless in the still air; to climb in haste, too, so as to reach the top before the deluge begins. In coming here this morning, I had imagined that the ascent would be made under a blue sky and in the glare of the sun; that the branches would be astir with gentle breezes, and that around me I should hear the sounds of birds, insects, and reptiles as they fled at my approach. But this mournful stillness daunts me; I was not prepared for this silence of waiting or for this black sky. My arrival wakens not a single sound, not a single movement, and even the sing-song of the monks, as they chant without ceasing at the foot of the temple, reaches me only very faintly, from the distance.

And now I have reached the first of the three platforms. Before me rises the second stage, of a height double that of the first, presenting stairways more abrupt, more guarded by smiles and rictus of stone. It is surrounded on its four sides by a vaulted gallery, a kind of cloister, immense and pompously magnificent, with its excess of carvings, its porticoes crowned with strange, elaborate frontals, with its narrow windows, the stone bars of which, already too massive, are brought close together as if the better to imprison you. All around the dilapidation is extreme. Within, the decoration is simpler than in the corridors of the base. The place is damp and dark, and there is an almost intolerable odour of bats; they cover the vault, these suspended sleepers.... At this height I no longer hear anything of the litany of the monks, and the silence is so profound that one scarcely dares to walk.

The second platform is surrounded like the first by a cloister, the façades of which are wrought with as much elaboration as the most patient embroideries. Here one might reasonably think that he was nearly there; but now the third stage rises, of a height double that of the second, and the monumental stairway that leads up to it, with its worn, grass-grown steps, is so steep that it induces a sensation of vertigo. The gods desire, no doubt, to make themselves more inaccessible in proportion as one endeavours to approach them. And verily the temple seems to grow higher, to stretch out, to reach up towards the darkling sky, and it is a little like those baffling dreams in which we strive madly to reach a goal which flies before us.... There should be four of these staircases, watched over by smiling Apsaras, one on each of the sides of the enormous pedestal; but I have not time to choose the best, for the shadow of the clouds grows ever deeper, and the storm is at hand. I mount, almost running, and the forest, the sovereign forest, seems to rise at the same

7

time; on every side it begins to stretch its circle to the horizon like a sea.

Here now is the third square platform, bordered also with its cloister, the façades of which are carved even more magnificently still. In high relief on the walls are the inevitable Apsaras standing in groups, and welcoming me with smiles of quiet mockery, the eyes half-closed. On this, the highest of the terraces, where I reach the bases of the towers, and the very doors of the sanctuary, I must be about a hundred feet above the level of the plains. And here the illusion is reversed. It seems now that it is the temple which has sunk into the forest. Seen from here it looks to be submerged, buried up to its middle in verdure. Below me, three graduated courses of cloisters, of high-crowned porticoes, of sumptuous vaults, scarcely broken by the centuries, have plunged, as it were, into the trees, into the silent expanse of trees, the tufts of which, in the distance, and as far as eye can see, simulate the undulations of an ocean swell.

The rain! A few first drops, astonishingly large and heavy, by way of warning. And then almost at once the general drumming on the leaves, torrents of water which descend with fury. Then, through a portico, the over-loaded frontal of which is in the form of flames and horns, running to take shelter, I enter at last what must be the sanctuary itself.

I expected an immense hall, where I should be alone, whereas it is only another gallery infinitely long but narrow, oppressive, sinister—in which I shudder almost at meeting, in the half-light of the storm and the barred windows, a number of motionless people—people eaten by worms, corpses and phantoms of gods, seated and foundering along the walls.

The majority are of human stature, but some are giantlike, and others are dwarfs. Some are of a dull grey, others of blood-coloured red, and here and there a little gilding, as in the masks of the mummies, shines still on certain of the faces. Many are without hands, without arms, without head, and a mass of excrement, the offering of our friends the bats, humps their back, deforms their shoulders. And when I raise

my eyes, how the sight fills me with disgust! For here, more
even than below, the stone ceilings are tapestried with these
little velvet pockets which hang suspended by their claws,
and want but the slightest noise to unfold and become a
whirlwind of wings. The interior of the thick, blackish
walls, void of any kind of ornament, are half concealed by
fine spun draperies, like funereal crapes, which are the work
of innumerable spiders. Without, I hear the storm raging.
Everything is inundated; the water streams in veritable cas-
cades. I breathe a warm vapour at once fetid and musk-
scented. In the long gallery the closeness of the walls and the
enormous size of the sandstone columns which mask the
openings induce a feeling of confinement; and this, notwithstanding that the circle of the horizon, seen between the
same window bars, supports the notion of altitude, serves as a
reminder that one dominates, from the height of this kind of
aerial prison, the infinite expanse of the sodden forest.

This, then, is the sanctuary which haunted many years ago
my childish imagination. I reach it at last only after many
journeyings about the world, in what is already the evening
of my wandering life. It gives me mournful welcome. I had
not forseen these torrents of rain, this confinement amongst
the webs of spiders, nor my present solitude in the midst of
so many phantom gods. There is a personage beyond, conspicuous amongst them all, reddish in colour like a flayed
corpse, with feet worm eaten and crumbling, who, in order
that he may not fall altogether, leans crosswise against the
wall, half-upturning his face with its scarred lips. It is from
him, it seems, that all the silence and all the unutterable sad-
ness of the place proceed.

A prisoner here for so long as the storm may last, I go first
of all to a window, instinctively, to get more air, to escape
from the odour of the bats. And between the rigid spindle-
shaped bars, I see sloping below me the architectural mass
which I have just ascended. On the sides of the ruins, all the
foliage bends and trembles, overwhelmed by the tumultuous
downpour. The legions of Apsaras, the great holy serpents,

the monsters crouching on the threshold of the flights of steps, seem to bow the head under the daily deluge, which, for seasons without number, has worn by dint of washing them. More and more I hear the water crackling, rushing in a thousand streams.

In order to discern the general plan of this third and highest platform, it would be necessary to see it from outside. But the light continues to diminish, as if it were the twilight instead of the morning; the horizon of the forests is completely hidden behind the opaque curtains of the rain, and it is clear that the storm will last for another hour at least. I have, perforce, to remain in shelter, and, in this persistent twilight of eclipse, feeling that I am followed by the cadaverous smiles of all this assembly of Buddhas, who are watching me, I proceed towards what must be the centre and very heart of Angkor-Vat.

I tread softly on the layers of dust and excrement, sprinkled with feathers of owls. The huge, hairy spiders, weavers of the multiple draperies, remain motionless and on watch.

Over and above that which falls unceasingly from the roof, little heaps of withered flowers and incense appear before all the idols, attesting that men venerate them still. But why do not people dust them a little when they come to visit them? And in what disorder, too, they have been left!—the small, the large, and the colossal, and higgledy-piggledy as after a rout. At the uncertain date of the sack of the town and the pillage of the temple they were all overthrown and dragged to earth. Subsequently the piety of the Siamese put them upright again, as best it could, but in a methodless grouping along the walls, those of sandstone against those of worm-eaten wood, which crumble to powder at the slightest touch, those which have lost their colouring side by side with those which still possess red robes and gilded faces. (And, lest they should forget a single one of them in their devotions, the pilgrims who come hither spend hours, it seems, in passing through the endless galleries where they repose.) Buddhist statues, already centenarian many times over, they were yet new-comers, quite recent intruders in this temple of a far more ancient cult. And having supplanted the images of Brahma, the primitive god of Angkor, they are now fallen in their turn, destroyed by time.

The flagstones are so carpeted with filth and ashes that the sound of my footsteps is smothered, and, without being heard by the thousands of little ears above, I make my way towards the darker end of the gallery, between the two rows of silent personages. Here, formerly, was the Holy of Holies, the place where the supreme Brahma was enthroned; but it has been walled up for an unknown period of time.

And before this wall—which, no doubt, still encloses the terrible idol, and perhaps preserves it as intact as a mummy in its sarcophagus—a Buddha of gigantic size, commanding and gentle, has been seated for centuries, with legs crossed and downcast half-closed eyes, for so many centuries that the spiders have contrived patiently to drape him with black muslins, hiding the gold with which he is adorned, and that the bats have had time to cover him as with a thick mantle. The swarm of horrible little sleeping beasts forms now a kind of padded daïs of brown plush above his head, and the rain, which continues to stream mercilessly outside, makes for him its plaintive daily music. But his bowed head, which I can distinguish in spite of the darkness, preserves the same smile as may be found on all representations of Him, from Thibet to China: the smile of the Great Peace, obtained by the Great Renunciation and the Great Pity.

Pierre Loti, *Siam*, 1913; translated from the French by W. P. Baines, 3rd edn., London: T. Werner Laurie, 1929, pp. 83–99.

2

A Visit to Angkor Thom and the Bayon

MALCOLM MacDONALD

Of all the enigmatic marvels of Angkor, the most intensely strange of all must be the Bayon, the great temple of Angkor Thom, built by Jayavarman VII at the end of the twelfth century. As one walks the terraces of this fantastical building, one has an eerie sense of being watched, before the eye takes in one after another the carved faces looking down at one out of the stone. It seems that the temple's plan was altered several times during construction, so that parts of the interior ended up consisting of many tiny dark rooms, which it is hard to imagine were ever used for anything. The sharp contrast between the creepy and unfunctional interior, and the brilliance of the exterior carved friezes, depicting battles and scenes of everyday life, accentuates the sense of excess. Coupled with the heavy atmosphere of decay and abandonment which hangs around the architectural achievements of the Khmer empires, this extraordinary piece of design leaves a lasting impression on the visitor.

The author of this piece is Malcolm MacDonald (1901–1981), the son of Labour leader Ramsey MacDonald, who spent many years in South-East Asia in the course of his distinguished career as a diplomat. When he wrote *Angkor* he was British Commissioner-General for South-East Asia, having already served as Governor-General of Malaya and Singapore (1946–8). He went on to be High Commissioner to India, and last Governor of Kenya (subsequently British High Commissioner, after having speeded the country to its independence). In all these appointments, he played a key role in facilitating the process of peaceful decolonization. He wrote a number of other books recounting his experiences in Asia and beyond, notably *Borneo People* (Toronto: Clark, Urwin, 1956), about the Iban of Sarawak, for whom he had a deep affection. (His kilt is still preserved as an heirloom by his adoptive Iban family in their longhouse up the Rejang River.) By all accounts a delightfully unstuffy person, he combined his exceptional talent for diplomacy with other skills, being particularly well known for his ability to walk on his hands. He did this sometimes in distinguished company, as a way of breaking through the crust of formality which tended to surround his position and which he found so uncongenial. In his memoir, *People and Places* (Glasgow: Collins, 1969), he describes an occasion in Singapore when he entertained the cellist Pablo Casals to dinner in his favourite backstreet Chinese restaurant after a concert. Challenged by Casals to prove his ability, he walked upside-down up and down the street, to loud applause from his guest and the huge amusement of the Chinese courtesans who lived on the top floors of the same street.

During his time as Commissioner-General, MacDonald made several trips to Cambodia, during which he visited Angkor. The first was in 1948, when, as he put it, he went 'to pay my respects to His Majesty King Sihanouk and to confer with him on Indo-Chinese affairs'. The dominant concern of British diplomacy in this period was to check the spread of Communism in the region. On a subsequent trip, he stayed at Sihanouk's small villa at Angkor, and was invited by his host to join him in water-skiing on the West Baray, an ancient reservoir constructed by Suryavarman I in the eleventh century. A crowd gathered to watch, and Sihanouk completed several laps 'with splendid dash', but Malcolm, who had only had one quick lesson in Singapore before the trip, showed off on one ski and ended up in the water.

J AYAVARMAN'S principal architectural achievement was the rebuilding of his capital. He raised Angkor Thom on the site of the old city, which had remained the seat of Imperial Khmer government almost continuously since the first Yasovarman founded his capital of Yasodharapura three hundred years earlier. In the intervening centuries it had experienced many changes as king succeeded king and their varying needs or tastes caused them to pull down old palaces, temples and streets and construct new ones in their places. Now the city was to receive its last transformation and take the final shape which its ruins in the Cambodian jungle indicate today.

The Chams had spared no effort at destruction when they sacked the place, but some of its stone buildings survived. For example, the temples of the Phimeanakas and Baphuon still stood, and these were incorporated by Jayavarman in his new plan. Much of the rest had to be reconstructed, though he adopted the general lay-out of the royal centre conceived by Suryavarman. It was a task well suited to Jayavarman's powerful, insatiable creative urge.

When Angkor Thom was newly completed it must have been a wonderfully impressive city. Its size was colossal. The moat surrounding it extended more than eight miles, enclosing completely the four sides of a square metropolis. This wide channel of water—probably stocked with crocodiles as an extra protection against enemies—formed the outer defence works of the capital. Immediately inside it rose a tall, massive wall built of stone, for Jayavarman learned when Yasodharapura was burnt how vulnerable is a fortress guarded only by wooden palisades. The inner side of the wall was buttressed by a high mound of earth, along the top of which ran a terrace for troops to man the ramparts.

The moat was crossed at five places by causeways leading to the five gates giving entry to the city. These causeways were bordered by their famous sculptured balustrades of *nagas* gripped by scores of giants and demons. The gateways were handsome, monumental structures spanning lofty arches, for they had to admit processions of elephants with retainers holding sunshades over the heads of princes lolling on the monsters' backs. The massive flanks of each gate were decorated by gigantic, three-headed stone elephants, and the towers above were adorned with four vast, smiling Buddhic faces. In magnificence these gates compare with any of the architectural creations of classical Greece or Rome.

The area within the walls was more spacious than that of any walled city in medieval Europe, and could easily have contained the whole of ancient Rome. Yet it is believed that this enclosure, like the Forbidden City in Peking, was only a royal, religious and administrative centre accommodating the court and the chief civil, ecclesiastical and military dignitaries. The rest of the population lived outside its walls in suburbs spreading perhaps beside two artificial lakes—the East and West Barays—and along the banks of the Siem Reap river as far as the shore of the Great Lake. In those places numerous bazaars were a scene of constant petty commerce, and beyond them stretched mile upon mile of peasants' rice-fields.

The regal centre of the capital was the Grand Plaza, already partly laid out by Suryavarman I. Jayavarman beautified it. To its Kleangs and Towers of the Cord-Dancers he added the most decorative feature of the place, the Royal Terrace. Its great length is covered with bas-reliefs on which elephants, *garudas*, lions, *devatas* and other creatures sport in multitudinous pageantry. Close by is another of Jayavarman's ornamental edifices, now known as the Terrace of the Leper King. Rows upon rows of figures of kings and queens, princes and princesses on its walls form the most concentrated assembly of semi-divine royalty in all Khmer sculpture. On the greensward above is the strange statue, of earlier date, which gives the place its name, for legend said that it represented a Khmer monarch who suffered from leprosy—though later scholarship alleges that the figure is that of neither king nor leper.

The Grand Plaza must have presented a splendid appearance when Angkor Thom was the proud, lively capital of an Empire. A wide, open space surrounded by noble buildings, it was the hub of the city. Along one side stretched the wondrously sculptured walls of the Royal Terrace and the Terrace of the Leper King. Flights of steps led through these to the lawns and pavilions of the royal gardens beyond, in the centre of which rose the glories of the palace. The stately Baphuon stood on a hill overlooking this splendour, and close by was another imposing imperial tomb, the Phimeanakas. Ranged opposite were the dozen Towers of the Cord-Dancers, and behind them more walled terraces with flights of steps led to the two Kleangs. At the ends of the Plaza were Preah Pithu and other temples and public buildings, and from it radiated in all directions the main streets of the city, with vistas of avenues, statues, pools and fountains. The place had a spacious dignity as fine as that of any civic centre on earth.

A stone's throw from the Plaza stood the Bayon, the temple

of temples in Jayavarman's new city. It was the most ambitious of his architectural conceptions, the most fabulous of his dramatic designs, the most astonishing of his megalomaniac dreams. In some ways its plan followed the hallowed Siva-ite tradition of Khmer sacred buildings. Though it has no moat, surrounding walls or outer enclosures, it seemed to be basically a pyramid temple raised in three steep, successively receding platforms. But this intention was then overlaid by the whim of the Buddhist king to make it an overwhelming exhibition of the worship of a supreme Buddhic divinity. In the place of spacious terraces bearing occasional towers culminating in five central sanctuaries, it is crowded with more than fifty towers which intrude everywhere on the terraces and reduce them to little more than corridors between these close-packed pinnacles. It is all very confusing.

Many details of the sculpture are attractive. Thus the shallowly cut figures of dancing *apsaras* on pillars in the lowest terrace are as engaging as could be, and they convey charmingly the light, gay natures of these heavenly creatures, who were said to have no mothers and fathers but to be born on the flying spray of ocean waves. The more fully rounded forms of *devatas* in niches beside doors and windows are also extremely gracious, and the bas-reliefs depicting contemporary Khmer life—which I have described in the last chapter—are vigorous. But all this decoration is too crowded. On the Bayon there is scarcely a square foot of space uncovered by assertive, bizarre carvings. The building is less a work of architecture than a colossal exhibition of sculpture. One French commentator, Commaille, who was an authority on decoration rather than architecture, wrote: 'It would be superfluous to insist on the beauty of the Bayon and its particular charm. The visitor will notice at once that this temple, although of dimensions less vast than its immense neighbour, Angkor Vat, is of a superior conception and that it is here that we must study the genius of the masters of Angkor. In a relatively restrained space the constructors of the Bayon have been able to enclose more marvels than in all the other Cambodian temples combined. . . .'

That is exactly what seems to me to be wrong with the Bayon. Into its comparatively small space it crowds more 'marvels' than can be seen in many other temples put together. Its over-ornateness is a mark of decadence.

Yet certain of its features are undeniably magnificent, in the fullest sense of the word. They combine beauty with power. They are works of genius—but one has an uneasy feeling that it is the genius which is akin to madness. Those features are the temple's fifty-odd towers, and they reveal the megalomaniac strain in Jayavarman's character.

As on his city gateways, so on every side of every tower appears a tremendous sculptured face of a divinity—more than two hundred exactly similar countenances with mysteriously half-closed eyes and enigmatically smiling lips. Crowned with jewelled diadems, and with ear-rings dangling from their elongated ears, whilst pearl necklaces depend around their necks, each one rises eight feet high. No masterpieces of sculpture anywhere are more compelling, more haunting, more hypnotizing. And perhaps part of their fascination springs from the fact that they are faces of Jayavarman himself, the once modest, humble priest who twice renounced the throne and then became the mightiest of all Khmer rulers; and whose head swelled incredibly until he imagined himself to be the living Buddha. The multitude of great carved masks on the Bayon's towers are all symbolic likenesses of the king-god himself. The temple was his supreme act of self-worship.

Many people regard it as the climax of Khmer art, the loveliest work of a race of superhuman builders, the noblest expression of a wonderful civilization. Some highly qualified critics think it finer than Angkor Vat. With respect, I cannot agree with them. As a fantasy the Bayon has never been excelled, but as a work of art it lacks pure beauty. Perhaps some of its sculpture is superior to anything of the kind in Angkor Vat, but as an architectural tour de force it has not the simplicity combined with mass, the austerity associated with rich decoration, and the strength allied with serenity of the earlier temple. It is a piece of extravagance, a sample of gorgeous decadence, a sort of 'folly'. Human vanity has never been more devastatingly exposed. And, leaving aside that mortal defect, as an essay in architecture it was overdone. The characteristic faults in its construction have caused some towers to crumble, and time and weather have also mellowed its forms, but even so its multitude of faces seems too blatant. I cannot help thinking that when the building was brand-new, and they peered through lowered eyelids with spick-and-span freshness on the world, they must have looked a trifle vulgar.

Malcolm Macdonald, *Angkor*, London: Jonathan Cape, 1958; reprinted Kuala Lumpur: Oxford University Press, 1987, pp. 119–24.

3
'Pagan as It Is Today'

V. C. SCOTT O'CONNOR

V. C. Scott O'Connor was the author of two valuable books about Burma, *The Silken East* (1904) and *Mandalay* (1907). The first of these focused on contemporary peoples and cultures of Burma, the second on history, through an account of twelve cities which had played important roles in past ages. O'Connor was a British colonial officer who travelled widely throughout the country during two periods of duty, from 1891 to 1895 and again from 1899. His enthusiasm and admiration for the country shines through his erudite yet exceedingly readable book. Widely read, he was also a keen observer of Burmese life, and took the opportunity to talk to many Burmese who had witnessed important historical events, or who were keepers of oral memory. His description of Pagan is highly evocative, for remarkably little has changed there (except for UNESCO's admirable restoration efforts) since the time when he wrote. Pagan is a broad plain beside the Irrawaddy River in central Burma, which from the eleventh to the fourteenth century gave its name to the Burmese state of which it was the capital. Buddhism flourished here, and much of the wealth from irrigated rice agriculture was concentrated in the building of temples. At its peak in the early thirteenth century Pagan, in O'Connor's words, 'must have been one of the most remarkable capitals the world has seen'. Sudden decline set in after 1287 when the city was sacked by the troops of Kublai Khan, though later kings, after moving their capitals elsewhere, continued to patronize the monasteries at Pagan and to build new pagodas.

At Pagan, an area of over a hundred square miles is covered with thousands of pagodas, of extraordinary beauty. Though 'steeped in an atmosphere of religion', Pagan was a secular capital as well as a holy city. Here, as at other great temple sites in South-East Asia, appearances are misleading, for all trace of secular buildings, made as they were of perishable timber, have vanished. O'Connor notes the tendency in Burma for the finest architecture (in the form of religious buildings) to 'exist side by side with the humblest kind of secular civilisation and prosperity' (p. 230); the builders of magnificent pagodas may well have dwelt in simple mat houses much like those of the contemporary small village of Pagan, Nyaung-u (which was moved by the authorities in the early 1990s, but which until then looked much as it did when O'Connor photographed it). In writing of the history of Pagan, he evokes the grandeur of the past, before contemplating the silence of the present: '... the cactus and the wild plum now grow where Anawrata once ruled in magnificence and splendour, and a dusty wheel-track runs through the grand gateway of old Pagan. A slow country cart, creaking along the ruts, toils alone now in the broad sunlight where of old there marched the processions of a king, and a breath as of utter desolation broods over a city which has been dead for six hundred years.'

THE steamers of to-day come to anchor at the village of Nyaung-u, which now stands for Pagān, of which in the past it was little more than a distant northern suburb. It is here that the British Magistrate resides, that justice is done, the revenue of the district collected; and Pagān, once the capital of an empire, survives now, in so far as it can be said to survive at all, as the capital of a subdivision of a District—something less than a *sous-préfecture*.

Down in the sands of the village there are mat cottages and a Post Office and a Bazaar, structures so frail and temporary that a few hours would suffice to extinguish them completely. On the neighbouring hilltops stand the Court House, the Magistrate's quarters, and the rest-house for the traveller. Here and there amidst these novelties stand the isolated dragons of once-existing pagodas, figures of Buddha which have lost nearly every trace of human semblance, and spires that are tottering to decay.

All that spreads to the north and east of these is classic soil, linked with the innermost history of Pagān. The country is a low plateau deeply intersected by ravines. In the full tide of summer there is no more desolate spot in Burma; but it has its season of beauty. When the rains come, its small acacias clothe themselves in rich foliage, and under their shelter spread meadows of yellow bloom and grassy glades.

The plateau ends abruptly in sheer cliffs overhanging the river, which swirls below. Old pagodas crown the cliffs, and lie buried to a third of their height in the ploughed fields. Monasteries perpetuating the tradition of the past still find a beautiful seclusion in places which are shaded by groves of trees and sheltered by cliff-ledges, but which yet command wide and noble views over the vast world of the river.

The most striking object in the near vista, as one makes one's way, is the Chauk-pa-hla Pagoda, built by King Narapati-sithu late in the twelfth century. It presents a brave front to time, its spire of slender beauty rising high in dazzling whiteness above the sands of the rivulet and the palm-clusters below. A wooden bridge leads over the ravine to the Shwé-thabeik, the pagoda of the Golden Alms-bowl, and a small monastery which shelters at its foot. The site is one of singular beauty, and if the existing tradition of the place be true, a monastery has stood here since the days of Anawrata, when his wife, a princess of Wethali, built the pagoda, and the caves in the near cliff face were dug for the first recluse....

A little way off, in the hollows that lie behind the monastery on its landward side, is the Kôndaw-gyi temple, with a figure of Buddha within and fine plaster work without. The latter is so fresh and beautiful where it still lingers that it is hard to believe that it is many hundred years old. Each line looks as though it might have been struck with the carving tool but a moment since. The border-device under the cornices consists of loops enclosing figures of Buddha.

Its near neighbour is the Thet-kya-muni Pagoda seven centuries old, with a figure within it seated on a throne, under a bawdi-tree, painted in green fresco. The dome is frescoed in a geometrical pattern with figures of Buddha; while the vaulted roof over the wings contains life-like vignettes of white elephants, ducks, hare, ostriches, and other creatures. The frescoes on the central vault contain vignettes of Buddha, much superior to those on the side walls. Inscriptions in square letters run beneath the frescoes. Large standing figures are painted, one on each side of the archway, which opens from the east into the central vault. The four exterior sides of the tapering cone of the temple are ornamented with plaster figures of the Buddha in semi-relief. Brick walls of solid construction make square courtyards round most of these pagodas.

Here under the dark vaulted domes of these ruined temples one may still come upon men at prayer, still hear the echo of their voices sounding the Litany of their faith. But others, and they are in the vast majority, are completely deserted, and the stalled ox and the passing leopard shelter where worshippers once thronged....

As one rides of a morning over the waste spaces of Pagān littered with the bricks of countless ruins, the sunlight still streams in at the ruined porches, bathing the lotus thrones and the superincumbent feet of Buddhas in rising waves of gold. Nearly all look east, and the constant sunlight enters in now, with its homage, as it did a thousand years ago, careless of the changes that have been since then. In the lonely ways, flanked with cactus and heavy with a fine white sand, the detritus of centuries, carts creak slowly on their way, voices come up over the barren *despoblado*, and from time to time as one nears the road his eyes are caught by the shimmer of silk and the passing face of a fair woman.

But the supreme note, as it always is at Pagān, is one of desolation and despair; of desolation in these vast spaces crowded with decaying spires and ruined walls, the dead bones of the past; of despair of all human progress, since it is liable to such sweeping cataclysms as this. The mat-hovels, the squalid hamlets, that now exist amongst the ruins are but a poor broken sequel to the old-time splendour of Pagān. . . .

And now, leaving lesser things alone, we may well turn up the pathway which leads to the Ananda Pagoda, the first of the great temples of Pagān. Built in the reign of King Kyansittha, the Ananda as a building has suffered little from the passage of nine hundred years. Kings no longer worship in it, ministers and nobles no longer make their way through its great portals from the neighbouring city. But the people of the countryside have not forgotten that it is a great shrine of their faith. The colossal images of the four Buddhas within are still brilliant with gold; its climbing spires without still gleam white in the sunlight, and no day passes without worship, and adoration within its walls. At the season of its annual festival the old building moves again with life. All day the bells clang, and tapers are lit, and one who peers into its dusk interior can trace in faint outline the forms of many worshippers, the flicker of innumerable lights; can hear the low murmur of prayer. At night the pilgrims lie asleep in the halls and vestibules, while the full white moonlight floods the cusped spire and stately façades of the temple. At such times one is tempted to doubt if any change at all has come over Pagān. But in truth the life that moves in it now is but a flicker to the great flame of adoration that burnt within it in the days of Kyansittha the King.

Of its architecture this only need here be said. Its plan is that of a perfect Greek cross, measuring two hundred and eighty feet across each way. Its walls are of such immense solidity that the temple within looks, not as if it had been built up of brick, but as though it were hewn out of a solid pyramid. Standing figures of the four Buddhas of the present world-cycle are enshrined within it, and each of them is lit from an invisible aperture above, as figures of the Virgin are lit in Roman Catholic churches in Europe. In niches left in the walls of its corridors there are images of Buddha and sculptured groups depicting incidents in his life. Of such images and groups there are several thousand, many of them admirably executed, within and without the temple. The square mass of the building is surmounted by six successively diminishing terraces, the last of which forms a base for the square mitre-like spire, which itself upholds like a jewel in its cusps the typical pinnacle of the Burmese pagoda. There is an exquisite harmony of design in this building, combined with enormous solidity and fine workmanship which seem destined to preserve it for many centuries to come.

A short way beyond it, and approached by a pathway which runs through a gap in the eastern wall of the fortified city, stand the That-byin-nyu and Gaw-daw-palin pagodas, which share with it the glory of being the finest structures in Pagán. The That-byin-nyu, rising to a height of two hundred feet, is loftier than any other building in the city. Its most striking feature is presented by its third terrace, which leaps up unexpectedly to a height of fifty feet, unlike the Ananda, whose terraces climb in regular succession to its summit. Within these walls of fifty feet, the great image of the temple is enshrined some seventy feet above the level of the ground.

The Gaw-daw-palin stands architecturally midway between its two fellows. The Ananda, more exquisite in detail than either of its companions, lacks something of the majesty of the That-byin-nyu. In the Gaw-daw-palin stateliness and harmony of proportion are combined.

Seen from a little distance, these great pagodas present an appearance of extraordinary beauty. Transfigured in the soft

light of a Burmese evening against a curtain of electric
clouds, they look as if for sheer perfection of form and outline they could not be surpassed; and it is impossible to resist
their absolute fascination.

V. C. Scott O'Connor, *Mandalay and Other Cities of the Past in Burma*,
London: Hutchinson & Co., 1907, pp. 234–64.

4
The Antiquities of Borobudur and Dieng

THOMAS STAMFORD RAFFLES

The Buddhist monument of Borobudur, in Central Java, with its
1,460 exquisitely-carved panels of bas-reliefs set around four con-
centric terraces, and its 504 life-sized Buddha-statues, is the largest
Buddhist sanctuary ever built. It was constructed over a seventy-
year period, from around AD 760 to 830. By around 1700, however, it seems that the Javanese had forgotten that their own
ancestors had built it, and believed that the deserted 'mountain'
was a place of ill omen. Early Dutch colonists showed little interest
in antiquities, and remained unaware of its existence. It took
Thomas Stamford Raffles, who for a brief and innovative period
(1811–16) was Lieutenant-Governor of Java, to initiate a survey
of Java's historical monuments, and when in January 1814 a local
person told him that a huge ruined temple was to be found in the
Kedu Plain west of Yogyakarta, he at once took steps to investigate
it. The team that he sent, under a Dutch engineer, H. C.
Cornelius, found the monument so engulfed in dirt and vegetation
that it took 200 men a month and a half to uncover it. Raffles thus
became responsible for one of the most remarkable archaeological
discoveries of the nineteenth century. This was forty-seven years
before Henri Mouhot related his discovery of Angkor, and was a
revelation for Europeans who until then had had no idea of the
sophistication of ancient South-East Asian civilizations. Raffles also
provided for European readers the first account of another fascinating site, Dieng. This mountain plateau in north central Java is a

24

volcanic site of dramatic boiling lakes and bubbling mud-pools, which is dotted with hundreds of Hindu temples. Constructed in the early eighth century AD, it is the oldest temple complex in Java.

IN the district of *Bóro*, in the province of *Kedú*, and near to the confluence of the rivers *Elo* and *Prága*, crowning a small hill, stands the temple of *Bôro Bódo*,* supposed by some to have been built in the sixth, and by others in the tenth century of the Javan era. It is a square stone building consisting of seven ranges of walls, each range decreasing as you ascend, till the building terminates in a kind of dome. It occupies the whole of the upper part of a conical hill, which appears to have been cut away so as to receive the walls and to accommodate itself to the figure of the whole structure. At the centre, resting on the very apex of the hill, is the dome before mentioned, of about fifty feet diameter; and in its present ruinous state, the upper part having fallen in, only about twenty feet high. This is surrounded by a triple circle of towers, in number seventy-two, each occupied by an image looking outwards, and all connected by a stone casing of the hill, which externally has the appearance of a roof.

Descending from thence, you pass on each side of the building by steps through five handsome gateways, conducting to five successive terraces, which surround the hill on every side. The walls which support these terraces are covered with the richest sculpture on both sides, but more particularly on the side which forms an interior wall to the terrace below, and are raised so as to form a parapet on the other side. In the exterior of these parapets, at equal distances, are niches, each containing a naked figure sitting cross-legged, and considerably larger than life;† the total number of which is not far short of four hundred. Above

---

*So termed by the people of the neighbouring villages. *Bóro* is the name of the district, *bódo* means ancient.

†These figures measure above three feet in height in a sitting posture and with the images found in the towers exactly resemble those in the small temples at *Chandi Séwu*.

The first ever published view of Borobudur. From Thomas Stamford Raffles, *History of Java*, London, 1817.

each niche is a little spire, another above each of the sides of the niche, and another upon the parapet between the sides of the neighbouring niches. The design is regular; the architectural and sculptural ornaments are profuse. The bas-reliefs represent a variety of scenes, apparently mythological, and executed with considerable taste and skill. The whole area occupied by this noble building is about six hundred and twenty feet either way.

The exterior line of the ground plan, though apparently a perfect square when viewed at a distance, is not exactly of that form, as the centre of each face, to a considerable extent, projects many feet, and so as to cover as much ground as the conical shape of the hill will admit: the same form is observed in each of the terraces.

The whole has the appearance of one solid building, and is about a hundred feet high, independently of the central spire of about twenty feet, which has fallen in. The interior consists almost entirely of the hill itself. . . .

Next to *Bóro Bódo* in importance, and perhaps still more interesting, are the extensive ruins which are found on *Gúnung Díeng*, the supposed residence of the gods and demigods of antiquity. This mountain, from its resemblance to the hull of a vessel, is also called *Gúnung Práhu*. It is situated northward and westward of the mountain *Sindóro*, which forms the boundary between *Kedú* and *Bányumas*, and terminates a range of hills running east from the mountain of *Tegál*. There are no less than twenty-nine different peaks of this mountain, or rather cluster of mountains, each of which has its peculiar name, and is remarkable for some peculiar production or natural phænomenon.

On a table-land about six hundred feet higher than the surrounding country, which is some thousand feet above the level of the sea, are found the remains of various temples, idols, and other sculpture, too numerous to be described in this place. A subject in stone having three faces, and another with four arms, having a ball or globe in one hand and a thunderbolt in another, were the most conspicuous.

The ascent from the country below to the table-land on which these temples stood is by four flights of stone steps, on four different sides of the hill, consisting of not less than one thousand steps each. The ascent from the southern side is now in many parts steep and rocky, and in some places almost inaccessible, but the traveller is much assisted by the dilapidated remains of the stone steps, which appear to be of the greatest antiquity. Time alone, indeed, cannot have so completely demolished a work, of which the materials were so durable and the construction so solid. The greatest part of this wonderful memorial of human industry lies buried under huge masses of rock and lava; and innumerable proofs are afforded of the mountain having, at some period since the formation of the steps, been in a state of violent eruption. Near the summit of one of the hills there is a crater of about half a mile diameter.

At no great distance from this crater, in a north-west direction, is situated a plain or table-land, surrounded on all sides but one by a ridge of mountains about a thousand feet above it. At some very remote period it was perhaps itself the crater of a vast volcano. On its border are the remains of four temples of stone, greatly dilapidated, but manifestly by the effect of some violent shock or concussion of the earth. The largest of them is about forty feet square: the walls are ten feet thick, and the height about thirty-five feet. The only apartment which it contains is not more than twenty feet square, and has only one entrance. The roof is arched to a point in the centre, about twenty feet high above the walls, so that the whole building was almost one solid mass of masonry, composed of the most durable cut stone, in blocks of from one to two feet long and about nine inches square. Yet these walls, so constructed, are rent to the bottom. It was particularly observable, that little or no injury had been done by vegetation, the climate being unfavourable to the *waríngen*, whose roots are so destructive to the buildings of the lower regions. The entablatures of these buildings still exhibit specimens of delicate and very elegant sculpture. Several deep excavations are observed in the neighbourhood. These, it is said, were made by the natives, in search of gold utensils, images, and coins, many of which have, from time to time, been dug up here.

The whole of the plain is covered with scattered ruins and large fragments of hewn stone to a considerable distance. In the centre are four more temples, nearly similar to those before-mentioned, but in a much better state of preservation, the sculpture being in many places quite perfect. Numerous images of deities are scattered about.

On a more minute examination of this plain, traces of the site of nearly four hundred temples were discovered, having broad and extensive streets or roads running between them at right angles. The ground plan of these, as far as it could be ascertained, with sketches of the different images, ornaments, and temples, which distinguish this classic ground, have been made by Captain Baker, who devoted three weeks to the accomplishment of this interesting object. At present I have it only in my power to exhibit a drawing of one of the temples, in the state in which it was found in 1815, with the same temple restored to what it originally was.

The whole of the country lying between *Gúnung Díeng* and *Brambánam*, in a line nearly crossing the central part of the island, abounds with ruins of temples, dilapidated images, and traces of Hinduism. Many of the villagers between *Blédran* and *Jétis*, in the road from *Bányumas* through *Kedú*, have availed themselves of the extensive remains to form the walls of their buildings. In the enclosures to several of the villages (which are here frequently walled in) are discovered large stones, some representing gorgon heads, others beautifully executed in relief, which had formed the frizes and cornices of temples, all regularly cut so as to be morticed together, but now heaped one upon another in the utmost confusion and disorder.

Along the fields, and by the road side, between *Jétis* and *Mágelan*, are seen in ditches or elsewhere, many beautiful remains of sculpture, and among them many *yonis* and

'One of the Temples on the Mountain Dieng, or Prahu', lithograph from Thomas Stamford Raffles, *History of Java*, London, 1817.

lingams, where they seem not only to be entirely disregarded by the natives but thrown on one side as if in the way.

Thomas Stamford Raffles, *The History of Java*, Vol. II, London: Black, Parbury and Allen, & John Murray, 1817; reprinted Kuala Lumpur: Oxford University Press, 1965, pp. 29–33.

5
'Boro Boedor'

E. R. SCIDMORE

An American visitor to Java in the 1890s, E. R. Scidmore wrote a spirited account of her travels which includes many glimpses of everyday life and culture. She visited Solo and Yogyakarta, climbed the summit of Mount Papandayang, and observed everything from plantation life to local markets and villages. A formidable traveller, who evidently derived huge enjoyment from her adventures, she was forthright about those details of life which surprised her in Java. She was shocked at the 'startling dishabille' of Eurasian women in Batavia who could be seen in public dressed in *sarong* and *kebaya* ('Only shipwreck on a desert island would seem sufficient excuse for women being seen in such an ungraceful, unbecoming attire'), stern on the table manners of Dutch colonial personnel, and their puffing of 'clouds of dense, rank, Sumatran tobacco-smoke', and withering in her recollections of a Muslim servant who made sandwiches for an extended train journey from Tjilatjap to Garoet—and was found at lunchtime to have eaten them all himself. On one occasion, a railway station attendant was about to make tea for them with lukewarm water. In a move which present-day travellers to Indonesia might well appreciate, she seized the offending kettle, penetrated a village kitchen, and put it firmly back on the fire till it boiled. She stood up to a Dutch official at Yogyakarta, who officiously declared her papers out of order, and found herself ordered to depart for Borobudur.

Scidmore provides for us a more richly detailed description of Borobudur, the full magnificence of which had, by the time she saw it, been fully revealed by excavations which had continued intermittently from 1814 until the early 1870s. Once it was uncovered, however, new deterioration from sun, rain, and plant growth rapidly set in, and the condition of the whole structure became increasingly shaky. The colonial government for long remained indifferent. They built a tea house on top of the monument, and as late as 1896, even permitted King Chulalongkorn of Siam, while on a trip to Java, to take home with him eight cartloads of sculpture as a memento of his visit. A first attempt at restoration was not undertaken until 1907, and even then, rain water continued to drain down through the inside of the hill and pour out through the reliefs at the base. It was the independent Indonesian government, with the help of UNESCO, who were ultimately to take responsibility for the complete rescue of this architectural masterpiece.

THE deep portico of the passagrahan commands an angle and two sides of the square temple, and from the mass of blackened and bleached stones the eye finally arranges and follows out the broken lines of the terraced pyramid, covered with such a wealth of ornament as no other one structure in the world presents. The first near view is almost disappointing. In the blur of details it is difficult to realize the vast proportions of this twelve-century-old structure—a pyramid the base platform of which is five hundred feet square, the first terrace walls three hundred feet square, and the final dome one hundred feet in height. Stripped of every kindly relief of vine and moss, every gap and ruined angle visible, there was something garish, raw, and almost disordered at the first glance, almost as jarring as newness, and the hard black-and-white effect of the dark lichens on the gray trachyte made it look like a bad photograph of the pile. The temple stands on a broad platform, and rises first in five square terraces, inclosing galleries, or processional paths, between their walls, which are covered on each side with bas-relief sculptures. If placed in single line these bas-reliefs would extend for three miles. The terrace walls hold four hundred and thirty-six niches or alcove chapels, where life-size Buddhas sit serene upon lotus cushions. Staircases ascend in straight lines from each of the four sides, passing under stepped or pointed arches the keystones of which are elaborately carved masks, and rows of sockets in the jambs show where wood or metal doors once swung. Above the square terraces are three circular terraces, where seventy-two latticed *dagobas* (reliquaries in the shape of the calyx or bud of the lotus) inclose each a seated image, seventy-two more Buddhas sitting in these inner, upper circles of Nirvana, facing a great dagoba, or final cupola, the exact function or purpose of which as key to the whole structure is still the puzzle of archæologists. This final shrine is fifty feet in diameter, and either covered a relic of Buddha, or a central well where the ashes of priests and princes were deposited, or is a form surviving from the tree-temples of the earliest, primitive East when nature-worship prevailed. The English engineers made an opening in the solid exterior, and found an unfinished statue of Buddha on a platform over a deep well-hole; and its head, half buried in debris, still smiles upon one from the deep cavern. M. Freidrich, in 'L'Extrême Orient' (1878), states that this top dagoba was opened in the time of the resident Hartman (1835), and that gold ornaments were found; and it was believed that there were several stories or chambers to this well, which reached to the lowest level of the structure. M. Désiré de Charnay, who spent an afternoon at Boro Boedor in 1878 in studying the resemblance of the pyramid temples of Java to those of Central America, believed this well-hole to be the place of concealment for the priest whose voice used to issue as a mysterious oracle from the statue itself.

A staircase has been constructed to the summit of this dagoba, and from it one looks down upon the whole structure as on a ground-plan drawing, and out over finely cultivated fields and thick palm-groves to the matchless peaks and the nearer hills that inclose this fertile valley of the Boro Boedor—'the very finest view I ever saw,' wrote Marianne North.

Three fourths of the terrace chapels and the upper dagobas have crumbled; hundreds of statues are headless, armless, overturned, missing; tees, or finials, are gone from the bell-roofs; terrace walls bulge, lean outward, and have fallen in long stretches; and the circular platforms and the processional paths undulate as if earthquake-waves were at the moment rocking the mass. No cement was used to hold the fitted stones together, and another Hindu peculiarity of construction is the entire absence of a column, a pillar,

'On the Second Terrace', one of Scidmore's evocative drawings of Borobudur. From E. R. Scidmore, *Java: The Garden of the East*, New York: Century, 1899.

or an arch. Vegetation wrought great ruin during its buried centuries, but earthquakes and tropical rains are working now a slow but surer ruin that will leave little of Boro Boedor for the next century's wonder-seekers, unless the walls are soon straightened and strongly braced.

All this ruined splendor and wrecked magnificence soon has an overpowering effect on one. He almost hesitates to attempt studying out all the details, the intricate symbolism and decoration lavished by those Hindus, who, like the Moguls, 'built like Titans, but finished like jewelers'. One walks around and around the sculptured terraces, where the bas-reliefs portray all the life of Buddha and his disciples, and the history of that great religion—a picture-Bible of Buddhism. All the events in the life of Prince Siddhartha, Gautama Buddha, are followed in turn: his birth and education, his leaving home, his meditation under Gaya's immortal tree, his teaching in the deer-park, his sitting in judgment, weighing even the birds in his scales, his death and entrance into Nirvana. The every-day life of the seventh and eighth century is pictured, too—temples, palaces, thrones and tombs, ships and houses, all of man's constructions, are portrayed. The life in courts and palaces, in fields and villages, is all seen there. Royal folk in wonderful jewels sit enthroned, with minions offering gifts and burning incense before them, warriors kneeling, and maidens dancing. The peasant plows the rice-fields with the same wooden stick and ungainly buffalo, and carries the rice-sheaves from the harvest-field with the same shoulder-poles, used in all the farther East to-day. Women fill their water-vessels at the tanks and bear them away on their heads as in India now, and scores of bas-reliefs show the unchanging customs of the East that offer sculptors the same models in this century. Half the wonders of that great three-mile-long gallery of sculptures cannot be recalled. Each round disclosed some more wonderful picture, some more eloquent story, told in the coarse trachyte rock furnished by the volcanoes across the valley. Even the humorous fancies of the sculptors are expressed in stone. In one rilievo a splendidly caparisoned state elephant flings its feet in imitation of the dancing-girl near by. Other sportive elephants carry fans and state umbrellas in their trunks; and the marine monsters swimming about the ship that bears the Buddhist missionaries to the isles have such expression and human resemblance as to make one wonder if those primitives did not occasionally pillory an enemy with their chisels, too. In the last gallery, where, in the progress of the religion, it took on many features of Jainism, or advancing Brahmanism, Buddha is several times represented as the ninth avatar, or incarnation, of Vishnu, still seated on the lotus cushion, and holding a lotus with one of his four hands. Figure after figure wears the Brahmanic cord, or sacrificial thread, over the left shoulder; and all the royal ones sit in what must have been the pose of high fashion at that time—one knee bent under in tailor fashion, the other bent knee raised and held in a loop of the girdle confining the sarong skirt. There is not a grotesque nor a nude figure in the whole three miles of sculptured scenes, and the costumes are a study in themselves; likewise the elaborate jewels which Maia and her maids and the princely ones wear. The trees and flowers are a sufficient study alone; and on my last morning at Boro Boedor I made the whole round at sunrise, looking specially at the wonderful palms, bamboos, frangipani-, mango-, mangosteen-, breadfruit-, pomegranate-, banana-, and bo-trees—every local form being gracefully conventionalized, and, as Fergusson says, 'complicated and refined beyond any examples known in India'. It is such special rounds that give one a full idea of what a monumental masterpiece the great Buddhist *vihara* is, what an epitome of all the arts and civilization of the eighth century AD those galleries of sculpture hold, and turn one to dreaming of the builders and their times.

No particularly Javanese types of face or figure are represented. All the countenances are Hindu, Hindu-Caucasian, and pure Greek; and none of the objects or accessories depicted with them are those of an uncivilized people. All the art and culture, the highest standards of Hindu taste and living, in the tenth century of triumphant Buddhism, are expressed in this sculptured record of the golden age of Java. The Boro Boedor sculptures are finer examples of the Greco-Buddhist art of the times than those of Amravati and Gandahara as one sees them in Indian museums; and the pure Greek countenances show sufficient evidence of Bactrian influences on the Indus, whence the builders came.

Of the more than five hundred statues of Buddha enshrined in niches and latticed dagobas, all, save the one mysterious figure standing in the central or summit dagoba, are seated on lotus cushions. Those of the terrace rows of chapels face outward to the four points of the compass, and those of the three circular platforms face inward to the hidden, mysterious one. All are alike save in the position of the hands, and those of the terrace chapels have four different poses accordingly as they face the cardinal points. As they are conventionally represented, there is Buddha teaching, with his open palm resting on one knee; Buddha learning, with that hand intently closed; Buddha meditating, with both hands open on his knees; Buddha believing and convinced, expounding the lotus law with upraised hand; and Buddha demonstrating and explaining, with thumbs and index-fingers touching. The images in the lotus bells of the circular platforms hold the right palm curved like a shell over the fingers of the left hand—the Buddha who has compre-hended, and sits meditating in stages of Nirvana. It was never intended that worshipers should know the mien of the great one in the summit chalice, the serene one who, having attained the supreme end, was left to brood alone, inaccess-ible, shut out from, beyond all the world. For this reason it is believed that this standing statue was left incomplete, the profane chisel not daring to render every accessory and attribute as with the lesser ones. . . .

When the British engineers came to Boro Boedor, in 1814, the inhabitants of the nearest village had no knowledge or traditions of this noblest monument Buddhism ever reared. Ever since their fathers had moved there from another district it had been only a tree-covered hill in the midst of forests. Two hundred coolies worked forty-five days in clearing away vegetation and excavating the buried terraces. Measurements and drawings were made, and twelve plates from them accompany Sir Stamford Raffles's work. After the Dutch recovered possession of Java, their artists and archæologists gave careful study to this monument of earlier civilization and arts. Further excavations showed that the great platform or broad terrace around the temple mass was of later construction than the body of the pyramid, that a flooring nine feet deep had been put entirely around the lower walls, presumably to brace them, and thus covering many inscriptions the meanings of which have not yet been given, not to English readers at least. Dutch scientists devoted many seasons to the study of these ruins, and Herr Brumund's scholarly text, completed and edited by Dr. Leemans of Leyden, accompanies and explains the great folio volumes of four hundred plates, after Wilsen's drawings, published by the Dutch government in 1874. Since their uncovering the ruins have been kept free from vegetation, but no other care has been taken. In this comparatively short time legends have grown up, local customs have become fixed, and Boro Boedor holds something of the importance it should in its immediate human relations. . . .

After the temple was uncovered the natives considered it a free quarry, and carried off carved stones for door-steps, gate-posts, foundations, and fences. Every visitor, tourist or antiquarian, scientist or relic-hunter, helped himself; and every residency, native prince's garden, and plantation lawn, far and near, is still ornamented with Boro Boedor's sculptures. In the garden of the Magelang Residency, Miss Marianne North found a Chinese artist employed in 'restoring' Boro Boedor images, touching up the Hindu countenances with a chisel until their eyes wore the proper Chinese slant. The museum at Batavia has a full collection of recha, and all about the foundation platform of the temple itself, and along the path to the passagrahan, the way is lined with displaced images and fragments, statues, lions, elephants, horses; the *hansa*, or emblematic geese of Buddhism; the *Garouda*, or sacred birds of Vishnu; and giant genii that probably guarded some outer gates of approach. A captain of Dutch hussars told Herr Brumund that, when camping at Boro Boedor during the Javanese war, his men amused themselves by striking off the heads of statues with single lance- or saber-strokes. Conspicuous heads made fine targets for rifle and pistol practice. Native boys, playing on the terraces while watching cattle, broke off tiny heads and detachable bits of carving, and threw them at one another; and a few such playful shepherds could effect as much ruin as any of the imaginary bands of fanatic Moslems or Brahmans. One can better accept the plain, rural story of the boy herders' destructiveness than those elaborately built up tales of the religious wars, when priests and people, driven to Boro Boedor as their last refuge, retreated, fighting, from terrace to terrace, hurling stones and statues down upon their pursuers, the last heroic believers dying martyrs before the summit dagoba. Fanatic Mohammedans in other countries doubtless would destroy the shrines of a rival, heretic creed; but there is most evidence in the history and character of the Javanese people that they simply left their old shrines, let them alone, and allowed the jungle to claim at its will what no longer had any interest or sacredness for them. To this day the Javanese takes his religion easily, and it is known that at one time Buddhism and Brahmanism flourished in peace side by side, and that conversion from one faith to the other, and back again, and then to Mohammedanism, was peaceful and gradual, and the result of suasion and fashion, and not of force. The old cults faded, lost prestige, and vanished without stress of arms or an inquisition.

E. R. Scidmore, *Java: The Garden of the East*, New York: Century, 1899; reprinted Kuala Lumpur: Oxford University Press, 1984, pp. 182–202.

6
Looking for the Ruins of Majapahit

HARRIET PONDER

Harriet Ponder was an Englishwoman who, moving to Java from Australia in the 1930s, 'fell in love with the place' and wrote two engaging books about it. Resisting the temptation to judge by appearances, she tried to learn as much as she could about local life, and wrote of many aspects of everyday Javanese life, as well as interesting herself in the history of the island. In this extract, she goes in search of the ruins of the great Hindu empire of Majapahit, which claimed authority over vassal states in Sumatra, the Malay Peninsula, Kalimantan, and East Indonesia during the thirteenth to fifteenth centuries. Majapahit also maintained diplomatic relations with Champa, Siam, Cambodia, southern Burma, and Vietnam, and sent missions to China. Both Buddhism and Hinduism were practised, syncretised somewhat in the cult of divine kingship, in which the king was regarded as 'Siwa-Buddha'. At the capital, great annual festivities were celebrated. In Javanese memory, Majapahit's greatness has never been forgotten, though, as Ponder's investigation shows, few material remains are to be found to bear witness to its former glory.

B UT most interesting of all these relics are those of Madjapahit, the greatest of the Hindu kingdoms that between them dominated Java for at least a thousand years, which is quite a chapter in a country's history when you reflect that it is as yet less than that since the Norman conquest of England! The actual remains of Madjapahit are sadly few and unimposing for the capital of a state which the records prove to have been of great wealth and importance. But the once great Hindu stronghold has left its mark in a curious fashion on the straggling *kampongs* that are now the only human habitations on the vast site it covered in its heyday. The builders of Madjapahit used brick rather than stone; and when the city had been sacked by its Mohammedan conquerors, and the temples and palaces abandoned or demolished, the peasants of the surrounding country, who crept back to their holdings when peace was restored, doubtless thought it a wicked waste that so many millions of bricks should be lying idle. That, at least, seems the most likely explanation of the fact that, instead of the split bamboo fences elsewhere universal in native villages throughout Java, here at Madjapahit all the compounds and gardens are enclosed by brick walls often further embellished with tall brick gateposts. These are set up without mortar, and are therefore very thick, so that the contrast between their solidity and the flimsy *bilik** houses behind them is oddly incongruous. Many of the irrigation ditches serving the surrounding ricefields are also lined with those same beautifully made bricks, all as sound and shapely as when they left their makers' hands anything from 500 to 1000 years ago.

The remains of Madjapahit are not very easy to find; and the stranger who follows the vague native directions given in response to inquiries is likely to take several wrong turnings before he discovers the byroad that leads from Trowelan, an inconspicuous *dessa* a few miles from the big modern sugar town of Modjerkerto. This road soon degenerates into a rough track; and it is here that the brick walls, by the mere incongruity of their existence in so obviously poor a place, attract attention, and offer their silent, incontestible evidence that this *kampong* is not quite as others are.

As my car bumped slowly along the uneven track, the inhabitants of the houses inside the brick walls came drifting out, as is the native way, full of curiosity to see what a stranger might be wanting here so far the main road; and in reply to my questions, and the offer of a cigarette, an unfailing key to Javanese good will, a dignified old man squatted himself on the running board and offered to show me the way. He took me first to a partly ruined red brick temple of much the same design as many of those in Bali, which latter in all probability were copied from those here, refugees from Madjapahit having fled to Bali when their country was overrun by conquerors. This temple, said my guide, was called Badjang Ratoe, and little was known about it; but he could show me better things if I would leave the car a little farther on and go afoot, for there was a stream ahead of us, and there the track ended. So to the end of the track we presently went, abandoned the car in the mud on the bank of the stream and, wading across, took to a slippery six inch path on the *bund* between two ricefields. Meanwhile I wondered as we slithered along whether in a few hundred years' time,

---

*bilik: woven bamboo.

perhaps, visitors from other lands might not be picking their precarious way along just such a path, guided by just such another *dessa* man, in search of the last traces of Batavia or Soerabaya! It is no more impossible, perhaps less so, than such an idea would have seemed to the inhabitants of Madjapahit in the fourteenth or fifteenth century, with a thousand years of power and glory behind them. Whereas the Dutch have been in Java less than 350 years, and their cities have been places of dignity and importance for little more than a century.

One of the earliest references to Hindu Java is contained in the *Chronicle of the Buddhist Monk Fa-Hian*,* who relates that he went in A.D. 400 overland from China to India and in A.D. 414 returned by sea via Ceylon, whence he set sail 'in a great ship with 200 persons on board, and a small ship in tow carrying provisions'. On the way they visited Java, which he calls 'Ya-vi-di', or 'Jawa-dwipa', and relates of it that 'all the people were of the Brahman religion, and he met only one or two Buddhists' on his travels through the country. Buddhism had therefore not yet gained the foothold it was destined to attain later; four centuries or so had yet to elapse after this Chinese monk's visit before the building of Boroboedoer.

It is to a Chinese source also, the records of the Yuan Dynasty, that we owe accounts of Kublai Khan's attacks on the coasts of Hindu Java in 1292 and 1293, at Soerabaya, Padjetan, and Toeban. The attempts at conquest were successful at first, but the enemy were beaten off eventually 'by the skill of the men of Madjapahit', who had 'great ships with Naga heads on the stem'. The same records contain many references to the importance and elaborate administration of Madjapahit, mentioning, among other interesting details, that good maps of the country were obtainable, and that there was a complete 'National Register' of the population! It is a little disconcerting to find that such a scheme was in full working order in a vanished Hindu state six or

*J. Legge (Oxford, 1886).

seven hundred years ago, which we have only now rather nervously organised in modern England!

However: *sic transit gloria mundi*. Madjapahit, once the centre and focal point of its Government Survey maps, is no longer even a name on ours. Lost among a maze of ricefields, located only through the good offices of a village native, the symmetrical sunken water temple towards which at last my guide waved a proud proprietary hand was indubitable proof of a splendid past, for it was worthy to be what legend claims for it, the bathing place of kings. Built on the plan beloved of Indian architects in their Golden Age, with intersecting squares and rectangles enclosing small square 'islands' carrying groups of miniature shrines, the enclosing walls rose from the water in projecting tiers, decorated with carved heads and floral designs. Parts of this outer wall were still quite perfect; in others they seemed to melt imperceptibly into the high grass bank that in its turn merged into the pattern of the surrounding fields, giving to this strange isolated relic of vanished glory a dreamlike unreality.

A sense of hallucination persists. Turn your back and walk ten paces away and this last tangible trace of Madjapahit has vanished; you are in the midst of the familiar ricefields, and it seems impossible that you should have seen anything so utterly irrational; turn back and there it lies: an elaborate, costly, carven bath, with decorated walls reflected in the gleaming water that they imprison, set in the midst of fields whose silvery surfaces mirror only the slim green spikes of newly planted rice: no more numerous, perhaps, than the human life that crowded the sites of these very fields only a few hundred years ago.

Harriet Ponder, *Javanese Panorama*, London: Seeley, Service & Co., 1942; reprinted Kuala Lumpur: Oxford University Press, 1990, pp. 238–41.

Cities and Towns

7

Floating Houses in Bangkok

JOHN THOMSON

John Thomson (1837–1921), an Edinburgh-born photographer, spent ten years of his life in South-East Asia and China. He travelled widely, recording everything that interested him. For three years he ran a photographic studio (one of the first) in Singapore, and subsequently in Hong Kong. These were very early days for photography, which, as Thomson himself recorded, was then 'an experiment not to be lightly undertaken', indeed the weight and bulk of the equipment, and the need to carry all the chemicals with one and develop glass plate negatives on the spot in a dark tent, by means of processes still primitive and difficult, must have added immeasurably to the challenge of journeys such as Thomson's. In spite of this he travelled to some very remote locations, including to Cambodia to photograph Angkor Wat, not to mention covering some 4,000–5,000 miles over four years in China. After his return to England, he remained to the end of his life an enthusiastic member of the Royal Geographical Society, campaigning vigorously to have explorers trained in photography, and becoming the Society's photography instructor in 1886. Besides his visual gift, Thomson wrote in a style both entertaining and informative about his experiences. The following anecdote not only gives us a vivid picture of life on the waterways of Bangkok, but also reveals some other unexpected South-East Asian hazards to the photographer.

IN Bangkok at least two-thirds of the native population pass their lives in their boats, or else in houses which float on the surface of the river. These floating houses are built upon platforms of bamboo, for the hard durable stems of this useful plant grow to great dimensions in that country, and offer special advantages in the construction of a raft. Thus the long hollow stem is divided naturally into a certain number of water-tight compartments, separated from each other by solid diaphragms of wood. The bamboo, too, will remain for a great length of time under water without deteriorating; and even should the stem by chance spring a leak in any one of its compartments, this still will not affect the buoyancy of the rest. It may have been from that fact alone that the Chinese derived the idea of building their boats in water-tight compartments. The bamboos of the foundation or raft are piled up one above the other, in longitudinal and transverse layers; these are then lashed together with ratan, and when sufficient buoyancy has been obtained to float the dwelling above, the platform is launched and moored in the stream. The raft, when moored, is fastened at each of the four corners to a strong pile which has been driven into the river bed for that purpose. The fastening consists of a loop of stout ratan rope, which will move or 'travel' freely up and down the pile, and thus the abode will rise or sink with the ebb and flow of the tide. When the raft has been got into position, the house is then erected above its surface, and may be constructed of teak-wood or bamboo, according to the taste or means of its proprietor. Not uncommonly the eaves, the windows, the panels, and the balustrading, are carved and varnished; often they are painted and gilt, so that they form highly picturesque objects on the water. As to the interior apartments, these are so comfortable and well arranged as to furnish a cool and suitable dwelling even to the most fastidious tastes. From a sanitary point of view these 'river dwellings' offer many advantages. Thus they do away with the need of a borough engineer, and the complicated systems of subterranean drainage which burden the rate-payers in

Europe. The Siamese, too, are much addicted to bathing, and like to have their water close at hand. These floating houses are generally moored close together in compact lines, and are difficult to deal with in case of fire—a calamity happily of rare occurrence. Not many years ago one of the houses in a long row having caught fire, the neighbours immediately cut it adrift, and let it go blazing down the stream. It was not long before it fouled a barque at her anchorage, and the latter was soon in flames and burnt to the water's edge. Floating houses are rather in the way of unskilful pilots, especially at points where the river narrows, and if the current is strong. I remember once lifting a part of the roof off one of these abodes with the bowsprit of a steamer. Two merchants, an engineer, and myself, having had a steam launch placed at our disposal, determined to visit the ancient capital of Ayuthia. We armed ourselves with a chart of the river, and took turn about at the helm, leaving the engines to the charge of our professional friend.

Things went on pretty smoothly during the first day, until at night we reached a district where the country was flooded, and it was difficult to keep to the main channel of the stream. About eight o'clock, when, of course, it was already dark, I found we were steering bow on for a green mount, which loomed up in the distance. By reversing the engines and altering the course we just cleared the obstacle, but having rounded and taken bearings, we discovered to our dismay that we were in the centre of a paddy (rice) field. Here we halted till daylight, and, enabled to regain the bed of the channel, soon after arrived in safety at our destination. Having examined the Kraal and the Sala or 'Grand Stand', whither the King repairs periodically to see the wild elephants driven in, and the most promising specimens secured, we took our way to the Royal Elephant Stables, where about a dozen of these huge animals are usually to be seen. Near to the river a splendid buffalo cow was feeding tethered to a stake, and with a calf at her heels; she looked up fixedly and steadily at the white faces of our party; so steadily, that I determined to photograph her. But the sight of the camera, and the mysterious dark tent, disgusted the brute more than ever, and she began to assume a disagreeably threatening look. 'Now,' I said, 'let one of you open out your umbrella suddenly, just as I am about to photograph, and we shall have an attitude of surpassing grandeur.' One of my friends, therefore, cautiously approached her and fired off his umbrella. This was too much for the buffalo, and, with a wild toss of her head, she broke the rope, and I just got a glimpse of her in full career, as she charged in the direction of her aggressors. The next moment I found that the owner of the umbrella had tumbled into an elephant midden, and though in a disagreeable position, was safe from harm. As for my China boy, he had consigned himself to the river, and only consented to crawl out of his place of refu ɜe on being informed that a huge alligator was at his heels. We started for home shortly after, and came down beautifully with the flood, but the steering required constant attention; and, finally, at a most unfortunate conjuncture, when we were just entering the city of Bangkok, we lost all command of the helm; the steamer would not steer; first she stuck her nose into the reeds on the bank, then she turned round with the flood, came out again into mid-channel, and at last crossed to the opposite shore, and carried the roof away from the floating house aforesaid. When we had leisure to look for the cause of this strange behaviour, we found that the steering-chain had got displaced. Things were put to rights at last, and we reached the jetty without further disaster.

John Thomson, *The Straits of Malacca, Siam and Indo-China*, London: Sampson Low, Marston, Low and Searle, 1875; reprinted Singapore, Oxford University Press, 1993, pp. 103–7.

8

Walks in Phnom Penh and Saigon (1871–2)

FRANK VINCENT

Frank Vincent (1848–1916) was the son of a wealthy Brooklyn merchant. He seems to have been one of those not infrequent adventurers of the nineteenth century who were virtual invalids at home, but displayed amazing stamina as soon as they departed on their travels. Escape from the restricting confines of respectable life at home must have had an exhilarating effect on their constitutions. Vincent, who had to leave Yale after two terms because of ill health, went on to cover an astonishing 355,000 miles over the next fifteen years as he travelled through Japan, China, South-East Asia, Scandinavia, South and Central America, and Africa, armed with his sketch book and camera. If he shared, inevitably, some of the ethnocentric prejudices of his day, he generally responded warmly to the people he met and the hospitality extended to him. He wrote many popular books and papers, and became a member of twenty scientific and literary societies. Vincent was in South-East Asia during 1871–2, as part of a world tour. He dined with governors and had audiences with kings (in Burma the King of Ava viewed him through a pair of binoculars and accused him of spy-. ing), visited Angkor Wat, and cooked for himself on a boat down the Tonle Sap from there to Phnom Penh. When he visited it, Phnom Penh was still a one-street town of bamboo houses, its one impressive feature the new palace built by King Norodom. Saigon too had only recently come under French control, and was comparatively undeveloped, the brand new Government House presenting a sharp contrast in scale and grandeur to the rest of the city.

ONE day we walked down the main road, past the palace, and turning to the west, soon found ourselves at the embankment which bounds *Panompin* [Phnom Penh] on that side, and although but a stone's throw from the most thickly inhabited part of the city, still so dense were the banana and cocoa-nut trees that not a house was visible. The parapet of earth is about fifteen feet high, and the same in width, being faced on both outer and inner sides with large bamboo sticks. Upon it are erected the telegraph poles and the wire which runs from the *Protecteur's* house here to Saigon; there is a branch line from the former to the palace, so that any *surplus* information or *proper* (i.e. for the King to know) news may be sent to His Majesty. But few houses stand without the embankment, and not more than a quarter of a mile distant is the virgin forest.

In rear of the centre of the city, upon a high artificial mound, stands a very old pagoda, some image-houses, small temples, and tombs. The pagoda is the only one at Panompin, and is in most wretched condition. In one of the image-houses was an immense gilded Budha, with mother-of-pearl eyes and finger nails; in another was the large gilded figure of a king, and a lofty four-sided shrine, containing four little Budhas. The pagoda and the great mound were built of diminutive bricks; from the summit of the latter an excellent view of that part of the river upon the opposite bank, including the custom house and the great Makong river, may be had. There are but two or three priests in charge of the old pagoda; in fact, there are but few priests and temples in Panompin, though the religion here—the Budhist—is the same as that professed by the Siamese. In the evening we went to the palace—there is a stand for musicians near the entrance—to hear the King's brass band. A selection of lively dance music, concluding with the Cambodian National Hymn, was played by the band—Manilla men—of fourteen piece.

Early on one morning of my stay at Panompin, Miriano, the interpreter, called to offer his services for a visit to some of the public and royal buildings within the palace enclosure. We first looked in at some of the machine shops, where, with French overseers, natives were working a saw-mill and a brass turning-lathe, and where there were forges for making metal vessels and musical instruments. Directly before the palace building is the private office of the King, a handsomely furnished little room where His Majesty receives all visitors on business; behind it are the reception halls, in process of erection and nearly completed. These buildings, built of brick, with tiled roofs and gaily ornamented in the Siamese style, are quite imposing.

The ambassadors' grand audience hall is a room a hundred feet in length, forty in width, and thirty in height, and extending through its entire length are two rows of massive square pillars; the ceiling is to be finished in blue and gold. Not far from this magnificent building is the supreme court—a *sala* open upon three sides, and having at one end, for the King's use, an elegant sofa, attached to which was a patent breechloading rifle and a Cambodian spear, to be used by His Majesty in case of emergency or necessity for self-protection. There exists what is called 'a board of judges', but no case of importance can be tried without the presence of the King, from whose decision there is no appeal. Near and parallel to the supreme court is the royal theatre—a large shed open upon three sides, the floor covered with mats, and with a miserably painted scene at one end, though it is not here that the plays are performed, as with us, a narrow gallery just beneath the roof being reserved for the *lacon* (theatricals); a *sala* near by is set apart for the ladies of the harem.

There are several small brick houses within the palace enclosure—the residences of princes, brothers of the King, and some of the higher nobles. In the barracks were about two hundred stand of arms—breech-loaders with sword-bayonets attached. In the King's stables there were three carriages—a barouche, a rockaway, and a buggy—not in very good repair—and a dozen or more horses. Among the latter were two beautiful greys, presented by H.I.M. Napoleon III. It is seldom that the King rides out, owing to the very important desideratum of properly constructed roads.

As previously stated, Panompin has but recently been made a seat of government; until within three or four years Oodong has been the capital of the kingdom of Cambodia. In 1860 M. Mouhot, the French naturalist, visited Oodong, and thus writes of its appearance, which corresponds with that of Panompin at the present day in many respects: 'On

approaching the capital the prospect becomes more diversi-
fied; we passed fields of rice, cottages encircled by fruit
gardens, and country houses belonging to the Cambodian
aristocracy, who come here in the evening for the sake of
breathing a purer air than they can find in the city. As we
drew closer to the gates I found the place to be protected by
a palisade three mètres high. The houses are built of bamboo
or planks, and the market-place, occupied by the Chinese, is
as dirty as all the others of which I have made mention. The
largest street, or rather the only one, is a mile in length; and
in the environs reside the agriculturists, as well as the mandarins and other Government officers. The entire population
numbers about 12,000 souls [in 1860].

'The many Cambodians living in the immediate vicinity,
and still more the number of chiefs who resort to Oodong
for business or pleasure, or are passing through it on their way
from one province to another, contribute to give animation
to the capital. Every moment I met mandarins, either borne
in litters or on foot, followed by a crowd of slaves carrying
various articles; some yellow or scarlet parasols, more or less,
according to the rank of the person; others, boxes with betel.
I also encountered horsemen mounted on pretty, spirited
little animals, richly caparisoned and covered with bells,
ambling along, while a troop of attendants, covered with dust
and sweltering with heat, ran after them. Light carts, drawn
by a couple of small oxen, trotting along rapidly and noisily,
were here and there to be seen. Occasionally a large elephant
passed majestically by. On this side were numerous processions to the pagoda, marching to the sound of music; there,
again, was a band of ecclesiastics in single file, seeking alms,
draped in their yellow cloaks, and with the holy vessels on
their backs.'

* * *

Saigon, captured by the French in 1861, and added to
their dominions, together with six provinces of Lower
Cochin China placed by treaty under a French protectorate,

is situated upon the right bank of the river of the same name, about twenty-five miles from the sea. From Chalen a large creek runs to the Saigon river, joining it about the centre of the city. The approach to Saigon is through an immense forest of the betel and cocoa-nut palm, banana and bamboo trees, and thick copses of others with names unknown, save to the professed naturalist. The first impressions one receives of the town are not at all flattering to its appearance. The only object that attracts the attention is a large three-storey brick building on the bank of the river, at one the town hall and an hotel. In the river, which is here not more than five hundred feet in width, are anchored several small French gunboats—intended for up-country service most of them— and, besides these, there are usually two or three large steamers in port (either one of the 'Messageries', or an English Hong Kong 'liner', or one running to Singapore and Penang, or the war vessel of some foreign power); farther down the river are anchored sometimes as many as twenty merchantmen, mostly of five to eight hundred tons burden and flying the flags of either France or Germany.

There are in Saigon very many hotels, or more properly speaking *cafés*, at which the most of the French residents appear to live. These *cafés* are not scrupulously clean; still one may obtain a modest room and fair meals at reasonable charges. The population—ten thousand at a guess—consists of Cochin Chinese, Chinese, Malabars, and French troops, civilians, and a few Europeans of other nationalities. Public affairs are administered by a Governor appointed by the Emperor and sent out from France, and assisted by a Legislative and Executive Council. The streets of Saigon are broad, and macadamised with brick (which makes a very disagreeable dust); in two of them, which run at right angles to the river, are stone canals for the more convenient loading and unloading of the small cargo boats of the country. The street which runs parallel and next to the river is lined with double rows of trees. Here, after sundown, it is the custom of the residents to promenade, while listening to the music of one of the regimental bands. The streets are lighted by oil lamps, and are drained by extensive gutters at the sides. There are no public squares, but there is a small botanical garden, tastefully laid out, but not kept in the best order; in it are some wild animals, among them two fine large tigers, captured in Cambodia.

The public buildings are few in number and not particularly grand in design or elegant in construction, with perhaps the exception of the Government House, recently completed. It is built of brick and stucco, is two storeys in height—about three hundred feet in length by one hundred in depth—and is situated in the centre of a large cleared space on the southern side of the town. The compartments of the interior embrace an elegantly plastered ball-room, rooms for the different offices of Government, an observatory, &c., with marble staircases and balustrades, laid floors, and frescoed ceilings. The appearance, however, of this elegant modern palace, with its grand staircases and pillars, which would appear to advantage in London or Washington, in the midst of a tropical jungle and surrounded only by a few bamboo huts is most droll. In one part of Saigon is a large nunnery and chapel inclosed by a lofty wall; there are also many small Roman Catholic chapels.

The European business houses are few in number— America not being represented—and trade is anything but brisk. As usual, the real life of the town is maintained by the Chinese, who do the work, keeping small shops of miscellaneous goods generally. . . .

In Saigon there are many schools for teaching Annamites the French language and the general rudiments of education; the children of Europeans are usually sent home to attend school. The army and navy at the disposal of the Governor-General is small, but sufficient to preserve order throughout the French provinces in Cochin China. There is an earthwork fortification at Saigon, which is garrisoned, I was told, by about three thousand men; it contains, moreover, a large quantity of provisions and war stores. The troops wear a blue blouse uniform with leather leggings and a white flat sun-hat (pith or cork); they are armed with breech-loading muskets and swordbayonets. The navy consists of ten or fifteen light-draught gun-boats (for river guards, and to transport troops to the various citadels throughout the country), the whole under the command of an admiral. The police system is very effective, Malays from Singapore having been enrolled and trained for that service.

Morals are at the low ebb usually found among Europeans in oriental towns—the French living at free quarters with Annamite girls, whom they puchase, when quite young, from their parents, $30 being considered a high price. The climate of Saigon is hot, being so near the equator, but it is generally considered healthy for temperately-living foreigners; the diseases are those incidental to the tropics everywhere—fevers, dysenteries, and cholera in its various stages. The French language is of course that in common use by all Europeans and even by the Annamites, who learn to speak it without much difficulty.

Frank Vincent, Jun., *The Land of the White Elephant: Sights and Scenes in Burma, Siam, Cambodia, and Cochin-China*, London: Sampson Low, Marston, Low and Searle, 1873; reprinted Bangkok: White Lotus, 1988, pp. 289–94 and 306–12.

9

Impressions of Luang Prabang in the 1860s

LOUIS DE CARNE

A member of the French Commission for the Exploration of the Mekong River (1866–8), Louis de Carné's life was tragically cut short by his adventures, for he contracted a disease in Indo-China which killed him at the age of 27. His account of his experiences had to be published posthumously by his father, who wrote as a preface a moving obituary to his son, describing how the 'putrid exhalations' of Laos had proved as fatal to him as to the great explorer Henri Mouhot a few years earlier, and to all the European missionaries who had ventured there. The object of this Expedition was to follow the Mekong to its source, with the aim of discovering whether it might prove a lucrative 'back door' trade route to South China. These hopes were unfulfilled, for fierce rapids make the river unnavigable. De Carné arrived in Luang Prabang in April of 1867, and has left us a charming account of it. After enduring great hardships, the team finally reached Yunnan in January 1868.

W E had at last come to a collection of houses and people meriting the name of a town. We had seen nothing like it since leaving Pnom-Penh. Without going the length of Mgr. Pallegoix, who sets down the population at eighty thousand, I am inclined to think M. Mouhot's estimate of seven or eight thousand a little under the mark. From the top of a knoll which serves for base to an elegant pyramid, you overlook a plain covered with thatched roofs, shaded by a forest of cocoa-trees. From this point, from which the eye embraces at once the whole panorama of the town, one hears the confused hum which rises from all centres of human activity, resembling, according to its intensity, the dull sound of waves dying on the beach; or, it may be, the hoarse roar of billows dashed upon the rocks by the storm. To the ear of the traveller, tired with vast solitudes, this confused murmur, in which all articulate words are lost, is a delicious harmony. The town of Luang-Praban, which is traversed for all its length by a great artery, parallel with the river, stretches along the two sides of a hill, bathed on one side by the Mekong, on the other, by the Nam-Kan. This little river throws itself into the great one by a sharp turn at the north-west end of the town. The side towards the Nam-Kan is not less peopled than that towards the Mekong. A crowd of filthy lanes abut on the principal street; some slope rapidly, or are made into stairs, and paved with brick, or even with blocks of rough marble, polished by the feet of the people. Macadamising is not altogether unknown. It is strange that the Laotioans have so wholly neglected to take advantage of the inexhaustible quarries of marble they have at hand, that when they have wished to use some in ornamenting, for example, the space before a pagoda, they should have thought of bringing it from Bangkok, to which, if we can credit a mandarin, who flattered himself that in giving us this detail he would excite our admiration, it had previously been brought from China.

Luang-Praban forms a kind of rectangle, which is bounded on three sides by running water. The fourth is shut in by a wall with five gates, which extends from the Nam-Kan to the Mekong. At the point where this wall, hardly visible under the growth which buries it, joins the great river, a little sanctuary, on the very bank, white, with a round roof attracts attention: it protects the footprints of Bouddha impressed on a rock. . . .

From the river-bank where he left the mark of one of his feet, the heavenly traveller, in visiting Luang-Praban, set down the other on the top of a little knoll, adorned now, in memory of the fact, with an elegant pavilion supported on ten pillars. The roof is covered with coloured tiles, and edged with bells which tinkle in the wind: the sacred footstep is in a grotto, at its side, and is covered with leaves of gold. From this picturesque spot, which is reached by a very steep stair, the view is magnificent. On one hand, stretch the great river and the mountains which border it; a gap in the mass of the first range lets the eye lose itself over distant undulations bathed in mist; nearer, you see the thatched roofs of the houses, and the tiles of the pagodas, the trees with waving plumes, and the tops of some pyramids; on the other side, the eye ranges along the valley of the Nam-Kan, which runs at the foot of the bluff, separating a great faubourg, planted, like the rest, with cocoas and palms, from the town.

It was on the banks of the Nam-Kan, not far from the village of Ban-Napao, that the king of Luang-Praban caused the body of M. Mouhot, who had come there six years before, and had died of fever, to be buried. This traveller had made himself beloved by the natives, who still hold his memory in respect; and the king himself paid a last homage to it, by furnishing, at his own cost, the material for a modest monument, which we raised over the tomb of our brave countryman. . . .

The pagodas are numerous at Luang-Praban, and there is some variety in the architecture. Each has a bonzery, and the yellow dress abounds in the streets. They are well supported; sometimes decorated richly, and not without taste. In one I admired an altar incrusted with blue glass, in imitation of enamel: on the blue ground, pleasantly lighted by the soft rays of evening, a rose in relief, full blown, with gilt petals, spread itself. In another pagoda, which rested on magnificent columns of wood, and was nearly circular, two of the most beautiful elephant tusks that could be imagined have been placed near the principal statue. The chord of the arc formed by these huge weapons of defence is a metre and seventy-six centimetres across. As a rule, gilding and vermilion are lavished on the ceilings and the pillars, and the altar is heaped up with so many statuettes and ornaments that it might be taken for a shopkeeper's display.

The services seemed regularly observed, and I was often present at the evening ones in the pagoda nearest our camp. The faithful, on their knees before a great statue of Bouddha, listened, with the attitude of meditation, to the prayers read by a bonze, giving the responses, themselves, at long intervals. Lighted tapers illuminated the building; sweetsmelling canes burned at the feet of the god; and a charming lacework of flowers, woven each day by the women and children, a perfumed and beautiful drapery, hung before the altar. The ceremony ended commonly with some notes of music: the women beat a small bronze timbrel; then went out to the porch, laid flowers on some sacred stones, and watered them, as they murmured their prayers. Not seldom they mingled grains of rice with the flowers; and I noticed that the poultry of the neighbourhood, into whom, perhaps, the soul of some bonzes, dead in a state of sin, had passed, had retained from their former existence a very exact remembrance of the hour of the offering. Besides the daily offices, the Laotians have also periodical fêtes, at some of which we had already been present. Those of spring, which we had seen begin at Paclaï, were celebrated at Luang-Praban with a noisy solemnity, in keeping with the size of the town and the number of the population. Naturally, young people take the greatest part in them. During the day, while the overpowering heat lasts, all is dull, for the Laotians themselves suffer by the sun; but hardly has this redoutable foe to pleasure disappeared behind the mountains of the right bank of the Mekong, than the air is full of din, from bursts of laughter and wild songs, to which the dogs add their voices. I had the curiosity to look on from a distance at these nocturnal rejoicings. The white light of the moon threw silver tints on the porticoes of the pagodas, on the pyramids, on the thatched roofs; the cocoas, the palms, and the light leaves of the clumps of bamboos defined themselves sharply against the clear sky; and though no perceptible air came to stir the atmosphere, the whole trembled before me like a dream, without my being able to seize the moving outlines of this magic picture.

Louis de Carné, *Travels in Indo-China and the Chinese Empire*, London: Chapman and Hall, 1872, pp. 149–53.

10

The Straits Settlements at the Turn of the Century

FRANK SWETTENHAM

When Frank Swettenham first embarked for Singapore as a young Straits Civil Service cadet in 1870, he travelled in an old second-hand paddle steamer which took over two months to make the journey. He rose rapidly to hold a series of senior posts in the western Malay States, eventually retiring as Governor of the Straits

Settlements in 1904. One of several outstanding figures in the colonial history of Malaya, he has been depicted as an egocentric and at times arrogant personality, but one who was undeniably charming. A man of his times, with an unquestioned faith in the British imperialist mission, he nevertheless claimed a strong sympathy with the Malays. He spoke Malay fluently, lived closely with the people, and developed a very deep knowledge of western Malaya. He had a considerable literary gift, and his collections of short stories, which draw on his experiences, reveal his affection for Malay people. *British Malaya*, his own account of the 'Residential System' he had helped to create, includes the following vividly impressionistic pictures of arrival at the three towns which formed the Straits Settlements (Penang, Malacca and Singapore)—an arrival by sea, which travellers of today rarely experience—and conveys something of the distinctive character of each of them.

W HAT strikes the traveller, as his ship rounds the northern end of Pinang, is the extraordinary beauty of the scene to which he is introduced with almost startling suddenness. On his right is the island, a vision of green verdure, of steep hills rising from the water's edge till they culminate in a peak 2500 ft. high. The sides of these hills are partly forest, partly cultivated, but everywhere green, with the freshness and colour of tropical vegetation washed by frequent rains. About the hills, at varying heights, are picturesque buildings nestling amongst the trees or standing on outcrops of grey rock. Down by the shore—a fascinating in-and-out shore of little sandy bays and little rocky promontories—there is a deep belt of palms, shading but not altogether concealing quantities of brown cottages. Then a broad ribbon of sand, sometimes dazzlingly white, sometimes streaked, or wholly tinted, with burnt sienna; and so the sea, a very wonderful summer sea, blue or grey or pale gold, under different conditions of sunlight, often chequered by great purple and indigo cloud shadows. Along the beach lie boats and nets set out to dry; black nets and brown nets, of immense length, stretched on a framework of poles; quaint objects and infinitely picturesque, but not more so than the fishing stakes, the upper half of which stand above the water, many fathoms from the shore, on the edge of every sand bank. That is what you see as you round the north foreland, by the loftily-placed lighthouse; and then, in a moment, there is the town, and the ship seems to be running into its main street. The white buildings and red roofs, which house a hundred thousand people, crammed closely together on the flat tongue of land that stretches, from the foot of Pinang Hill, right out into the Strait which divides it from the mainland, just as though the island were ever trying to get its foot back on to the opposite shore. And when the red roofs cease to catch the eye as a mass, they twinkle at you, here and there, from out the foliage of garden and orchard, till all is merged in green and purple against the background of that great hill.

Close in shore, beside the busy quays, are hundreds and hundreds of strange craft, a very forest of masts and rigging rising from acres of fantastically coloured hulls, of every form and every nationality the Further East produces. There are Chinese junks, small and great, with painted eyes on their low, narrow bows, and quaint erections on their high, wide sterns; there are Malay schooners, and fast boats, and fishing boats, things so small and so crank that only an amphibious creature, like the Malay, would trust himself in them. There are huge, unwieldy cargo boats, manned by natives of Southern India, and propelled by immense heavy sweeps when there is no wind to fill their single square sail. There are wicked-looking Bugis vessels from Celebes, low in the water, with black hulls, fine lines, brown canvas or yellow palm-leaf sails; clumsy old craft from Sumatra and the Malay States; Chinese junks, piled high with firewood or palm thatch; long rakish Chinese fishing boats, loaded with dark brown nets; scores and scores of every eastern boat that swims, navigated by black and brown and yellow men, in every kind of dress and undress known from Japan to Jeddah.

These form the inner line, five or six boats deep, stretching as far south as the eye can reach. Then there are steam launches, of every colour and size, and every degree of cleanliness or dirtiness, rushing or crawling about the harbour, some full of passengers, some empty; while a few ride silently at anchor, here and there, amongst the crowd of small coasting steamers, which puff and squeal arrive or depart, take or discharge cargo, or simply rest between two voyages. And last the outer line, where, in midstream, a few large steamers and sailing vessels strain at cables. But,

> There is another shore, upon the other side,

the shore of Province Wellesley, distant from the nearest point of Pinang, about two miles. Far to north and far to south, an endless grove of palm trees fringes the strip of yellow sand, which is sometimes land and sometimes sea. Behind the palms are acres of rice fields, villages, hamlets, and isolated huts; then low hills, forest, and higher hills; range upon range in ever rising steps, till the eye loses count in heat waves, mist, and distance. Nearly due north, a little inland, and distant about thirty-five miles, stands the sharp peak of Gunong Jerai, five thousand feet high. Almost in a line with this mountain, some hazily-blue islands seem to swim on the surface of the sea. Looking south, the coast line of Pinang curves, crescent-wise, to its extreme point, and in the land-locked space of water are islands, large and small, clad like the rest in green. What is called the South Channel is not often used now except by coasting steamers, but the approach to Pinang is even more attractive by this route than by the North Channel. The beauty of the place comes more gradually, sinks deeper into the appreciation, and leaves a picture of form and colour, a sensation of real warmth and real life, which only the East can offer. This feeling will be intensified if the traveller is fortunate enough to see what I have tried to describe under the glamour of a moonlit night.

Yet the pride of Pinang is the Hill, and those who reach the summit will not regret the effort. Looking westward, the eye travels over a wide expanse of jungle—covered slopes, and foot hills, pierced by narrow cultivated valleys, till it rests on the 'measureless expanse of ocean'. One may gaze for hours, fascinated by the ever-changing effects of sunlight and shadow playing on the mirror of the sea. Northward lie the islands, coast, and sharply outlined peak of Kĕdah; while to the south are lower ranges of the main hill, the rice fields and the sinuous coast line of Pinang. Due west is the ship-board view reversed, only softened by height and distance. There are the woods, with their half-hidden dwellings, heading up to a flat but ever-narrowing plain, completely covered by white, red-roofed buildings, broken here and there by groups of dark trees. Then the shining stretch of water, carrying its burden of ships and boats, the smaller craft looking like queer black insects; and last, the long coast line of Province Wellesley, with its palms and rice fields and winding rivers, the whole bounded by successive ranges of blue hills, the most distant summits lost in clouds.

Seventy miles south are just visible some islands off the coast of Pêrak, and the traveller who means to see Malacca, and prefers a journey by ship to one by rail, will appreciate their beauty on closer inspection. Mail steamers do not call at Malacca, so the voyage from Pinang, about two hundred and fifty miles, must be made in some humbler vessel. She will probably reach the roadstead before dawn, and the passenger will have the advantage of landing at the ancient port in the early morning. Even small vessels cannot get within less than two or three miles of the shore, and whilst covering that distance in a launch or more probably a Malacca boat, the visitor will first be struck by the curious spectacle of a town with its legs in the sea. The reason is that the houses which face the main street of Malacca have their backs to the shore, and the space between road and sea is so narrow that the Chinese, who love deep, narrow houses, have built out over the water; this end of the building being supported upon high pillars of a peculiar red stone called laterite. The effect is strange but picturesque, and from the Malacca River, where Albuquerque and his men performed such deeds of valour, to the northern end of the town, every house on the sea side of the long main street has one foot on land and one in the sea.

On the south side of the river, and close to it, is the landing-place; further south still, a long pier with the end still in very shallow water. Beyond the fact that a sea-wall protects a broad strip of close green turf, with great ansenna trees planted at intervals along its edge, while a small hill, crowned by the ruins of an ancient church, shows well above the trees, there is nothing particular to be seen from the boat. Quite near the landing-place, and close to the left bank of the river, is the old Dutch Stadt House, a very solid old world building, approached by flights of steps. The house is built round a square, stone-paved courtyard, with a double flight of stone steps leading up to the side of the hill, on the summit of which are the walls of the roofless old Portuguese church. There is also on this hill the house of the Resident Councillor of Malacca, with a most attractive garden of very ancient date. The view from the hill is enchanting, whether one looks southward over the orchards and villages to Gunong Lêdang, called Mount Ophir, or westward to the hill which has been appropriated by the Chinese as their fashionable burying-place; or over the dark red roofs of Malacca town, across the rice-fields and cocoanut groves to Cape Rachado in the north. Drive along any road in Malacca and you can feast your eyes on a picture which is typical of cultivated Malaya at its best. On either hand there will be rice fields: emerald green when newly planted, golden with ripe grain, or brown when fallow. These are studded by topes of lofty palms shading a few brown huts. The distance is always shut in by hills of a marvellous blue. But of all roads the most lovely is that which runs along the very edge of the coast, passing through palm groves and villages, with vistas of rice fields and blue hills on one side and on the other spaces of water, green or blue, grey or blood-red, molten silver or black, under the varying conditions of sunlight and shadow, of eastern day or eastern night. There are no Malay villages, no country scenes, more picturesque than those of Malacca; and if the visitor chances to meet a wedding party in bullock carts, or a Malay funeral procession; if he witnesses a fleet of fishing boats putting out at sunset, or homing at dawn; and has eyes to see and to appreciate the colours, the movement, the strange people with their strangely beautiful surroundings, the scene will live in his memory for all time.

Singapore is 120 miles south-east of Malacca, a few miles north of the southernmost point in Asia; the island stands sentinel at the narrow gate which divides the Straits of Malacca from the China Sea. A dozen ocean-going steamers pass into or out of its harbours every day, and most of these vessels call at no other port in the Straits. By good fortune, it commonly happens that, owing to the dangers of navigation in such narrow seas, one arrives at dawn and leaves at sunset. In either case, the most unobservant must be struck by a scene as beautiful as it is unusual. Long before making the Karîmun Islands (which are thirty-five miles from Singapore, on the right as you come from the west), the coast of the Malay Peninsula has been visible; a low coast covered by mangroves growing out into the water. Ten miles from the narrow entrance to the harbour the vessel passes between the mainland (and later the shores of Singapore) and a succession of small islands, which gradually converge till they seem to bar further progress. Just when the space of water has so narrowed that the forts and guns, on either side of the channel, become visible to the practised eye, the bow of the vessel swings to the left, through jade-green eddying waters, and she slowly forces her way along a channel so narrow that it will only just admit the safe meeting of two large steamers. Still there are islands, quantities of islands, large and small, but only large by comparison. They are covered with foliage, with gardens, with cool pleasant-looking bungalows, with barracks and other military buildings. Near the water the soil, where you can see it, is more red than brown, and the rocks, where they come through the soil, are much more red than grey. But the water is always green, and clear, and swirling; it looks and is very deep, and the foliage of the islands is repeated on its surface, in dark green reflections. Then the passage widens somewhat, the shore of Singapore becomes one interminable line of wharves, against which lie an almost unbroken chain of ships, flying every known flag, but mostly the red ensign of Britain. The wharves, the warehouses, the docks, the coal-sheds, seem parts of some gigantic manhive, where men of every colour, in every conceivable garb, load and unload, gather and stack and store, every imaginable human production, from locomotives and lanterns, to mail bags and matches, pianos and pickaxes. Behind the ships, and wharves, and docks, and warehouses are roads, with a ceaseless traffic of people, carts, and carriages; then villages and green hills, chequered by houses and gardens. Across the waterway there are still islands, far as the eye can reach; but they are curving seawards, and whilst those nearest are covered, or partly covered, by buildings and chimneys, or groups of Malay huts straggling off the land right out into the water, as though they had walked there on stilts, there are others green with pineapples or jungle, and others still, away in the distance, like opals on the shining surface of the water. It is a thousand to one that the vessel, which brings the stranger from a distance, will tie up alongside the wharves, and he will then enter the town by a drive along a dusty, crowded road. The more excellent way is that of the small steamer which, skirting the long line of wharves, makes for the roads and gives the traveller the best and most comprehensive view of the Lion City, Queen of Far Eastern Seas.

Between the docks and the town, a bold headland, crowned by a battery, juts out into the water, and forms the southern horn of a crescent which embraces the whole city; till the land curves round to a far distant point, where a thick grove of palms faintly indicates the northern horn. Singapore from the Roads is very fair to see. From Mount Palmer (the fortified headland), to the Singapore River—that is, about one-third of the crescent—there is an unbroken mass of buildings, shining and white, facing the sea. The next third is green with grass and trees, through which are caught glimpses of public buildings and the spires of churches, backed by low hills, on one of which, in the distance, stands white and stately the Governor's residence. The remaining third is again covered by closely packed houses, seen indistinctly through a forest of masts. The space enclosed by the beach and a line drawn from horn to horn of the crescent, would contain about 1500 acres of water, and that is the real harbour of Singapore. Native craft, mainly Chinese junks, great and small, with hundreds of other vessels of every form, and size, and rig, lie crowded together in the northern half, while the southern half is occupied by numbers of small coasting steamers. Outside, in the deeper water, four or five miles from shore, is the man-of-war anchorage. As for launches and cargo boats, fishing boats, passenger boats, and pleasure yachts, their name is legion, and their goings to and fro, day and night, are ceaseless. The Singapore river is so tightly packed with hundreds of small craft that it is difficult enough to preserve a fairway to admit of passage. On shore it is the same; the place is seething with life, and, to the unaccustomed eye, the vehicles to be met with in the streets are almost as strange as the boats in the harbour; while such a medley of nationalities, such a babel of languages, surely finds no parallel in all the world. Of colour and life there is enough to satisfy the greediest; of heat and dust and strange smells there are usually too much for the western visitor. Only the extraordinary novelty of the scene, the wonderful colouring, the unusual interest, will banish every other feeling—for a time.

Each of the three Settlements, which together form the Straits Colony, has attractions of its own, peculiar to itself, though all have much in common. Pinang has its hill, with that glorious view, and it also has Province Wellesley, where one can see the Malay and his rice fields, but not quite as they are to be found in Malacca. There is a romance of age, of experience, of a full life lived, which remains with Malacca to-day as the heritage of her history. Malacca has drifted out of the stream of endeavour, away from the struggle for riches and greatness. She has drifted into the back waters of Time, and her attractions, for the dreamer, the lover of beauty and the student, may be greater than those of her sisters. Singapore has a history too, far more significant than and as full of thrilling incident as that of Malacca; but of her former glory not a trace is left, not a stone remains to recall her ancient greatness, and little more than tradition to establish the fact that it ever existed. Yet it did exist, seven or eight hundred years ago, and perhaps not then for the first time; and to-day it has come again, with new life, to flourish as never before. No stranger will approach this far eastern fortress, these wharves, and docks, and coalsheds, weaving stories of its long-forgotten past; his eyes will glean unmeasured delight from the rich colours of ever-changing landscape and seascape, the countless islands and the wonderful harbour, half circled by a sunlit shore. But his mind will carry away an impression foreign to the east, a sense of hurry, of movement, of boats driven fast through the water, by steam or sail, of straining oars propelling deep-laden barges, of bustling crowds jostling each other in the streets, of white and yellow, brown and black men, intent on something that matters, that makes for money. That is the new Singapore, where the traveller and his kind are the only idlers.

Frank Swettenham, *British Malaya: An Account of the Origin and Progress of British Influence in Malaya*, London, 1906; reprinted London: George Allen and Unwin, 1948, pp. 2–11.

11
Kuala Lumpur at the Turn of the Century

NG SEO BUCK

Ng Seo Buck was born in Swatow, China in 1893, and came to Kuala Lumpur at the age of nine. He was educated at the Victoria Institution, where he subsequently became a teacher in 1910. During the 1920s he became Headmaster of Kajang High School, and from 1948 worked for Radio Malaya as Liason Officer for

Schools. Looking back, at the time this article was written, the author recalls half a century of change in a city that was still in its infancy when he first arrived in it. A number of the streets he mentions still exist but have been renamed since that period. The High Street (probably the oldest street in town) is now called Jalan Tun H. S. Lee, Foch Avenue is now Jalan Cheng Lock, Rodger Street is Jalan Hang Kasturi, Market Street is Leboh Pasar Besar, Batu Road is now Jalan Tuanku Abdul Rahman, while the Padang has become Merdeka Square.

I arrived in this town in April, 1902. I can never forget my emotions when I first came here. Coming as I did from a two-thousand-year-old backward village in China, in my boyish mind, I had a sensation akin to that of John Keats when he first looked into Chapman's Homer.

Cities, like people, have their individualities. Some are commonplace and soon forgotten; others make a striking impression on even the passing stranger. Although what pleases one often fails to interest another, the majority of travellers agree that the older buildings and more massive structures of a city—its temples, churches, mosques, theatres —have a most attractive personality. Some have fallen into decay, some have become obscured from public view owing to changes in town planning. Indeed, there must be something lacking in a man, who, after living in Kuala Lumpur for fifty years, cannot retain in his memory, vivid pictures of some of the major changes in the metropolis.

The first landmark of this town—the K.L. Railway Station was not as majestic looking as it is today. The impressive Railway Offices were not there when I first came to K.L., nor was Sulaiman Building. Hotel Majestic was not even dreamed of. Sulaiman Bridge did not exist. The Klang River, which it spans, was not running in its present bed. This was the result of deviation for purposes of averting floods which, before the deviation of the river, were a yearly occurrence. In its natural course the Klang River flowed round the back of the Technical College in High Street. A stranger to the city ought to be told that the Technical College was the original home of the Victoria Institution. At the far end of the playing field stood the Headmaster's house. The house has been demolished now. It laid the scene of Somerset Maugham's novel 'Under The Casuarina Tree' which was later adapted as a film.

What is now the Central Police Station in High Street used to be the offices of the Chinese Protectorate with the first floor used as quarters for the interpreters.

Lee Rubber Building was then the site of the Capitan China's garden with his Court of Justice adjoining it. The shop houses opposite were the residence of the Capitan China and his seven or eight wives. There was no through traffic in High Street in those days. What is now Foch Avenue was the railway track on which Singapore mail trains were run. At one and the same time, if a train happened to pass, traffic in Rodger Street, High Street, Petaling Street and Sultan Street was held up by railway gates. Luckily traffic in those days was not heavy—a few rickshas, a few bicycles and perhaps one or two horse gharries on either side of the railway gates.

Another landmark of the town is the Chinese temple in High Street. Hemmed in on all sides by shop houses in High Street, Pudu Street and Rodger Street this temple, known as Soo Ya Miow, is now obscured from view. Before the shop houses were built, it would catch the eye of even the most sophisticated visitor. Once in seven years a grand thanks-offering service was held here. Kuala Lumpur was then on holiday, especially for those who had faith in the many wooden idols within the temple. Kowtowing to these monuments created by a mind destitute of cultural common-sense, the devotees came to ask for health, wealth, longevity and love charms, a typical example of Chinese culture debased by superstition.

Around the corner is K.L.'s boast—the Central Market. Of course it is a very recent structure. Delapidated, filthy, vermin-stricken cow sheds stood on the site before this modern, imposing structure was built. One night, a friend who was a perfect stranger to this town, while driving past it, asked me if it was a medical college! Medical study was at the back of his mind.

Here is the Mercantile Bank and here stood the dwelling houses—three in a row—of one of the descendants of Captain Yap Ah Loy. The one at the corner of Rodger and Market Streets was a druggist shop in which medicine prescribed by the gods of the High Street Temple was dispensed. They alone knew how to decipher the code used in the prescription printed on yellow paper.

On the site of Hongkong Bank across the road, stood a small shrine known to all as Datoh. I think it was the grave of a mystical Malay and most Chinese turned it into a place of worship. What is now John Little's consisted of a row of mud houses selling salt fish. Whiteaways had its small beginnings in Old Market Square somewhere near the present Straits Times office, and Robinson's began in Market Street, where the Caxton Press is. I may be wrong here unless Robinson's took over from Bonds Ltd. Very little changes have been noticed in the Government Offices, but King Edward VII's bust and Swettenham's statue were non-existent. The Spotted Dog was housed in very much smaller buildings thatched with attap. It sheltered the Prince of Wales—now Duke of Windsor, in 1922, when that august personage was on his goodwill tour. The Padang would be turned into a Lake when the Klang River swelled its banks.

There were very few places of amusement in those days. The theatre hall in Petaling Street—where the Madras Theatre now stands—and the Sultan Street Theatre Hall, replaced by the Rex, were vermin-stricken halls in which Cantonese Wayang played year in and year out. Occasionally a Teochiew Opera or a *bangsawan** would give a fortnight's performance in either of the halls. Men who could afford it spent most of their leisure in the licensed opium dens, or in the licensed gambling booths in Petaling Street, High Street,

---

*bangsawan: a Malay or Peranakan theatrical performance.

70

Ampang Street and Batu Road. All sorts of chance games were indulged in ranging from *fan-tan*, dice-throwing, *p'ai-kow* to *chap-ji-ki*. Those who made money spent it in one of the licensed houses of ill-fame many of which, including Japanese brothels, were situated in Petaling Street which was a veritable Yoshiwara.

What were the means of transport? For short distances there was the *jinricksha* and for distances over five miles there was the horse gharry—a sort of big box on four wheels drawn by a horse not much more active than Don Quixote's Rosinante.

The first bicycle—a penny-farthing—was introduced by Bachi, a son of Captain Yap Ah Loy. His Hainan boy rode it and when he did so, many small street urchins would run after it. You will smile when I tell you that His Lordship Justice Sercombe Smith had to come to office in a two-man-power single-seater ricksha, with one to pull and one to push. This sight was most impressive because the puller and the pusher were clad in khaki uniform with red fringes and they had *towchang** coiled round their heads.

In days that are dead but not forgotten, K.L. streets were paved with laterite. During the dry season and on a windy day almost every one wore khaki clothes. The streets were illuminated by flickering kerosene oil lamps and most streets had their stand pipes from which the inhabitants drew their daily supply of water. Prisoners, with chained feet and guarded by an armed policeman, swept the streets early in the morning and semi-nude Indian labourers did all the road repairs. In the shopping quarters very few European ladies could be seen. When they did come out they were clad in Victorian dresses, fully veiled and gloved with their skirts trailing along the ground. Chinese women wore black silk dresses or blue; white was taboo because it was a sign of mourning; Japanese women donned their highly coloured kimonos with a big bow behind and were veritable Madame

towchang: Cantonese term for a head-cloth.

71

Butterflies; Malay women were '*ber-tudong*' (veiled). On social grounds the East and West were miles and miles apart. Most Government officials and business men wore closed coats with high collars, known as '*tutup*', and tropical helmets.

Children went to school bare-footed and in the primary classes boys had to learn English and colloquial Malay side by side. The Barnes Report is by no means a new discovery.

There is one more thing I should like to mention. Our first museum was situated in a plank house on Bukit Nanas. Later on that same building became the Education Office. It was in that office that I sat for the Cambridge Preliminary Examination in 1907.

These are some of the impressions which remain indelible in my mind and will remain in it as long as I live. Modern K.L. is interesting because all development is interesting, but what gives the city its greatest, its most baffling charm, are the ever-present reminders of a yesterday more strange and fascinating than today—a yesterday when there was so much tranquillity, and so much contentment.

Ng Seo Buck, 'Some Recollections of Kuala Lumpur Fifty Years Ago', *Malayan Historical Journal*, 1/1 (1954): 29–32.

12
Singapore in the 1860s

JOHN CAMERON

John Cameron, who was editor of the *Straits Times*, gives us a picture of Singapore 46 years after its founding and on the eve of its passing from the Government of India to the Colonial Office in London. The reference to 'Malayan India' in the title must therefore have seemed a little old-fashioned even at this date, but there is nothing quaint about Cameron's assessment of the commercial and political importance of Singapore, to which he devotes the greater part of the book. He prophesied (rather accurately, as it turns out) a great future for Singapore so long as it retained its advantage of being a duty-free port. He clearly wanted his British audience to gain a better appreciation of their tropical colony, claiming rather improbably that its landscape 'surpasses in loveliness that of Ceylon and Java'. Still, his Singapore was one where 'magnificent tropical forest runs down to the very water's edge' (a forest still full of tigers, who regularly carried off human victims), and where, Cameron tells us, the night winds carried the breath of 'lovely forest perfumes', detectable more than a mile from shore; where from the mass of small craft plying the harbour you could purchase for a dollar and a half a 'whole boat-load' of the most beautiful corals 'of all tints and hues'; where Orchard Road was still an orchard, and where the sharpest contrasts still existed between the living conditions of those who survived the exploitations of the coolie trade, and the Europeans in their elegant bungalows.

THE first thing that strikes the stranger on landing as remarkable is this appearance of bustle and activity, heightened by the motley character of those who compose the crowd. The street leading from the landing-place to Commercial Square, the great business centre of the town, is a rather narrow one, with a constant stream of Chinese, Malays, Klings, Parsees, and Mussulmen, pouring one way and the other. . . .

But the place itself is no less Oriental in appearance than its inhabitants, though considerably less so here than at the native parts of the town lying further back. Commercial Square, which, ever since the settlement rose into importance has been the principal locality for the European houses of business, is about 200 yards from the landing, but completely shut in from a view of the sea. It is built round a reserved piece of ground, turfed over with green sod and tastefully laid out with flowers and shrubs, which afford to the eye a pleasing relief from the glare of the whitewashed walls of the square, while the open space ensures good ventilation to the neighbourhood. The square itself is some 200 yards long by fifty broad, and many of the houses, or

rather godowns (the latter term being used to denote mercantile establishments), which surround it, are of very elegant
design. They are all built of brick and plastered over, but as
both labour and materials have at no period since the settlement of the place been costly, their construction and finish is
good. Some of the finest now standing are twenty or thirty
years old. They are two stories high, lofty, and with heavy,
overleaning eaves; and the lower part of the front wall is
composed of a series of arches or pillars inside of which a
verandah runs from building to building....

In the centre of the square is the telegraph-office, connecting New Harbour with the town, and at one end of
it is the favourite stand for hack-gharries, which, with their
drivers, form by no means an ornamental feature of the
town. Four of the buildings fronting the square are occupied
by banks, each with an English proprietary, and the everlasting chink of dollars to be heard on passing these establishments is almost deafening. All the cashiers in the banks, as,
indeed, in mercantile establishments generally, are Chinamen, who count and, at the same time, test the genuineness
of dollars with remarkable exactitude and rapidity, by pouring them from one hand to the other. By the ring which the
dollars give in falling, they are able at once to detect base
metal and even light coin. These men keep their cash
accounts not in the English but in the Chinese character, and
it is remarkable that they are never known to be incorrect.

Till within the last year, the European business was almost
entirely confined to this square, but a good deal of it is likely
to be deflected to the sea frontage immediately in advance,
where, upon land recently recovered from the sea, a fine terrace of godowns is being built, some of which are already in
occupation. These buildings are being constructed as nearly
uniform as possible, and though they are not, individually
considered, finer than some of the old ones in the square,
still, viewed together, they will most probably form the finest
part of the commercial half of the town....

On the eastern bank of the river for a considerable way up

there are no houses, the land having been reserved for Government purposes, but the green grass and the foliage which surround the public offices erected close by, form a very pleasing contrast to the thickly-packed buildings opposite.

The river is alive with boats of all sorts, Chinamen with their shoe-boats, Malays with their sampans, or fast-boats, and Klings with their tongkangs. The first two craft are used for the conveyance of passengers and their luggage; the last, which are far the most numerous, are employed in bringing up and down the river the cargoes of ships in the harbour. The latter contain from ten to fifteen coyans* each, and so numerous are they, that they generally lie three or four abreast along the entire western bank of the river, from its mouth to Elgin Bridge above. I have never counted them, but should say that very seldom indeed are there less than 500 of these small craft to be seen at one time in this first reach of the river. To each of these boats, taking one with another, there is a crew of not less than three men, which would give a floating population of at least 1,500 men; and the expression is by no means improperly applied, for most of these men live and sleep in their boats, and at night time the effect of this part of the river is considerably heightened by the innumerable lights which glimmer from under the attap† or kajang‡ awnings of this little fleet.

The crescent of buildings which I have described, and which is about a quarter of a mile long, is termed Boat Quay, from the fact of nearly the entire river frontage opposite them being taken up with the loading and discharging of cargo boats. Here it is, at present at least, that three-fourths of the entire shipping business of the island is effected, and from morning till night may be seen the landing of huge cases, casks and bales of British manufactures, as well as machinery and iron-work of all descriptions; and no sooner are the boats

---

*A coyan is about two tons English.
† *attap*: palm-leaf thatch.
‡ *kajang*: bamboo or wickerwork matting.

which bring these emptied, than they are filled up again with bales of gambier, bundles of rattans, tin, bags or cases of sago and tapioca, bags of pepper, and boxes of spices. It is, indeed, impossible to view these operations and not realize the fact that Singapore possesses a commerce and commercial importance altogether disproportioned to its size and population. Here alone there must be landed and shipped not less than 30,000*l.*-worth of goods per diem, throughout the entire year, and this is allowing some 5,000*l.* or 6,000*l.*-worth more to be landed and shipped from the private wharves possessed by a few godowns on the western side of the town....

The whole of the native part of the town, the chief business division of which lies behind Commercial Square, and the river frontage I have described, are very much alike in appearance. The buildings are closely packed together and of a uniform height and character. The style is a sort of compromise between English and Chinese. The walls are of brick, plastered over, and the roofs are covered with tiles. The windows are of lattice woodwork—there being no glazing in this part of the world. Under the windows of many houses occupied by Chinese are very chaste designs of flowers or birds in porcelain. The ridges of the roofs, too, and the eaves, are frequently similarly ornamented, and it is no unusual thing to see a perfect little garden of flowers and vegetables in boxes and pots exposed on the tops of the houses. Underneath run, for the entire length of the streets, the enclosed verandahs of which I spoke before, and in a quiet observant walk through these a very great deal may be learned concerning the peculiar manners and customs of the trading inhabitants. The principal street for native shops leads from Commercial Square towards the country. For a quarter of a mile after leaving the square, but before crossing the river, this is a great thoroughfare. Being narrow, it is nearly always crowded, and the buildings fronting it are occupied entirely by Chinese and Klings....

There is probably no city in the world with such a motley

crowd of itinerant vendors of wares, fruits, cakes, vegetables, &c. There are Malays, generally with fruit; Chinamen with a mixture of all sorts, and Klings with cakes and different kinds of nuts. Malays and Chinamen always use the shoulder-stick, having equally-balanced loads suspended at either end; the Klings, on the contrary, carry their wares on the head on trays. The travelling cookshops of the Chinese are probably the most extraordinary of the things that are carried about in this way. They are suspended on one of the common shoulder-sticks, and consist of a box on one side and a basket on the other; the former containing a fire and small copper cauldron for soup; the latter loaded with rice, vermicelli, cakes, jellies, and condiments; and though I have never tasted any of their dishes, I have been assured that those they serve up at a moment's notice are most savoury, and that their sweets are delicious. Three cents will purchase a substantial meal of three or four dishes from these itinerant restauranteurs. . . .

The court-house and the town-hall stand close together on the east bank of the river. The former is thirty-five years old, but not a bit the worse for its age. It is a large graceful building with a fine display of pillars and porticoes, and by its size and elegance shows that as far back as the date of its foundation the old Company had foreshadowed the greatness to which Singapore would arise. It is now used as the treasury, the land-office, and the resident councillor's office; only a small outer building connected with it is appropriated to the use of the Court of Judicature, and which is scarcely large enough to afford accommodation to its thirteen licensed practitioners.

The town-hall is of modern construction, having been commenced about four years since by public subscription of the merchants. It was to cost just 20,000 dollars, though when finished it was found that no less than 50,000 dollars had been spent upon it; but it is a pretty building, and the money has not been grudged. It is of a mixed style of architecture. The lower hall has been neatly fitted up as a theatre by the Amateur Corps Dramatique, and the upper hall is used for public meetings and other public purposes.

Close to both these buildings are some fine old trees which throw a grateful shade all around, and from this the esplanade extends in a broad belt of beautiful turf along the beach as far as the institution buildings. The esplanade contains about nine acres, and it is wonderful how green the grass keeps throughout the year. The institution buildings were erected by Sir Stamford Raffles, and are consequently older than any other public building in the place. The purpose of the institution is a most worthy one. It was endowed by the Company for educational purposes, and a yearly sum is still granted for its maintenance.

To the line of buildings fronting the beach on this side of the river, extending from the church for a quarter of a mile eastward, more perhaps than to any other feature, Singapore owes its pretty appearance, viewed from the harbour. These, as I have said before, though the finest of them are hotels now, were once the residences of the early merchants, and are large and of elegant construction; they each cover a considerable space of ground and have compounds or gardens around. It is a very fine sight from the beach to see these houses lit up at night, the brilliant argand lamps in use shedding a flood of light round the lofty white pillars and colonnades of the upper stories, while the lower parts of the buildings are hid by the shrubbery of the gardens in front. Every door and window is thrown open to admit the cool night breeze, and gathered round their tables, or lolling about in their easy chairs, may be seen the wearied travellers or residents, with the strange and often grotesque figures of their native servants flitting about with refreshments. Indeed, on a fine starry night, standing there, on the sea-wall of the bay, with the stillness around only broken by the gentle ripple of the wavelets at one's feet, it is not difficult while gazing on the houses, the lights, the figures, and the heavy-leafed shrubbery in front, to imagine oneself amid the garden palaces of the Arabian Nights....

The greatest number of European residences are about two miles out, but some are twice that distance. Those nearer town, where ground is more valuable, are built tolerably close together, with perhaps one or two acres to each; those at a greater distance are more apart, generally crowning the summits of the innumerable little hills, which are such a geological peculiarity of Singapore, and surrounded by ten or fifteen acres of ground, either covered with patches of jungle, or planted with nutmeg and fruit trees....

The residences are built very similar to one another, and generally of brick. Bungalows, a term often applied to any style of dwelling-house in the East, are, properly speaking, only of one story, elevated some five or six feet from the ground upon arched masonry. A moderate-sized building of this description might be 90 feet long, 60 or 70 deep, usually a parallelogram in form, but sometimes varied in shape to suit the arrangement of the rooms inside. The walls from the flooring to the roof are seldom less than fifteen feet high, which gives a lofty ceiling to the apartments, and the roof is covered with tiles. The most striking feature of these buildings, however, is the broad verandah which runs right round the house about eight or ten feet in width, resting on the plinths of the pillars that, extending upwards in round columns with neatly moulded capitals, support the continuation of the roof which projects some four feet beyond the pillars, forming deep overhanging eaves. On to the verandah, which is surrounded by a neat railing, all the doors of the bungalow open, and as these also serve the purpose of windows, they are pretty numerous; they are in two halves, opening down the centre like cottage doors at home, with the lower panels plain and the two upper ones fitted with venetians to open or close at pleasure. From the centre of the building in front a portico projects some twenty-five or thirty feet, and generally about twenty-five broad, covering the carriage way and a broad flight of stone steps leading from the ground to the verandah. The pillars and walls are chenammed* to a snowy whiteness, the doors are painted a light green, the tiled roof in time becomes a dark brown, and the whole forms a very pleasing picture, especially in its contrast with the foliage around.

Those residences which are not bungalows have no peculiar local denomination. They are two stories high, and very similar in construction to the others.

The interiors of all the houses are lofty, for in addition to the side walls being seldom less than fifteen feet high, the ceilings of the principal rooms are alcoved. There are numerous columns and arches inside as well as outside, and the Chinese builders make very neat cornices to the doorways and ceilings. The rooms are never papered, but the entire plasterwork—ceilings, walls, and pillars—is kept beautifully white with chenam. The floors are matted, not carpeted, and the apartments not overcrowded with furniture. The wooden doors leading from room to room are usually thrown open, there being silk screens on hinges attached to each doorway, which, while they maintain a sufficient privacy, admit of a free ventilation throughout the house. From the ceilings are suspended a very liberal supply of hanging argand lamps, which, when lit up, give a brilliant effect to the rooms. Punkahs are used in the dining-rooms, but not in the sleeping apartments, as is the case in India.

The kitchen, stables, and servants' rooms are always built at a good distance from the house, and connected with it by a covered passage. There is little remarkable about these, except perhaps in the internal arrangements of the kitchens, which, though for the use of Europeans, are thoroughly oriental in their character. There is no fireplace, but in the centre of the room a table of solid brickwork is built with slabs of stone or brick tiles laid on the top; at one end of this a small circular chamber is built to serve as an oven; a strong

*chenam: A Tamil word for whitewash made from lime.

80

fire is placed inside, and when the brickwork is thoroughly heated, the fire is raked out, and whatever dish is required to be baked placed inside and the aperture closed up, the heat given out from the bricks being sufficient to cook it in a short time. The rest of the table is divided into a series of little fireplaces, over which proceed the ordinary processes of cooking. Wood or charcoal only is used as fuel.

The grounds around the European residences are for the most part tastefully kept. A couple of gardeners cost eight or nine dollars a month, and to such good effect can nature be cultivated that the expenditure is seldom begrudged. The beauty of the hedges, which are either of bamboo or of wild heliotrope, and the greenness of the grass, are features not often seen in a tropical climate, but which are particularly noteworthy about Singapore. The grass is a very coarse, short, thick sort, and so vigorous is it of growth that a considerable body of men are maintained throughout the year at the public expense to keep the roads clear of it. Few of the private gardens as yet yield much fruit, owing to the fact of the greater part of the grounds around Singapore not many years ago having been laid out with nutmegs, a crop which made magnificent returns for many years, and then suddenly gave way from some unknown disease or blight. Fruit trees, however, are now growing up in their place.

The roads leading from one to another of these residences, and from them to the town, are very pleasant walks or drives, according as it may be morning or evening. Of those leading into and out of town, Orchard Road and River Valley Road are the two chief. The former is the approach to the greater number of houses, and has the most traffic; it is, besides, probably the prettier of the two. Shortly after leaving town it follows the windings of a small stream of anything but pellucid water, in which the dhobies, or washermen, are busy from morning till night, on Sabbaths and on week-days, in shower and in sunshine, beating away at the soiled linen of the clothed section of the population. The process is common in India, but certainly quite strange to Europe. The men, generally strong, stalwart Klings or Bengalese, naked to a strip of cloth round the loins, stand up to their knees in the bed of the stream with a flat slab of stone in front of them. They seize the pieces of clothing one by one—if it is a shirt by the tail, if a pair of pants by the legs—dip them into the stream, swing them over their heads, and bring them down with their whole force on the stone slab. This operation is continued with each piece till it is thoroughly cleaned. A great deal of damage is, of course, done to the clothes by this process; it is especially fatal to buttons; but on the other hand, it undoubtedly secures a matchless whiteness.

Beyond these dhobie lines, Orchard Road runs for about a mile in a straight line through a valley lying between a series of little hills, from the summits of which the residences I have described look down; but it is only at intervals that these can be seen. The road on either side is lined by tall bamboo hedges with thick shrubbery behind, and broken only here and there by the white portals at the entrances of the private avenues leading from it, or occasionally by a native hut or fruit shop. Many years ago, too, angsana, wild almond, jambu, and weringan trees were planted along both sides at equal distances, and these have now grown up to their full proportions, closing overhead, forming a complete shade to the road, and giving the appearance of a very beautiful vista extending along its entire length.

John Cameron, *Our Tropical Possessions in Malayan India*, London: Smith, Elder and Co., 1865, pp. 51–72.

13

The Dutch Lifestyle in Batavia in the 1790s

JOHN BARROW

Sir John Barrow, whose accounts of his travels made him famous in his day, had a distinguished career as Second Secretary of the Admiralty during the years 1803–45. He had not yet achieved this position, however, when he set sail as a member of the Macartney Mission to China in 1792–3. Originally published in 1806, *A Voyage to Cochinchina* provides a lively first hand account of Java and Vietnam which reached a wide audience of his contemporaries. He has left us an extraordinarily vivid, and critical, picture of the peculiar style of Dutch life in Batavia shortly before the collapse of the Dutch East India Company's rule. Barrow's collection of mortality statistics chillingly illustrate the deadly price paid by the Dutch for having built Batavia in a malarial swamp, laced with canals to remind them of home. (Like his contemporaries, though, Barrow believed malaria to be caused by the foul vapours given off by stagnant water; not until 1897 was it proved to be mosquito-borne). He is sharply observant of the social distinctions of Batavia, and writes in a mordantly critical tone of Dutch luxury, overdress and lack of exercise. Although the English of this period were also heavy eaters by today's standards, they obviously could not match the extent of Dutch overindulgence at the table—the dinner which he describes was just a prelude to a much more serious supper which was served later, after a nap. His account reveals just how little the Dutch had permitted themselves to adapt their habits to a tropical climate; it was not until much later, in the late nineteenth and early twentieth century, that they were to adopt a more locally-influenced lifestyle.

I N making choice of the present site of the city of Batavia, the predilection of the Dutch for a low swampy situation evidently got the better of their prudence; and the fatal consequences that have invariably attended this choice, from its first establishment to the present period, irrefragably demonstrated by the many thousands who have fallen a sacrifice to it, have nevertheless been hitherto unavailing to induce the government either altogether to abandon the spot for another more healthy, or to remove the local and immediate causes of a more than ordinary mortality. Never were national prejudices and national taste so injudiciously misapplied, as in the attempt to assimilate those of Holland to the climate and the soil of Batavia. Yet such has been the aim of the settlers, which they have endeavoured to accomplish with indefatigable industry. An extended plain of rich alluvious land, with a copious river serpentizing through it, in a stream of so easy and gentle a current that the water with great facility was capable of being conducted at pleasure; a tract of country holding out such easy means of being intersected by canals and ditches, and embellished with fish ponds; of being converted into gardens and villas, where draw-bridges for ornament and *trek-schuyts** for pleasure and convenience could be adopted, presented temptations too strong for Dutch taste to resist. Nothing, however, can possibly be more gratifying to the eye than the general appearance of the country which surrounds Batavia. Here no aridity, no sterility, no nakedness even partially intervene between the plantations of coffee, sugar, pepper, rice, and other valuable products, which are enclosed and divided by trees of the choicest fruits. In the immediate vicinity of the city, the extensive gardens of the Dutch, embellished with villas in the Oriental style, furnished with every convenience that a luxurious and voluptuous taste can suggest, are charming to behold from a little distance, but do not improve by a nearer acquaintance. The vitiated taste of Holland, delighting in straight avenues, trimmed hedges, myrtles and other evergreens cut into the *walls of Troy*, and flower-beds laid out in circles, squares, and polygons, are no less offensive to the eye than the numerous ditches and fish-ponds, from their stench and exhalations, are injurious to the health, besides being the nurseries of an innumerable host of frogs and mosquitoes. . . .

Batavia, though not of an extraordinary size, nor em-

---

trek-schuyt: a towboat or barge.

bellished with buildings that are worthy of particular notice for elegance of design or magnificence of dimensions, may nevertheless be considered to rank among the neatest and the handsomest cities in the world. The ground plan is in the shape of a parallelogram, whose length from north to south is 4200 feet, and breadth 3000 feet. The streets are laid out in straight lines, and cross each other at right angles. Each street has its canal in the middle, cased with stone walls, which rise into a low parapet on the two margins. At the distance of six feet from this parapet wall is a row of evergreen trees, under the shade of which, on this intermediate space, are erected little open pavilions of wood, surrounded with seats, where the Dutch part of the inhabitants smoke their pipes and drink their beer in the cool of the evening. Beyond the trees is a gravelled road from thirty to sixty feet in width, terminated also on the opposite side by a second row of evergreens. This road is appropriated for the use of carriages, horses, cattle, and, as particularly pointed out by proclamation, for all *slaves*, who are strictly prohibited from walking on the flagged causeway in front of the houses, as they are also from wearing stockings and shoes, in order that their naked feet may be the means of making their condition notorious. This *trottoir* or footway is at least six feet wide; and as the breadth of the canals is generally the same as that of the carriage road, the whole width of the Batavian streets may be considered to run from 114 to 204 feet; and the city is said to contain twenty of such streets, with canals in the middle, over which they reckon about thirty stone bridges. The trees that embellish the streets are of different kinds, but the most common are two species of *Callophyllum*, called by botanists the *Inophyllum*, and the *Calaba*, the *Canarium Commune*, or canary-nut tree, the *Guettarda Speciosa*, with its odoriferous flowers, and the free, elegant, and spreading tamarind tree.

In the style and architecture of the public buildings there is little to praise and much to condemn. The Dutch, both at home and abroad, have hitherto resisted, with an obstinacy which indeed on most occasions influences the conduct of this nation, the introduction of the Greek and Roman models of architecture. The large octagon church is considered by the inhabitants as a master-piece of elegance in its design, and of neatness in the execution; and is carefully pointed out to the notice of visitors. The annexed engraving will enable the reader, in some measure, to form a judgment how far its merits are correspondent to the high notions they bestow on it. The inside, however, is fitted up with great neatness, and a magnificent and fine-toned organ occupies completely a side of the octagon. The pulpit of teak wood is a laborious piece of workmanship, which is executed in a good style of carving. The expence of finishing this church is calculated to have amounted to eighty thousand pounds. The other public buildings consist in a Lutheran and a Portugueze church, a Mahomedan mosque and a Chinese temple; the stadt-house, the spin-house, the infirmary, the chamber of orphans, and some other institutions of inferior note; beside a very convenient and extensive market for butchers' meat, poultry, fish, grain and vegetables. The private houses of the inhabitants, and particularly of those in the service of the East India Company, are generally of great dimensions; the rooms are lofty, the doors and windows large. Most of the wood work and the furniture within are painted of a light chocolate brown, and all the mouldings are gilt. The ground floors are flagged with smooth blue stones or square brown tiles which, being frequently washed in the course of the day, communicate a refreshing and an agreeable coolness to the lower apartments. . . .

The mortality of Europeans in Batavia is far beyond what is known in any other settlement, exceeding, in the best of times, that in the most fatal of the West India islands. Of persons newly arrived the usual calculation is that three in five will die the first year; and, of the remaining survivors, the mortality is never considered to be less than from nine to twelve in the hundred, which is the usual proportion of seasoned Europeans, exclusive of infants. Among these, likewise, are not included either troops or seamen. The havock which this pernicious climate, added to their debaucheries and irregular conduct, occasion among these thoughtless people, is truly deplorable. The register of deaths in the military hospital in 62 years amounted to 78,000 persons, or 1258 every year; and as the establishment of European troops seldom exceeded 1500, and was generally less than half that number, it may fairly be concluded that every soldier who has been sent out to Batavia has perished there, which is I believe literally the fact. . . .

On our first visit to Batavia, we were received with great ceremony at the gates of the castle by the old Governor *Van Alting*, accompanied with the *wel edele heeren*, composing the Council of India. On this occasion we all suffered greatly from the heat of the climate. It happened to be about the middle of the day, when the sun was vertical, and not a breath of wind stirring; the mercury in Fahrenheit's thermometer at 89° in the shade; when, after abundant ceremony in the open air, we were introduced into a close narrow room, with a couple of windows at one end, nearly filled with fat 'sleek-headed men', dressed in suits of velvet stiffened with buckram. In this narrow room, and mixed among these warmly clad gentlemen, we were seated round a table covered with crimson velvet, on chairs whose corresponding cushions were stuffed with feathers. And though the very appearance of the furniture alone was enough to induce a fever, two or three little chafing-dishes with live coals were set on the table, for the accommodation of those who were inclined to smoke a pipe of tobacco, which, with wine, spirits, and cakes, were handed round to the company.

The ceremony of our introduction being ended, we proceeded from the castle to the country-house of *Van Weegerman*, the second in council, to which we were conveyed in small carriages, each drawn by a pair of ponies, and driven by a black coachman, who, mounted on a high box, with a large three-cornered hat and an enormously long whip, formed no unimportant part of the equipage. The distance we had to travel was only about a mile beyond the city gate. We entered his villa by a draw-bridge thrown across a moat, with which it was surrounded, and which was intended as well for ornament as defence. Behind the house was a considerable piece of ground laid out with much formality into a sort of pleasure garden intersected, rather injudiciously it would seem in such a climate, with fish ponds and canals or, more correctly speaking, with puddles and ditches of dirty water. The ground was well stocked with all kinds of tropical fruits, and many rare plants peculiar to the island. Orange trees of a large size, shaddocks and mangoes were loaded with fruit; and every individual of the vegetable world seemed to flourish with a vigorous luxuriance, except a few sickly European plants, which were here and there seen drooping in pots. On observing to our host how very bountiful nature had been to this island in the distribution of some of her choicest stores, he replied, '*Ya mynheer het is wel waär.*' 'You are very right, Sir, we have abundance of everything; and yet,' continued he, '*het is een vervloekt land,*' 'it is an accursed country, to say the best of it, where *we eat poison and drink pestilence at every meal.*' In what this poison and pestilence consisted will best appear by a short description of *Van Weegerman's* dinner.

We had scarcely set foot in the house when a procession of slaves made its appearance, with wine and gin, cordials, cakes and sweetmeats; a ceremony that was repeated to every new guest who arrived. After waiting a couple of hours the signal for dinner was given by the entrance of three female slaves, one with a large silver bason, the second with a jar of the same metal filled with rose water for washing the hands, and the third with towels for wiping them. The company was very numerous and, the weather being remarkably close, the velvet coats and powdered wigs were now thrown aside, and their places supplied with short dimity jackets and muslin night-caps. I certainly do not remember ever to have seen an European table so completely loaded with what Van Weegerman was pleased to call *poison* and *pestilence*. Fish boiled and broiled, fowls in *curries* and *pillaws*, turkies and large capons, joints of beef boiled and roasted and stewed, soups, puddings, custards, and all kinds of pastry, were so crowded and jumbled together that there was scarcely any room for plates. Of the several kinds of dishes there was generally a pair: a turkey on one side had its brother turkey on the other, and capon stared at capon. A slave was placed behind the chair of each guest, besides those who handed round wine, gin, cordials, and Dutch or Danish beer, all of which are used profusely by the Dutch under an idea that, by promoting perspiration, they carry off in some degree the effects of the poison and pestilence. After dinner an elegant desert was served up of Chinese pastry, fruits in great variety, and sweetmeats. There were not any ladies in company. Van Weegerman being a bachelor had no females in his house, except his haram of slaves amounting to about fifty in number, assorted from the different nations of East, and combining every tinge of complexion from the sickly faded hue of a dried tobacco leaf to the shining polish of black marble. A band of Malay musicians played in the viranda during dinner.

John Barrow, *A Voyage to Cochinchina in the Years 1792 and 1793*, London: Cadell and Davies, 1806; reprinted Kuala Lumpur: Oxford University Press, 1975, pp. 171–207.

14
Makassar in the 1850s

ALFRED RUSSELL WALLACE

Alfred Russell Wallace (1823–1913) shares the fame of Charles Darwin as the co-discoverer of the theory of evolution, while in *The Malay Archipelago* he gave us one of the great travel books of all time. The son of an unsuccessful solicitor, Wallace came from an unprivileged background. He was a self-taught biologist, who had to make his way in life through his own effort and determination.

Wallace travelled as a private individual, sometimes accompanied by his assistant, Charles Allen, at others only by two or three servants hired locally. He financed himself partly by selling some of his vast collection of specimens to wealthy European collectors. After an earlier expedition to Amazonia in 1848–50, he embarked on a journey through island South-East Asia that was to last 8 years (1854–62) and cover 14,000 miles. On the way he collected 125,660 specimens of mammals, reptiles, birds, butterflies, beetles, and shells, including great numbers of previously unknown species. Wallace's independent formulation of the theory of natural selection began during a malarial attack in Sarawak, as (like Darwin) he pondered the implications of Malthus's Essay on Population. By the time he finished his journeys in the archipelago, he was still only thirty-five years old, though his health had been weakened by many attacks of fever during his years of travel.

Wallace came to the Celebes [Sulawesi] in 1856 and spent the months of September to November in the countryside around Makassar [now Ujung Pandang]. His description of what at that time was still a small town of one street makes a startling contrast with today's teeming urban centre of 900,000 people. From here, he struck out into the countryside, enlarging his collections with birds, insects, and some of the brilliant butterflies for which South Sulawesi is still famous. None of the local villagers, he tells us, had seen a European before, and Wallace, a likeable person, was upset to find that wherever he went, 'dogs barked, children screamed, women ran away, and men stared as though I were some terrible cannibal monster'. Nowadays, people are more friendly, though in remote areas children are quite likely to *follow* you screaming, so perhaps Wallace did not realize the relative advantages of his position. Intermittent fever continually interrupted his work, and as the rainy season approached he decided to return to town. He visited again the next year on his return from the Aru islands.

MACASSAR was the first Dutch town I had visited, and I found it prettier and cleaner than any I had yet seen in the East. The Dutch have some admirable local regulations. All European houses must be kept well whitewashed, and every person must, at four in the afternoon, water the road in front of his house. The streets are kept clear of refuse, and covered drains carry away all impurities into large open sewers, into which the tide is admitted at high-water and allowed to flow out when it has ebbed, carrying all the sewage with it into the sea. The town consists chiefly of one long narrow street, along the seaside, devoted to business, and principally occupied by the Dutch and Chinese merchants' offices and warehouses, and the native shops or bazaars. This extends northwards for more than a mile, gradually merging into native houses, often of a most miserable description, but made to have a neat appearance by being all built up exactly to the straight line of the street, and being generally backed by fruit trees. This street is usually thronged with a native population of Bugis and Macassar men, who wear cotton trousers about twelve inches long, covering only from the hip to half-way down the thigh, and the universal Malay sarong, of gay checked colours, worn round the waist or across the shoulders in a variety of ways. Parallel to this street run two short ones, which form the old Dutch town, and are enclosed by gates. These consist of private houses, and at their southern end is the fort, the church, and a road at right angles to the beach, containing the houses of the Governor and of the principal officials. Beyond the fort again, along the beach, is another long street of native huts and many country houses of the tradesmen and merchants. All around extend the flat ricefields, now bare and dry and forbidding, covered with dusty stubble and weeds. A few months back these were a mass of verdure, and their barren appearance at this season offered a striking contrast to the perpetual crops on the same kind of country in Lombock and Bali, where the seasons are exactly similar, but where an elaborate system of irrigation produces the effect of a perpetual spring.

Alfred Russel Wallace, *The Malay Archipelago*, London: Macmillan, 1869; reprinted Singapore: Graham Brash, 1983, pp. 162–3.

15

Life in Early Nineteenth Century Manila

PAUL PROUST DE LA GIRONIERE

Adventures of a Frenchman in the Philippines, which appeared in several editions, both in French and in English, was probably the most widely-read book on the Philippines in the nineteenth century. Its author, a Breton doctor, went there in the 1820s, purchasing a large estate of 2,400 hectares, called Jalajala. He proceeded to distinguish himself as a pioneer of new and scientific agricultural techniques, growing coffee, indigo, sugar, rice and other crops as well as rearing livestock. His vigorous narrative fascinated the reader of that time with its string of picaresque adventures, the extent of which also caused some people to doubt the author's veracity. There is in fact some evidence that a few of the more exhilarating exploits, such as the single-handed capture of a giant man-eating crocodile, were actually borrowed from his acquaintances. Still, his stories sufficiently captured the imagination that a British naval officer, who sought out de la Gironière on a visit in 1856, records that 'The good folks of Manchester, so I was told, had caught a bright idea and sent out some "Gironière" pocket handkerchiefs, with prints of the author, performing many of the exploits recorded by himself, and illustrative of his work generally; but the only result was, that those who knew him thought them funny, and those who knew him not, could not see the fun of them, and neither party bought any'.[1] In spite of an evident degree of literary licence, however, there is much accurate background detail in his book, as for example in his portrait of life in Manila, as well as in his account of political events.

Life was not all derring-do and comic incident. Like so many others who spent long periods in South-East Asia in those early days (or for that matter those who stayed at home), his life was touched with tragedy, for he lost his brother, his adored wife, his sister-in-law and finally his small son to fevers. He moved to Calauan by 1859 in order to establish a sugar mill, and had appar-

---

[1]Henry T. Ellis, *Hong Kong to Manila and the Lakes of Luzon, in the Philippine Isles, in the Year 1856*, London: Smith, Elder and Co., 1895, pp. 94–5, cited in Benito J. Legarda y Fernandez's preface to Gironiere, 1972.

ently adopted native dress out of sympathy with the local people. This project failed, and de la Gironière may have died there (or possibly in Paris) in 1865.

MANILLA and its suburbs contain a population of about one hundred and fifty thousand souls, of which Spaniards and Creoles hardly constitute the tenth part; the remainder is composed of Tagalogs, or Indians, Mestizos, and Chinese. The city is divided into two sections—the military and the mercantile—the latter of which is the suburb. The former, surrounded by lofty walls, is bounded by the sea on one side, and upon another by an extensive plain, where the troops are exercised, and where of an evening the indolent Creoles, lazily extended in their carriages, repair to exhibit their elegant dresses and to inhale the sea breezes. This public promenade—where intrepid horsemen and horsewomen, and European vehicles, cross each other in every direction—may be styled the Champs Elysées, or the Hyde Park, of the Indian Archipelago. On a third side, the military town is separated from the trading town by the river Pasig upon which are seen all the day boats laden with merchandise, and charming gondolas conveying idlers to different parts of the suburbs, or to visit the ships in the bay.

The military town communicates by the bridge of Binondoc with the mercantile town, inhabited principally by the Spaniards engaged in public affairs; its aspect is dull and monotonous; all the streets, perfectly straight, are bordered by wide granite footpaths. In general, the highways are macadamized, and kept in good condition. Such is the effeminacy of the people, they could not endure the noise of carriages upon pavement. The houses—large and spacious, palaces in appearance—are built in a particular manner, calculated to withstand the earthquakes and hurricanes so frequent in this part of the world. They have all one storey, with a ground floor; the upper part, generally occupied by the family, is surrounded by a wide gallery, opened or shut by means of large sliding panels, the panes of which are thin mother-of-pearl.

The mother-of-pearl permits the passage of light to the apartments, and excludes the heat of the sun. In the military town are all the monasteries and convents, the archbishopric, the courts of justice, the custom house, the hospital, the governor's palace, and the citadel, which overlooks both towns. There are three principal entrances to Manila—Puerta Santa Lucia, Puerta Real, and Puerta Parian.

At one o'clock the drawbridges are raised, and the gates pitilessly closed, when the tardy resident must seek his night's lodging in the suburb, or mercantile town, called Binondoc. This portion of Manilla wears a much gayer and more lively aspect than the military section. There is less regularity in the streets, and the buildings are not so fine as those in what may be called Manilla proper; but in Binondoc all is movement, all is life. Numerous canals crowded with pirogues, gondolas, and boats of various kinds, intersect the suburb, where reside the rich merchants—Spanish, English, Indian, Chinese, and Mestizo. The newest and most elegant houses are built upon the banks of the river Pasig. Simple in exterior, they contain the most costly inventions of English and Indian luxury. Precious vases from China, Japan ware, gold, silver, and rich silks, dazzle the eyes on entering these unpretending habitations. Each house has a landing-place from the river, and little bamboo palaces, serving as bathing houses, to which the residents resort several times daily, to relieve the fatigue caused by the intense heat of the climate. The cigar manufactory, which affords employment continually to from fifteen to twenty thousand workmen and other assistants, is situated in Binondoc: also the Chinese custom house, and all the large working establishments of Manilla.

During the day, the Spanish ladies, richly dressed in the transparent muslins of India and China, lounge about from store to store, and sorely test the patience of the Chinese salesman, who unfolds uncomplainingly, and without showing the least ill-humour, thousands of pieces of goods before his customers, which are frequently examined simply for amusement, and not half a yard purchased. The balls and entertainments, given by the half-breeds of Binondoc to their friends, are celebrated throughout the Philippines. The quadrilles of Europe are succeeded by the dances of India, and while the young people execute the fandango, the bolero, the cachucha, or the lascivious movements of the bayaderes, the enterprising half-breed, the indolent Spaniard, and the sedate Chinese, retire to the gaming saloons, to try their fortune at cards and dice. The passion for play is carried to such an extent that the traders lose or gain in one night sums of 50,000 piasters (£10,000 sterling). The half-breeds, Indians, and Chinese, have also a great passion for cock-fighting; these combats take place in a large arena. I have seen £1,500 betted upon a cock which had cost £150; in a few minutes this costly champion fell, struck dead by his antagonist. In fine, if Binondoc be exclusively the city of pleasure, luxury, and activity, it is also that of amorous intrigues and gallant adventures....

The military town, so quiet during the day, assumes a more lively appearance towards the evening, when the inhabitants ride out in their very magnificent carriages, which are invariably conducted by postilions; they then mix with the walking population of Binondoc. Afterwards visits, balls, and the more intimate reunions take place. At the latter they talk, smoke the cigars of Manila, and chew the betel, drink glasses of iced *eau sucrée*, and eat innumerable sweetmeats; towards midnight those guests retire who do not stay for supper with the family, which is always served luxuriously, and generally prolonged until two o'clock in the morning. Such is the life spent by the wealthy classes under these skies so favoured by Heaven. But there exists, as in Europe, and even to a greater extent, the most abject misery, of which I shall speak hereafter, throwing a shade over this brilliant picture.

Paul Proust de la Gironière, *Adventures of a Frenchman in the Philippines* (French edn.), Paris: Au Comptoir des Imprimeurs–Unis, 1855; revised 9th edn, Manila: Burke-Mialhe/Filipiniana Book Guild, 1972, pp. 13–18.

Palaces

16
The Palace of Mandalay

V. C. SCOTT O'CONNOR

O'Connor (see also Passage 3) seems to have been particularly
happy at Mandalay, and has left us a glowing and vivid account of
the exquisitely carved wooden architecture of the palace buildings.
After Mandalay fell to the British, their officers had turned the
Queen's Lily Throne Room, with its gilded teak pillars, into the
'Upper Burma Club', and used the Great Hall of Audience as a
Church. O'Connor confesses that he could not bring himself to
regret his times spent in the beautiful Throne Room, even while
recognizing 'the undoubted enormity of our being there'. Later, in
1901, Lord Curzon, Viceroy of India, had the Club and Church
removed and ordered the palace buildings preserved as a national
monument. He also had the famous Lion Throne removed from
the dilapidated Audience Hall and presented it to the Calcutta
Museum. One of his motivations was his concern about the danger
of fire—which, ironically, was to cause the destruction of the
palace buildings at the end of World War II. The Lion Throne was
thus saved, and was returned to Burma after Independence.

THE Palace from which we have set out on every journey to the city is the centre to which our steps return.
It is because there was a king in Burma that the palace
was built, and it was because the palace was built that
Mandalay came into existence. The two are inseparably associated, and without the Palace the City would be of little
interest.

Yet the palace upon a first acquaintance can only bring disappointment. It is described in such words of magnificence by its own people; it left such a mark upon the minds of those who came to it as Ambassadors and Envoys in the days when it was wrapped in the mystery of kingship; it claims

'A Corner of the Palace', Mandalay, showing the delicacy of timber architecture within the Palace, nearly all of which was later destroyed by fire. From V. Scott O'Connor, *Mandalay*, London: Hutchinson & Co., 1907.

so obviously to stand for the highest achievement in the national architecture, that a feeling of disappointment on first beholding it is inevitable. For when all is said the world is entitled to expect something exceptional of a palace, wherever it may be; but most of all in a country of which the palace is the centre, as the palace of the kings of Burma was meant to be. Here, if anywhere, it would be reasonable to look for the highest expression of the national power. But one who comes on a brief visit with such expectations, had better, in the cause of unbroken illusions, stay away. It is only with time, with the growth of sympathy, that the charm and beauty of the palace steal on one. Only when one has lived within its precincts, and listened to the music of its spire, and seen the sun flame on its golden eaves, and the moonlight at play upon its walls, does he come to care for it and appreciate its character.

To live in it day after day, to see the cheery people come and go, lost in admiration of its wonders, as country people wander through The Tower—to sit by its dark canals or walk alone in its silent chambers, to see old Ministers of the King, gentlemen of the most perfect manners, walking reverently through it with their shoes in their hands, while commoner folk go clad; that is the way to know this poor old tottering, gorgeous, beautiful, superficial, palace of Mindon Min.

Let us make such acquaintance with it as is possible on paper.

It is built on a raised platform that is nine hundred feet long and five hundred feet across, and it consists of one hundred and twenty buildings, nearly all of which are of wood. In intention it is a Hall of Audience, the living-place of the King, and the abode of all his women. Complicated at first sight, it is essentially simple in plan. For a line drawn across it, the Mayapin, distinguishes clearly between all of it on the east which men might enter, and that portion of it on the west exclusively reserved for women, and one man only, the King. The eastern third, with its eight ceremonial thrones, its lofty spire known as 'The Centre of the Universe', and its really noble Hall of Audience, is by far the most important portion.

Entering then by the winged stairs guarded by monstrous guns, on which traces of the old gilding still survive, we find ourselves in the midst of a colonnade of golden pillars, which culminates in the great throne of the King. To the right and left similar colonnades stretch away, supporting a triple roof. Here we are at once upon the site of the most splendid, the most ceremonial portion of the palace.

Seated upon his Lion Throne, and lifted high above his prostrate people, the King of Burma here gave audience three times a year to feudatory princes and great Ministers of State and the members of the Royal Family. The spectacle, described by more than one eye-witness, was of extraordinary interest and splendour. Nearest of all to the throne, in a kind of cradle, there sat bent in homage the Heir-apparent. Behind him the Princes of the blood, and to right and left, amidst the golden pillars, the Ministers of State in purple and gold. The wings were crowded with lesser people. The sunlight swept in through the golden aisles upon the prostrate multitude unrestrained by any walls.

The King's approach was announced by the sound of distant music, the marshalling of a guard of musketeers, and the sudden sliding back of the latticed doors of the throne, behind which his figure was seen slowly mounting a stair, under the burden of his jewelled coat and golden helmet. He was accompanied, as of right, by the chief Queen, and of favour by one of his little daughters. Even upon the throne at the most solemn of royal ceremonies, the child, as children in Burma always are, was happily privileged.

The audience began with the chaunting of a hymn by the Court Brahmins, clad in white and gold. There followed a recitation by one of the 'Messengers of the Royal Voice', of the Kings alms, and then each of the princes and noblemen assembled knelt down in homage and renewed his allegiance to the King, and announced through an officer of the Court the presents he had brought to place before His Majesty. The further business of the day was then transacted according to the humour of the King.

Tradition is so powerful at all Courts, and notably at all Eastern Courts, that it seems probable that the last King of Burma held his audience of his people in the great hall, much as his predecessors did fifteen hundred years before him. Certainly five hundred years ago the ceremony of reception cannot have been very different from that which has been described above, if we are to judge from the account of one, a prince of the blood royal, who made a presentation before his Sovereign.

'At the time of the presentation,' he writes, and the words are written upon stone, 'the Heir-apparent knelt on the right side of the throne, Thonganbwa of Maw was on the left, and Thirizeyathu, the Governor of Taungdwin, was between them and in a line with them, while the Court officials were in their proper places behind. His Majesty then commanded Naratheinga, a secretary, to approach, and, after having questioned him as to the particulars of the boon prayed for, granted it to the Governor and his wife, and to confirm the gift, poured out a cup of water and celebrated it by the beating of drums and cymbals.'

'When their Majesties were seated,' observes an Ambassador of England, present three-quarters of a century ago, 'the resemblance of the scene which presented itself to the illusion of a well-got-up drama, forcibly occurred to us; but I may safely add, that no mimic exhibition could equal the splendour and pomp of the real scene.'

V. C. Scott O'Connor, *Mandalay and Other Cities of the Past in Burma*, London: Hutchinson & Co., 1907, pp. 80–8.

17

'A Description of the Palace of the King of Siam'

GUY TACHARD

During the latter half of the seventeenth century, the Thai King Narai strove to cultivate ties with France as a means of counterbalancing the growing influence of English and Dutch traders in the region, and, he hoped, of eventually recovering greater control over trade himself. To this end, he had initiated an exchange of Embassies with France in 1670. In 1684, two Thai officials went to the court of King Louis XIV, accompanied by a Jesuit, Fr. Vachet. Although Narai's motivations were really political and economic, Fr. Vachet misleadingly persuaded Louis that the King could easily be converted to Christianity. Louis then dispatched as ambassador to Siam the Chevalier de Chaumont, a man of rigid religious convictions, accompanied by six Jesuit priests, one of whom was Guy Tachard. They arrived at the capital, Ayutthaya, in October 1685, and were granted an audience with the sovereign, of which Tachard has left us an interesting account. Not much was accomplished by the undiplomatic Chaumont, nor were future efforts more successful. Tachard was to accompany two further missions, in 1687 and 1698, but misunderstanding and suspicion only deepened, and the next King, Phra Phrecha, coming to the throne in 1688, expelled most of the French from Siam. After the failure of his efforts in 1698, Tachard left Siam for good; he died in India in 1712.

Although his book has been described as 'not an altogether objective description of Thailand and of what actually happened during the Embassy's stay',[1] Tachard's was the first comprehensive account of Thailand by a European, and therefore remains of great historical interest. Some further architectural details concerning the palace at Ayutthaya are also to be gleaned from the account of another member of the embassy, the Abbé de Choisy, who wrote: 'We have come from the palace; it is a curious place, of which I shall have the plan. Within its walls are five or six palaces with

[1] H. K. Kuloy, 'Introduction to the 1981 Edition', *Voyage to Siam*, Bangkok: White Orchid Press, 1981.

101

broad courtyards surrounded by separate buildings of importance and roofed with calin, a sort of resonant tin, very shiny, and above each building is a golden pyramid.... After walking a lot we reached the King's temple. I thought I was in a church when I went in. The nave is supported by big thick columns devoid of architectural ornament. The columns, the walls, the vault, all are gilded. The choir is closed off by a kind of highly decorated rood screen.'[2] Tachard's description of the spectacle of a royal audience must have fascinated his contemporaries, and still makes a vivid impression on the reader.

THE Palace of the King of *Siam* is of a vaft* Extent, but in the Architecture there is nothing that is regular nor like to our Building. It consists of spacious Courts encompassed with Walls and containing some Piles of Building; on one side are the Apartments of the Kings Officers, and on the other a great number of Pavilions, where the Elephants are. There are a great many Pagods in it also, both great and small, which though irregular, make still an Object pleasing enough to the Eye. When we came to the first Gate of the Palace all alighted, and my Lord Ambassador went and took the Letter out of the Triumphant Chariot, and gave it to the Abbot *de Choisi*.

In this manner we entered into the first Court of the Palace, where on one side were fifty Elephants of War harnessed with Gold, and on the other two Regiments of Guards, to the number of eight hundred Men drawn up in Batalia. From thence we advanced into the second Court, where were eight Elephants of War more, and a Troop of threescore *Mores* on Horseback; they were armed with Lances, and had a very good Meen. In the third Court were sixty Elephants, with Harness richer than the first, and two

---

[2] Abbé de Choisy, *Journal du Voyage de Siam fait en MDCLXXXV et MDCLXXXVI*, Paris S. Mabre-Cramoisy, 1687.

*The old English 'f' in the original text has been converted to modern English 's' in the remainder of the passage.

Regiments of Life-Guards that made two thousand Men under their Arms. Upon entering into the fourth Court, which had one half the Pavement covered with Mats, we found two hundred Soldiers who wore Sabres adorned with Gold and *Tambag,* called by the *Portugues, Os Bracos Pintados,* because their Arms are painted Red. These Soldiers are the Rowers of the Kings *Balon,* and as it were, the Guards of the Channel. In two Halls more forward there were five hundred *Persians* of the Kings Guard sitting on the Ground cross-legg'd, because in the Kings Palace no Man is suffered to be upon his Legs, unless he be going, and all the *Siam* Soldiers were squatted upon the Tail, holding their Arms betwixt their joyned Hands.

The fifth Court into which we entered, was covered with fine Mats, on which lay prostrate all the *Mandarins* of the third, fourth, and fifth Order, and at a little distance those of the second Order were in the same Posture upon Persian Carpets. Having passed amongst all the *Mandarins,* and crossed so many Courts, we came at length to the foot of a pair of Stairs, where on the Right-hand were two Elephants covered all over with Gold, and on the Left, six Persian Horses, part of whose Saddles and Stirrups were of maffie Gold, and their Harness set with Pearls, Diamonds, Rubies and Emeralds. My Lord Ambassador stopt there, and the Gentlemen going up to the Hall of Audience, where the King was not come as yet, sate down upon Persian Carpets over against the Throne, at twenty Paces distance, as it had been agreed upon. This Throne, to speak properly, is no more but a large Window raised seven or eight foot higher than the half Pace, and answering to the middle of the Hall. On the Right and Left-Hand were two great Parasols of Cloth of Gold, consisting of seven or eight Stories, whose Staves were of beaten Gold, and so high that they almost touched the Ceiling. The Bishop of *Metellopolis,* the Abbot of *Lyonne,* and *Monsieur Vachet,* state in the Hall in the same manner as the Gentlemen did, near the Seat which was prepared for the Ambassador. In that Hall the Princes, Ministers and *Mandarins* of the first Order lay prostrate, to the Right and Left, according to their Rank and Quality.

There are three sorts of Princes at the Court of *Siam*; the first are the Princes of the Blood Royal of *Camboie*, and other Kingdoms that are Tributary to the King of *Siam*. The second are the Princes of *Laos*, *Chiamay*, and *Banca*, who have been taken in the Wars, and some others that have voluntarily put themselves under the Kings Protection. The third are those whom the King has raised to the Degree of Princes; every one of them had before them great Cups of Gold and Silver, which are the Badges of their Dignity, and they lay prostrate with profound Silence, expecting the coming of the King. Sometime after all were thus placed, a great Noise of Trumpets, Drums, and many other Instruments was heard, and then the Throne was opened, and the King appeared sitting on it. But he was to be seen only to the Girdle, the rest being hid by the Front of the Window. All the prostrate *Mandarins* rose up upon their Knees, and having their Hands joyned over their Heads, made profound Inclinations of Body, and knocked their Foreheads against the Ground: The King wore a *Tiara* all shining with precious Stones. It is a long Cap ending in a Point like a Pyramid, encompassed with three Rings of Gold, at some distance from one another. On his Fingers he wore a great many large Diamonds that cast a great Luster, his Vest was Red on a Ground of Gold, and over that he had a Gaze of Gold with Buttons of big Diamonds; all these Ornaments, together with a brisk Air, full of Life, and always smiling, made him look with a great deal of Gracefulness and Majesty.

No sooner was the Ambassador advertised by the Noise of the Instruments that the King was come, but he entred the Hall, followed by the *Abbot de Choisi* and the Lord *Constance*. Having advanced four Steps, and looking upon the King, as if that had been the first time he had perceived him; he made a Bow to the Ground, a second he made in the middle of the

Hall, and a third when he was come near to the Seat that was prepared for him. The King answered every Bow he made by an Inclination of body, which he accompanied with a serene and smiling Countenance.

Guy Tachard, A *Relation of the Voyoge to Siam, Performed by Six Jesuits Sent by the French King, to the Indies and China in the Year 1685*, London, 1688; reprinted Bangkok: White Orchid Press, 1981, pp. 165–8.

18
An Audience with the Emperor of Annam at Hue in 1875

BROSSARD DE CORBIGNY

Brossard de Corbigny's account of his mission's audience with Emperor Thu-Duc of Annam [Central Vietnam] is of considerable historical interest since they were among the first Europeans to be conceded this honour. As he himself mentions, previous missions had been turned away, or prevented by a curtain from seeing the person of the Emperor. British efforts at diplomacy in Vietnam had often been even less successful. In 1875 the French had just taken over the kingdoms of Nam-Ki and Gia-Ding in South Vietnam, and were poised to take over Tonkin [North Vietnam]. These areas they viewed as more profitable for development than Annam, with their large navigable waterways, mineral resources, and extensive rice lands. By the terms of the treaties which this mission aimed to secure, Emperor Thu-Duc was to cede three provinces to France in exchange for French protection and assistance against Chinese pirates. The French were to provide Thu-Duc with a certain number of ocean-going steamers, a hundred cannon and a thousand rifles, though de Corbigny expresses the opinion that even these would not be sufficient to rid Hue of pirates. The Emperor, de Corbigny tells us, though treated as divine, was kept in great isolation by his mandarins, which prevented him exercising any effective political power. The niceties of etiquette essential to

105

the occasion were a matter of acute anxiety to the mandarin delegated to look after them, while the question in French minds was whether they would be required to make obeisances before the Emperor. It was agreed, however, that they should merely give the French salute at the beginning and end of the proceedings, and that since it would be an open air audience, they would not be required to remove their hats. Their interpreter was Fr. Hoang, a local convert to Catholicism. While de Corbigny was not able to see or report on the innermost parts of the palace, his description certainly conveys the ritual uses of royal space for impressive displays of power and wealth. All went well at the audience, and next day the Emperor showed his approval by sending a box of lychees under four royal umbrellas.

13th April. At about two o'clock, our *tam-tri*,* accompanied by servants of the king, came in search of our copy of the treaty; red cloth litters were brought for us, and each of us, French and Annamite, in ceremonial dress, did his best to make himself comfortable in these conveyances. At the head of our procession went the treaty, borne beneath the royal shade of four yellow umbrellas; another escort brought up the rear; lancers made a hedge around us, and behind them came the local inhabitants who rushed up to have a look at us. . . .

The boats soon brought us upriver, and we passed in the same order through the outer fortifications of the imperial city. After the exterior gate, one crosses an esplanade about two hundred metres in width, separating the first two lines of fortifications, and we alighted near a small room carpeted in red; it is an outbuilding of the military barracks and magazines. Tea and sweetmeats awaited us here.

Today we will not proceed further than a few paces from here, to the Ngô-mon gate, the main entrance of the second surrounding wall; but tomorrow, the day of the audience, we shall meet the king within the third line of fortifications.

*De Corbigny describes the *tam-tri* as 'mandarins appointed to guide, protect, and, I suppose, spy on us a little during our visit'.

From our resting-place one can see the grand esplanade stretching around the base of the walls, free of any structures; the interior face of these walls is sloping and dressed with large stones. At the centre of the southeast side towers the yellow-painted keep, visible from outside. Not many cannons; the parapets with their thatched roofs hid them from our view. After we had waited for a quarter of an hour, the king's delegates were announced to us. There were two of them, in full costume, bearing with them the Annamite treaty. Their features were so stamped with solemn emotion that it was only with difficulty that I could recognize, beneath that mask of ceremony and his great brocaded robes, the same Ki-vi-ba who on normal occasions would break from time to time into such an abrupt, ringing laugh....

At last the copies of the two treaties were signed, the seals attached, and the two processions moved towards the paved esplanade of the Ngô-mon gate. Three bridges lead to it; the gate itself has three main entrances and two side entrances. Above these entryways, the ramparts are crowned by galleries which dominate the square. The king, we were told, had positioned himself behind some lowered blinds, to take a look at us without being observed. Each procession, entering from opposite sides, came to a halt at the centre of the square. Umbrellas were lined up at the foot of the walls; around the gate, the king's servants held lighted incense burners, screens, fly-swats, etc. Two rows of mace-bearers in red completed the ceremonial guard. The ambassadors soon advanced towards each other, uttered some words of ceremony, and exchanged their respective treaties. The first Annamite ambassador then announced to us that his colleague would pay us a visit that evening, being charged with the duty of briefing us on the rules of court etiquette for the next day's audience, then each retired slowly to his own side. We climbed back into our litters, and our porters, at a jog trot, soon brought us back to our boats....

14th April. We arose early today, so as not to delay, since the sun would already be hot, the moment fixed for our departure. Just as yesterday, and in the same costume, we presented ourselves at the gate of the fortifications; but this time it was together with our French escort that we passed through the thick defensive wall. This fortress is the only serious defensive position that Thu-Duc has at his disposal. It was built by commandant Ollivier, under Gia-Long, after the French style. Its walls would make it difficult to beseige without artillary, but on the other hand the large number of useless spaces that it encloses would prevent it resisting a blockade which would be easy to establish in the plains and branches of the river which surround it. It is built on an island edged on one side by the river itself, and on the three others, by sizeable canals navigable by boats. At the foot of the walls runs a moat; two or three humped stone bridges bestride this on each side, and give access to the interior via the gates in the walls, which are twenty to thirty metres thick. One then comes to the esplanade, where we stopped yesterday evening, and which we found today filled with soldiers on parade, in uniforms of all colours. We left our infantry detachment at the barracks, and continued as far as the Ngô-mon gate, preceded by our ten sailors. There we got out of our litters, and the umbrellas were closed, since one does not use them beyond the second row of battlements. In front of the gate, a curious spectacle drew our attention: along the whole length of the esplanade, long rows of soldiers were drawn up facing each other, leaving space in the centre for an array of the king's carriages. Behind the soldiers, the parade elephants, in their armour, were arranged in two rows; they had palanquins on their backs, which were like square-shaped armchairs from which great draperies hung down on either side. Their mahouts, seated on their necks, kept them motionless, and behind these on their backs sat another man holding a tall, gaudily-coloured parasol. There were around twenty of them. Among the unhitched carriages, in the centre, was one which particularly caught the eye; it was a kind of gig, all red and as though transparent: it looked like a great paper lantern on little wheels. Another, with four wheels, green and yellow, looked like an ancient stage coach. We were told that it dated from the current reign, but the style was French, and of a period at least a century ago. Its white horses in their yellow harness stood beside it, they too sheltered by the royal umbrellas.

After passing beneath the Ngô-mon gate, the first thing we saw was his Majesty's two largest elephants, like motionless sentinels; they stood on guard, in full caparison. From their chest and sides hung great yellow draperies embroidered with dragons in every colour. On their backs they carried the royal palanquins, held in place by red cords with golden knots. They had golden rings on their tusks, and their front feet bore bracelets of the same material. Their heads were all harnessed with interlaced red ornaments. As a sign of their privileged royal status, these two mounts each had a blue-robed mandarin as mahout, and on his rump a page bearing an ornamented yellow umbrella. We next passed between lines of soldiers armed with shields, drawn up along an avenue of trees. To the left, two white horses, the king's mounts, were standing in line with them. To the right some ponds, surrounded by pierced balustrades, were apparently crocodile pens. Here, as in China, the tail of these ugly beasts is considered a delicacy. Between the crocodile pens, two huge, fantastic, gilded tigers sat on pedestals; their teeth were bared and their bulging enamelled eyes flashed at us above some large vases of blue porcelain. At the end of the avenue, the mandarins of the four lowest ranks stood with their backs to the third defensive wall, forbidden to those of their petty importance. Here on the left we came to a halt, in a vestibule, waiting for the moment of our presentation.

While we were being served tea, our poor *tam-tri*, in a voice strangulated by fear, repeated to each of us the advice he had given us the previous evening, concerning the positions we were to take up, the manners to be observed, the words to be exchanged. At the same time Fr. Huang, in order to accompany us further, dressed himself in court robes; there he was, transformed in an instant into a mandarin, with a square cap on his head, a long robe embroidered with cranes, an ivory board in his hand, and a grave expression on his face.

At last everything was ready; we were ushered through a low gateway into a courtyard filled with musicians; some had guitars made from python-skin, others a kind of violin, ivory shawms or trefoil-shaped cymbals. Their orchestra contained an entire family of gongs and drums, but, among so many instruments each more Chinese than the last, the one which we had formerly naïvely supposed to have come direct from Peking itself to take the place of the regimental bass drum, the 'Chinese Hat'* in fact, was completely lacking from this cacophonous collection. One more artistic illusion shattered!

Here we were before the great gate of the third defensive wall; its doors were red, ornamented with furiously contorted golden dragons; there was a roof over it, the frame of which was in the same style. Turning to the left, we were led beneath the gallery that ran around the edge of the great paved courtyard in which the royal audience would take place. Seated in the shade, we had plenty of time to observe the parade put on in honour of the interview. To our left, at the end of the gallery, the princes, drawn up in a group, regarded us with curiosity. They were dressed in robes of yellow silk with wide sleeves, and wore fine gilded caps on their heads; their features were fine, their complexions rather fair and smooth; one could see at once that their manners differed from those of the other dignitaries. Close to them was the great open gallery which faced the entrance to the courtyard. This was to be occupied by the king. A covered arcade also ran along the other side of the square courtyard opposite us. In this huge paved courtyard, beneath a dazzling sun, fluttered a thousand banners carried by soldiers drawn up along each side of the surrounding wall; before them stood other rows of screen-bearers, umbrella-bearers and

---

*'Chinese Hat' refers to a kind of musical instrument consisting of a stick with a copper top and small bells attached.

lancers of all kinds. At the front were aligned the highest-ranking mandarins, motionless, numbering about a hundred on each side, displaying in the sunlight their multi-coloured embroidered robes. In front of these, finally, stood pages holding lighted incense-burners. In the corners of the court-yard, two bands of musicians completed this varied gathering with its rainbow of colours. The ranks stood motionless; but the banners, the flags, the parasols fluttered in the wind, and the sunshine accentuated unexpected contrasts. In the centre, the great silk robes of the mandarins shimmered with the rich sheen of their Chinese embroidery. We felt how for-tunate we were to be enjoying, beneath the clear tropical sky, the rare spectacle of the court of the king of Annam in full ceremonial dress.

There was another moment of waiting benea:h the arcade, a moment during which our escorts were in such an agony of anxiety that one of them, overcome, no longer knew which one of us he was speaking to. At last we were led, between the multi-coloured ranks, as far as the row of grand dignit-aries; from there we could make out, in the centre of the courtyard, our little square carpets of yesterday evening, laid out before the throne.* At the same instant, a great shout rang out, and cannons were fired in the distance, signalling the arrival of His Majesty.

The red gates swung open at the same moment, and we could hear the melodies of the bands posted in the entrance-courtyard. This concert, less painful to our ears than we had at first anticipated, lasted only a few minutes; it ceased as soon as the king had taken his place; we saw him approach close to a table, and in spite of the bright light which dazzled us and the shadow cast by the gallery beneath which he was standing, one could make out his slightly wan face, his long, thin beard, and his rich costume of the imperial yellow.

The master of ceremonies himself then advanced before

---

*It had been arranged that the squares of carpet would indicate where they were to stand during the audience.

His Majesty and prostrated himself on his knees, with his face to the ground, then, still on his knees and with his hands joined together, he requested permission to introduce the French ambassador. The king replied through an announcer that the audience was open, and we advanced to take up our places on the carpets. After bowing to His Majesty, our ambassador extraordinary explained the purpose of his journey, said that he came in the name of the French government, asked after the health of the king of Annam, presented him with the grand ribbon of the Legion of Honour, and offered him gifts, as a mark of satisfaction in the exchange of treaties enacted the previous day. These words, translated by our mission's interpreter, were repeated to the king by two successive intermediaries, in spite of the fact that he had heard them perfectly well; then the decoration and the list of presents was placed on the table in front of him. He then responded with thanks, and in his turn requested news of the President of the French Republic (words which must have sounded strange for this oriental autocrat). His precious words were repeated twice more by the same intermediaries, and finally the ambassador replied and expressed his thanks. The king then withdrew to his apartments, followed by his pages bearing fans. We bowed to him as he departed; it remained only for us to retire ourselves.

Considering the mystery which surrounds the sacred person of this demi-god in the eyes even of his faithful subjects, such an interview could only have been a considerable effort on His Annamite Majesty's part, and one understands why these audiences do not end with a more intimate conversation, as has already been the case in Siam and Japan. If Thu-Duc had given us full satisfaction that day, it had not always been so in his rare audiences with the French. Once, indeed, a curtain had veiled the sacred personage from the eyes of those present. So there had been progress today, and all had gone off well. Still, a trivial enough incident had, we were told, caused a frown of the royal eyebrows: two of the princes lined up on the lower edge of the dais had permitted themselves to smile when they saw that we did not wear our hair coiled in a bun. As punishment for such a serious breach of etiquette, Thu-Duc had cut off their salary for a full year and deprived them of their rice ration. One does not make jokes at court. . . . As for the functionaries who had taken part in the ceremony, they received only compliments; they were even rewarded, the next day, in recognition of their services.

Brossard de Corbigny, 'Huit Jours d'Ambassade à Hué' ('An Eight-Day Diplomatic Visit to Hue'), *Le Tour Du Monde*, Paris (1875): pp. 55–61.

19
The Harem of the Sultan of Brunei in the 1860s

SPENSER ST JOHN

Sir Spencer St John, a lover of exploration in wild and unmapped places, spent thirteen years in Sabah, Sarawak, and Brunei, and made two pioneering ascents of Mt. Kinabalu together with Hugh Low. His *Life in the Forests of the Far East* also includes an exciting account of his ascent of the Limbang River to its headwaters. Both adventurous and gentlemanly, he talked his way through many dangerous encounters during his explorations of Borneo. Though not a naturalist like Low, he was a keen observer of ethnographic detail, and he writes in a way that is generally realistic and balanced, largely without condescension if occasionally revealing a typical prejudice of the day concerning the 'improveability' of indigenous peoples. His account of the women's quarters of the palace of the Sultan of Brunei provides a counterpoint to the more high-flown descriptions of some of the more exquisite of South-East Asian palaces and reveals the life led by the royal wives to have been rather less than luxurious.

THOUGH it is not my object to give an account of the Malays, I will enter slightly into the condition of the women. In Brunei, the wives and daughters of the sultan and of the nobles are much more concealed than holds with the Malays in other parts of Borneo, and one can only describe a harim from hearsay. It is nothing like the gorgeous palaces of Western Asia; the sultan's house consists of a long building like a rough barn, raised on posts in the water, and is perhaps seventy feet long by thirty in breadth. It is one story high, though in the roof are some rough attics: in this residence he keeps his wives, his concubines, and his female slaves; so jealous is he that no one shall see them, that when the house requires repairs, he will work with his own hands rather than permit the labourers to enter the inner rooms: the only man in whom he has confidence is a very old decrepit pañgeran, who assists him in the work. He has seventy women confined in this small space: his principal wife has a large room, elegantly hung with silk hangings, and well matted; she is permitted luxuries denied to all but three or four favourite concubines. The other unfortunates are allowed a little rice, salt, firewood, and water, and once a year a cheap suit of clothes; for everything extra they must depend on their families or their lovers.

The palace is, as I have said, like a rough barn, but the flooring is simply slips of a palm stem, tied together with rattans, and can be opened with facility; through the interstices every kind of refuse is thrown, to be carried away by the current.

This offers temptation to the bold lover, who comes in the dead of night, and by the signal of a white rag hung through the floor, knows the coast is clear: sometimes the girls get bold, and as they are all in league to deceive the sultan, they can occasionally leave the house without being discovered. The daughters of the late Muda Hassim, in 1859, absented themselves for three weeks and were not found out. . . .

The women are fond of making vows, and to that practice I am indebted for my only glimpse of a Bornean harim. During my first expedition to Molu, my boat snapped on a snag, and I was left to return through the jungle. The report spread that I was dead, and various vows were made; among others, the wives and daughters of some of the rajahs made a vow, if I returned in safety, I should visit them and be showered over with yellow rice for good luck's sake. The pañgeran consented, thinking I was dead; but, on my safe return, the ladies insisted upon carrying out their vow; they were anxious to see a white man within their walls.

The nobles came and asked me; I at first declined, but, on being pressed, consented. The whole place was very paltry; about twenty middle-aged women were present, while a crowd of young girls, half hidden by a curtain, occupied the lower end of the room. On my displaying the most perfect indifference as to whether I saw them or not, they gradually emerged. I observed no pretty faces, and constant confinement to the house had rendered their skins of a very light yellow. I am afraid we were mutually disappointed, as the only remark I heard them make about me was, "How very dull his eyes are"; and so they were compared to their flashing black ones.

Spenser St John, *Life in the Forests of the Far East: Travels in Sabah and Sarawak in the 1860s*, London: Smith, Elder & Co., 1862; reprinted Singapore: Oxford University Press, 1986, Vol. II, pp. 262–6.

20
'Visitors' Day at the Palace, Djocjakarta'

JAN POORTENAAR

Jan Poortenaar, a Dutch artist of the 1920s, and his wife, Gertruida van Vladeracken-Poortenaar, planned themselves an 'art journey' through Indonesia together with their daughter. Everywhere they went, Jan painted, while Gertruida gave a series of concerts which no doubt helped to finance their travels, and together they produced a lively book of their impressions. The trip was conceived as 'a quest of beauty and interest, with some little air of the Troubadour about it; for had we not songs for sale?' Jan carried introductions to the Sultans of Yogyakarta and Solo, and was permitted to paint the court dancers of each. Gertruida rose to the challenge of giving concerts on stages where the performer had to compete with bats, mosquitoes, buzzing beetles, *tokkeh*s [large and loud geckos], crickets, dogs, and pianos full of ants' nests down which, in accordance with time-honoured Dutch colonial custom, glasses of beer had been poured at the end of a night's festivities. The result was an intensely personal narrative, written with a deft touch both comic and poetic. The impressionistic style well suits a description of the faded elegance of the palace of Yogyakarta.

TO see the Kraton, the Palace of the Sultan! A palace of the Arabian Nights, nay, a veritable town of palaces the Kraton must be, and now this fairy tale of the Orient is to become reality. We shall enter the mighty gateways, where sentinels, immobile and aloof in their task, guard the Holy; we shall cross courtyards shadowed by high waringin trees, and the palace walls will close in the silence, secretly, majestically, grandly. In this maze of apartments and buildings the inhabitants are counted by thousands. There beats the heart of Javanese music, lives the gamelan, the forgers, the wayang both as shadow show and acted, and also the finest dancing of the noble serimpis and bedoyos. Imposing Pendoppos* will we find in gardens full of flowers.... But now the imagination pauses, for where, in the omnipresent green which the East proved itself to be, especially in the dry season, would we find the riches of blossom with which we had invested those courts? Reluctantly we abandon the vision of an Oriental Versailles or Hampton court, but still we cling to the thought that the gateway to Ancient Java is to open for us. Up then, to see the Kraton, the Palace of the Sultan.

'The omnibus leaves at a quarter to nine, sir.'

'———?!'

---

*pendoppo [pendopo]: open audience hall, with a high roof on wooden pillars, and without walls.

'The omnibus of the Hotel. It is the easiest way to get there, or you must. . . .'

Whatever the alternative is we bow to the conventional method, and the omnibus accordingly it is. Thus to see the Kraton proves to begin: being brought to the Resident's office with other tourists; secondly: waiting until more sheep flock to this unromantic fold; and finally, at a stroke of the clock, the official appears who is to guide the polyglot company, and away we go. By omnibus!

At last we stop before the Kraton itself. Here watchmen stand, with long lances, in the official court dress, the bunched-up sarong, the Javanese jacket, the curling plait. We enter the wide aloon-aloon, the forecourt, and the hetero-geneous crowd of us stare at the heterogeneous pile of buildings. The old cannons sleep. The guide explains things in Dutch, which pleases us because since his father and his father's father were also in the Kraton as servants to the late Sultan he may know more about it than the English-speaking Hindoo from a hotel who has constituted himself guide to a dozen Americans. This gentleman's explanations sparkle with humour; and when we compare his English stories with those of the Dutch rival to which we listen with our other ears, we decide that the strange narratives of the old Buddhism or the more piquant details of life at the Kraton are as speculative as the European exchanges on after-war finance.

The long pilgrimage through the buildings has not the saving grace of humour, nor of beauty. Dilapidation, oriental neglect and carelessness everywhere, and the poorest set of buildings we have set eyes upon. Not even picturesque dis-order reigns. In a crude shed which looks like a stable to the European eye, we see—the Sultan's gamelan, and in a corner a heap of gold payongs* and spears.

Another door: the state coaches, of which the finest are

---

*payong: umbrella; also emblem of dignity, gilt wholly or partially according to the rank of noble.

covered with rather perished canvas. The mustiness of a cellar-atmosphere mixes with incense smoke which servants prepare continually from the burning of coco-fruit peel. Then again gardens, great courts with palm plants in majolica pots.

A single fine pendoppo, disgraced by European paraffin lamps and equally vulgar armchairs with curly legs and plush covers, is the next attraction. Thank heaven all this is doomed. The present Sultan, Hamengku Buwono VIII, has a project for restoring everything in Javanese style, and the execution of his plans has commenced. The lamps will disappear from the beautifully carved, gilded, and painted ceiling, and, indeed, when we visited the hall subsequently, the hideous chairs had already gone.

Here and there servants linger, servants 'who only stand and wait', it would seem. Or are they there to keep an eye upon the visitors? They examine each other's hair without the least embarrassment, they chatter and whisper; further on women sit giggling and playing cards; to the stranger under the sidelong scrutiny of these many eyes the atmosphere seems full of intrigue. We are shown the banqueting hall where three hundred guests can sit; and also we see the wall against which in the old days sentenced criminals were stabbed. In front of it is a raised place where the seated Sultans exercised their particular privilege of watching these spectacles. The guide's flow of humour is in full flood at this point; tipping time is getting near.

At many corners watchmen stand with lances, but the points are cased in leather. Others have a rifle, but it is some sort of harmless, old civic-guard's weapon. The sentinel is so unconcerned with his that it rests against a specially erected wooden stand. Two captains of the watch on their hassocks converse intimately over a cup of tea. Polonius gossips with Polonius. Five servants sit behind them.

Stairs, walls and courts with caged birds precede the spectacle of the Sultan's elephant. He stands under a roof with one foreleg tied so closely to a big pole that he cannot move it other than by shoving around the pole. That is what he does now, therefore; to-day, to-morrow, the day after to-morrow. Once a week, on Saturdays, he has his day off; he is taken for an airing and allowed to bathe in the brook. But to-day is not Saturday, and so he stands pathetically and shoves round as he will do for many years until the rope has worn this pole almost through, as it has worn one near by.

A new guard arrives, parades past with slow pace, dull greyheads, goodly bespectacled little men with a plait coming from under the head-dress. They also carry and put aside the lances with their leather sheaths; they also sit down quietly, they also chat listlessly and commence to drink tea.

The elephant propels itself around its pole endlessly. . . .

Round a corner we stay behind; we are permitted to, says our guide. We yearn for the aloon-aloon, for space and open air, and delivery from this oppressive silence. True, the great court is a bare, dusty desert, but the wide-spreading waringin trees cut to shape are protecting payongs outstretched above the balustrades which surround them; emblems, it is said, of the protective power of the Sultan and as exalted as he. They make the enormous space look majestic, but they cannot obliterate the impression of the realities of the Kraton as we have seen it.

In spite of all it is here that the culture of Java still lives and blooms unseen, as, unseen by the casual visitor, the old tree still brings forth its blossoms. How many branches it has lost in the passing of time, but its flowers are still pure and princely, and such as have not thrived for centuries in any Occidental court. The dance, the wayang, the gamelan and the batik remained, though the ruler's secular power decayed. No longer may he lead his armies; no longer stately ambassadors move in imposing procession across the now empty aloon-aloon. Years have elapsed since the last building was added to the intricate structure of the Kraton; now, scarcely any attempt is made to repair the ravages of decay; mildew, moss, dirt or weeds gather on the perishing wood and crumbling stone. For many ages the energy of the people was spent within the Kraton's walls; intellectually and materially all possessions of the people were vested in the Ruler, that truly Eastern Potentate. And for ages the whims and caprices of that All-Mighty One dissipated the wealth, until at last even his bullying servants could no longer extort money from his subjects, could no longer levy tribute upon the impoverished and exhausted mass of the people. The Shiva made room for the submissive Mohammedanism, and the servile attitude towards the All-Destroying God changed later into the submissiveness of the slave to the divinely empowered king, to whom year after year tribute in full measure was paid without question and without thought of injustice.

Now the free energy of the people has died, but with it too has gone the power of these tyrants who for so long lived as parasites on their subjects. Even the show of power, the ancient decorum and greatness of gesture, are but the pale shadow of what they have been.

Around the palace walls live the population in extreme poverty. Such dejection is not found in the islands outside the Principalities. For although the wild, seafaring Madura population, the Batak of the Sumatra highlands, and the Dajak of Central Borneo live in little better condition, it seems with them to be rather their natural and primitive existence, lightly and carelessly led. Here, however, the old oppression still marks the mien of the people.

Nevertheless, and in spite of all their antiquated social arrangements and wide-spread poverty, the Principalities have a culture and a refinement of race, and of the arts which remind one of the aristic efflorescence of the Medici, a culture which subtly penetrates all classes of society, a culture more valuable than material welfare, and one such as Europe has not known for centuries, whilst its art has become increasingly a stranger in its own land.

It is thus that the visitor sees the Kraton on Fridays, and thus he muses there. For the Kraton on a visitors' day is a stage seen in daylight, emptied of its actors and its accessories. One evening the still scene shall live anew for us. We have

120

been invited to assist at the exercise of the dancing girls. Our carriage halts where the street ends against the high wall, we enter the great gate opening on the wide, dark courtyard. A single, solitary lamp gleams in the black silence, and soon we stand before the main gate, where left and right the watchmen are posted under small pendoppos. We show our invitation and are permitted to pass. The dimly lighted pathway brings us to another high, dark gateway, its gate closed. When one of the watchmen gently knocks the heavy door slowly swings ajar; a whisper passes to and fro; quietly the door closes again. The watchman explains that someone within has gone to inform the Sultan's brother of our coming. We wait on in the darkness, and after a little while the gate is slowly opened again. Permission has been given for us to pass. When the door has fully opened we see in the dim, vague light of a little lamp the watchmen behind it with their huge, drawn swords and Javanese spears, their shadows gigantic on the white walls. We follow our guide, and soon from a large pendoppo a black silhouette appears against the lights behind, and the Sultan's brother, Pangeran Hadisooryo, welcomes us and bids us follow him. Across the marble floor, shining under the lights of lamps, chairs and tables have been placed for the European visitors.

At our left the instruments of the gamelan stand and wait; nothing else breaks the clear expanse of the wide floor. In the darkness outside rustles the rain. Now, noiselessly on their bare feet, some of the players come like shadows in the dim light, and crouch on their hassocks behind their instruments. Simultaneously from our right, crouching as they creep forward, the dancers appear; phantasmal. No noise disturbs the utter silence. The sarong they wear pulled up high under the arms so that it leaves the shoulders and arms bare; they wear no ornamental trimmings. The smallest and youngest, children still, remain at the extreme right, but in the centre of the hall, close to where we have taken up our position, the four serimpi dancers crouch, pale and yellow in the golden light of the lamps against the dark brown and gilt of the wooden wainscoting. Now the gamelan begins, and all the dancers rise and sway to and fro with the soft music, wherein it seems the rustling of tropic leaves is interwoven with the murmur of rain.

Who has heard a bird begin to sing in the dead stillness of a summer night before the dawn appears? Some decisive notes lightened and made lovely by a first essay of swift sound, then an echo from afar, till the long tones repeat from every side, and suddenly, again, again another bird will take up the strain, pouring out his own bright cascade of clear music. Thus the gamelan begins, and in perfect unity with its rhythm the arms of the dancers rise and fall like palm leaves stirred by the dawn breeze. Their hands write strange hiero-glyphics on the air, like necromancers conjuring unearthly spirits, slowly following the flowing lines of some secret and ethereal script.

After a while the fine fingers draw the dagger, the Javanese kriss which they each wear like some exotic stamen at their girdles. Crouching servants hand over shields, but both these and the weapons are of buffalo leather, explains the Pangeran who sits at our sides, so that the dancers cannot harm one another. Later, in the same highly conventionalised way, they handle pistols, always as though they were plucking and pre-senting flowers. No change of expression enlivens the still faces. What thoughts, we wonder, drift and die behind the lowered eyelids?

When, after a while, we chat with the Pangeran and ask him amusedly whether the pistols are charged and meant for us, he abandons his official demeanour for a time, and laughs heartily and drinks our health light-heartedly in the Tokayer, the wine which has been brought in the meantime in true court fashion by a long, silent, obsequious procession of ser-vants. And so the human East dispels our dream.

Jan Poortenaar, *An Artist in Java and Other Islands of Indonesia*, London: Sampson Low, Marston & Co., *c*.1928; reprinted Singapore: Oxford University Press, 1989, pp. 62–8.

21
A Meeting with the Raja of Goa, Celebes

ALFRED RUSSELL WALLACE

Like St John, Wallace here provides us with a record of one of the less grandiose palaces of the region. The rulers of South Sulawesi's various kingdoms lived in pile-built timber palaces which were built according to the same basic plan as ordinary houses, only much enlarged. Few of these structures still survive. The photograph (p. 124) shows the Raja of Goa's house, after 1880, as photographed by Woodbury and Page, a photo studio based in Java. Although slightly later, and therefore possibly not the same house, it would almost certainly be a perhaps somewhat larger version of the one visited by Wallace.

O N returning home to Mamájam (as my house was called) I had a slight return of intermittent fever, which kept me some days indoors. As soon as I was well, I again went to Goa, accompanied by Mr. Mesman, to beg the Rajah's assistance in getting a small house built for me near the forest. We found him at a cock-fight in a shed near his palace, which however he immediately left to receive us, and walked with us up an inclined plane of boards which serves for stairs to his house. This was large, well built, and lofty, with bamboo floor and glass windows. The greater part of it seemed to be one large hall divided by the supporting posts. Near a window sat the Queen squatting on a rough wooden arm-chair, chewing the everlasting sirih and betel-nut, while a brass spittoon by her side and a sirih-box in front were ready to administer to her wants. The Rajah seated himself opposite to her in a similar chair, and a similar spittoon and sirih-box were held by a little boy squatting at his side. Two other chairs were brought for us. Several young women, some the Rajah's daughters, others slaves, were standing about; a few were working at frames making sarongs, but most of them were idle.

And here I might (if I followed the example of most

Residence of the Raja of Goa, I-Kumala also known as Abdulkadir Muhammad Aidid (r. 1844–93). The covered steps leading up to it and the five tiers of the gable triangle are indications of rank. (Koninklijk Insitituut voor Taal-, Land- en Volkenkunde).

travellers) launch out into a glowing description of the charms of these damsels, the elegant costumes they wore, and the gold and silver ornaments with which they were adorned. The jacket or body of purple gauze would figure well in such a description, allowing the heaving bosom to be seen beneath it, while 'sparkling eyes', and 'jetty tresses', and 'tiny feet' might be thrown in profusely. But, alas! regard for truth will not permit me to expatiate too admiringly on such topics, determined as I am to give as far as I can a true picture of the people and places I visit. The princesses were, it is true, sufficiently good-looking, yet neither their persons nor their garments had that appearance of freshness and cleanliness without which no other charms can be contemplated with pleasure. Everything had a dingy and faded appearance, very disagreeable and unroyal to a European eye. The only thing that excited some degree of admiration was the quiet and dignified manner of the Rajah, and the great respect always paid to him. None can stand erect in his presence, and when he sits on a chair, all present (Europeans of course excepted) squat upon the ground. The highest seat is literally, with these people, the place of honour and the sign of rank. So unbending are the rules in this respect, that when an English carriage which the Rajah of Lombock had sent for arrived, it was found impossible to use it because the driver's seat was the highest, and it had to be kept as a show in its coach-house. On being told the object of my visit, the Rajah at once said that he would order a house to be emptied for me, which would be much better than building one, as that would take a good deal of time. Bad coffee and sweetmeats were given us as before.

Alfred Russell Wallace, *The Malay Archipelago*, London: Macmillan, 1869; reprinted Singapore, Graham Brash, 1983, pp. 167–8.

22

A Stay with the Raja of Magindanao
in August 1775

THOMAS FORREST

Thomas Forrest (*c*.1729–1802) was a British merchant seacaptain who travelled and traded widely through the Indonesian Archipelago. He began his career as a midshipman at the age of sixteen, and by 1760 had become an independent merchant making several exploratory voyages around the coasts of Java, Bali, and Sulawesi. He rose to become Commander-in-Chief of the British East India Company's Marine in 1770, and was closely involved in surveying to find the Company a more satisfactory site than the malaria-infested Bencoolen for their headquarters, and seeking to establish advantageous trading relations in areas not yet controlled by the Dutch. The main purpose of his voyage to New Guinea and the Moluccas in 1774–6 was to search for sources of cloves and nutmeg. It was made in a small ship of ten tons, the *Tartar Galley*, manned by a mixed crew of Malays, Indonesians, Filipinos, Indian Lascars, and Europeans. Forrest writes in a factual manner about many aspects of local custom, technology, and political organization. His refreshing lack of condescension may possibly reflect, not just his own temperament but a more eighteenth-century vision of other peoples as 'nations'—accepted as different without necessarily being inferior—by comparison with the increasingly racist assumptions which came automatically to so many later colonial writers. A remarkably sympathetic and keen observer, he showed consideration for cultural differences both among his crew and the peoples he visited. When ashore, he sometimes hunted wild pig for meat, but never brought it on board ship out of deference to the Muslims in his crew. Forrest, willingly removing his shoes before entering the palace, compares himself to the ancient Romans—a marked contrast to the British of a later date, who were adamant in their refusal to comply with this custom in India and Burma. He notices that the gaps between the floorboards, of split *nibong* palm wood (a very dense wood, widely used as a building material in South-East Asia), allow an updraft of cool air to be drawn through the house as warm air rises—one of several design features enhancing natural ventilation in pile-built

South-East Asian structures. The prestigious display of stored wealth in the form of Chinese jars and other prized items is a feature that also has parallels in some other South-East Asian societies. The chocolate must have been introduced to the Philippines from Mexico by the Spanish.

ABOUT four in the afternoon, it was fignified* to me, that Rajah Moodo[†] desired my company to visit the Sultan. We crossed the Melampy in two large canoes, strongly joined, though somewhat separated, by transverse planks. This floating stage carried over above forty persons.

The Sultan's palace is a tenement about one hundred and twenty foot long, and fifty broad. The first floor rises fourteen from the ground. Thirty-two strong wooden pillars support the house in four rows, eight in a row. The intercolumniation, or filling up between the two outer rows, is excessively slight; being of sticks so put together, that both light and air intervene. Through some windows cut low, are pieces of iron cannon pointed outward. Above six foot, which height the slender sticks do not surpass, the tenement is well matted all round. In the lower part nothing was kept, but boats under cover, with their furniture.

The first row of pillars inward, is about ten foot within those which support the outside, and covered with scarlet broad cloth to the top; where at the height of about twenty foot from the first floor, they sustain the beams and rafters, on which rests a substantial, though light roof, made of the sago tree leaves. From the tops of the inside pillars, palempores[‡] with broad white borders extending them, were smoothly expanded, and made a noble cieling.

A moveable slight partition divided the whole into two unequal parts. The first part being about one third of the

---

*The old English 'f' in the original text has been converted to modern English 's' in the remainder of the passage.

[†]Rajah Moodo [Rajah Muda]: a viceroy.

[‡]*palempore*: a cloth of flowered chintz, almost certainly Indian.

whole, was well floored with planks on strong beams: here were six pieces of cannon mounted. The inner apartment was not floored, but covered with split aneebong [*nibong*], a kind of palm tree, in pieces going the whole length of it, about five inches broad, and placed half an inch, or an inch asunder. This contrivance of floor for the inner apartment, seemed preferred to the solid floor of the outer, as admitting the fresh air from below; and covered, except in the passage, with matting, and a few carpets, it rendered the palace remarkably cool.

Between the two farthest pillars of the farther apartment stood the bed, on a stage of plank, a foot high, which projected about two foot behind the bedstead: this was covered with mats, and proved a convenient seat all round, except on the back part.

From the roof depended the tester, to which were fixed three rows of curtains; the inmost of white calico, the next of blue, the outermost combining breadths of silk, of the most contrasted colours.

Towards the head of the bed were arranged yellow pillows or bolsters; some as large as an ordinary bale of English broad cloth, some smaller, and all filled, with the plantain dry leaves, which made them light. Their ends of scarlet cloth were embroidered with gold. Of the pillows, some were shaped like prisms, and lay necessarily on a side. I imagine those large pillows are sometimes used to lean against, tho' no such use was made of them at that time; they lying then all near the head of the bed, which was about eight foot square.

That side of the inner apartment, which was opposite the bed, had much the appearance of a china shop. Below stood a range of about thirty china jars, each capable of, at least, twenty gallons; above them, a shelf supported another row of less capacious jars; the next shelf exhibited a row of black earthen water pots, with brass covers, in which the water contracted a coolness for the refreshment of guests. A fourth shelf, attainable only by a ladder, held salvers and cuspadores.

Towards the farther end ran a cross row of shelves, containing similar furniture, the largest jars being always the lowest: behind, were the retired apartments. Opposite the row of shelves, that went partly along the hall, stood two rows of red coloured china chests, one upon another, the lower row the larger; but each containing chests of equal size. A ramp of masonry was the ascent, but only to one door of this vast apartment. A palisade of strong posts surrounded three sides of it, the river washed the fourth.

Rajah Moodo was accompanied by one of his natural brothers; there was also Muttusinwood, an officer of polity, called sometimes *Gogo*, as in the Molucca islands: Datoo Woodine, an officer who superintended the prows and vessels belonging to Rajah Moodo; with some *Manteries**[*] and *Amba Rajahs.*[†]

In the outer hall were drawn up about twenty of the Bisayan guards, with the Spanish serjeant at their head.

The Sultan sat on the ground, in the inner hall, filling the center of a square, well spred with mats. Rajah Moodo was seated about eight foot from him, towards the door. The company was ranged before the Sultan and Rajah Moodo, and on the latter's right hand, making two sides of the square above mentioned. The third side, being open, displayed afar the Sultana Myong, and some ladies sitting by the foot of the bed. Near the fourth side, a curtain of party coloured silk was dropt, the Sultan's back being towards it. I had the honour of being seated on Rajah Moodo's right hand, and next to me sat the Spanish Envoy.

One of the company was Marajah Pagaly,[‡] the Sultan's natural brother. Topang, and his brother Uku, presently came in; the former gaily drest, in new silver brocade: nobody there was so fine. . . .

Out of respect to this assembly, I left my shoes at the

---

*Mantery, a kind of justice of peace.
†Amba Rajah, protector of the people's privileges.
‡Pagaly Mama, signifies brother; Pagaly Babye, sister.

door;*as did the Spanish Envoy. I had lately been accustomed to do so at Rajah Moodo's; but it was never required of me. They, who walk with slippers, always leave them without, when they are to sit down. . . .

Eight or ten large yellow wax candles being lighted, and put into brass candlesticks, before each person was placed a large brass salver, a black earthen pot of water, and a brass cuspadore.†

The salver was loaded with saucers, presenting sweet cakes of different kinds, round a large china cup of chocolate. My chocolate and the Spanish Envoy's, appeared in glass tumblers; and our water pots were red. The same distinction was observed at Rajah Moodo's, to us Christians.

About ten o'clock, as several had retired, and Rajah Moodo was talking with the Sultan, in the Magindano tongue, I got up also to go away. Leave is taken with a small ceremony; a lifting of the right hand to the head, with a small inclination of the latter.

Thomas Forrest, *A Voyage to New Guinea and the Moluccas, 1774–1776*, London: G. Scott, 1780; reprinted Singapore: Oxford University Press, 1969, pp. 230–6

---

*Among the Romans, it was usual for each guest to leave his slippers or sandals, with a slave, when he went in to supper. One merry instance may suffice, translated by the hand to which we have before been indebted. Mart. Ep. XII. 88.

Bis Cotta foleas perdidiffe fe queftus,	That his sandals he lost twice poor Cotta complain'd,
Dum negligentum ducit ad pedes vernam	While a negligent slave at his feet he retain'd;
Qui folus inopi præftat, et facit turbam:	Who, remiss as he was, made up Cotta's whole train:
Excogitavit homo fagax, et aftutus,	So he shrewdly bethought, nor bethought him in vain,
Ne faccre poffet tale fæpius damnum;	That he might no more suffer a damage so odd,
Excalceatus ire cœpit ad cœnam.	He resolv's to proceed to his supper unshod.

†An utensil well known by those who smoak tobacco, or chew betel.

Temples

23
Burmese Pagodas

R. TALBOT KELLY

Commissioned to produce a book on Burma, Kelly, a British artist
and writer, travelled around the country for seven months in the
first years of the twentieth century. He covered 3,500 miles and
was much impressed by the beauty of Burma and the 'happy picturesqueness of its people'. His seventy-five delicate watercolours,
illustrating the book, capture the soft quality of light in Burma. He
enjoyed the hospitality of British colonial friends, traders, miners,
teak foresters, and others and explored a wide variety of landscapes,
travelling by river, railway, and pony. Here he comments on that
most ubiquitous element of the Burmese landscape—the Buddhist
pagoda.

IT is in their religious buildings, however, that we recognise the chief expression of their art sense, where,
influenced by their environment and imitating the ex-
uberance of nature, they are elaborate in design and lavish in
their decoration. Their plaster-work is excellent, and teak
carving almost unique. They are fond of introducing human
and animal forms into their carvings, from life-sized figures
of dancing men and women to the innumerable little effigies
of beloos, nats, and other supernatural forms which decorate
the eaves and cornices of the kyaungs. In the pagodas, guarded
by griffins which have always a highly decorative feeling, a
common form I noticed was that of the peacock perched

131

upon a crocodile, no doubt emblematical of the triumph of beauty over what is vile, in which perhaps is also implied a religious parallel.

I remember that on landing at Rangoon a friend remarked to me that I would soon 'become sick of pagodas', and certainly the great number one sees on the Irrawaddy and throughout the country generally almost justifies such a remark, every point of vantage apparently being utilised by the Burman upon which to build his temple. It must be acknowledged that they add considerably to the beauty of the landscape, but apart from any pictorial value they may possess, I must say that, far from becoming tired of this continuous succession of temples, I found my interest grow rather than diminish upon fuller acquaintance.

At first sight one temple or pagoda is much like another, and it is a graceful object at that, but on comparing the various periods and styles, what a difference is noticeable! All more or less conform to the graceful zedi form of design, yet no two are alike. The plinths are sometimes square, again octagonal or polygonal, receding in successive stages—each differently ornamented—to the base of the dome. This again is built in stages, each representing in conventional form some familiar object, such as the rice bowl, the twisted turban, a plantain bud, etc, until the finial is reached, itself almost always enriched with ornament of individual character, and surmounted by the gilt 'ti', which is hardly ever the same in two pagodas. A comparison between the Shwe Dagon in Rangoon, the Shwe-Tsan-Dau at Prome, and the unique bell pagoda at Bhamo will soon demonstrate this. Further, the treatment of the panels, which often lend interest to the plinth, the guardian leogryphs and votive vases, the emblematical tree rising from its architectural base, and the hundred odd architectural and artistic adjuncts which combine in forming any given pagoda are all as distinctive as are the different types of humanity. Moreover, each is beautiful, and far from being 'sick of pagodas', my only regret is that I had not sufficient time at my disposal more fully to study and

'Platform of the Shwe Zigon Pagoda—Pagan', from R. Talbot Kelly, *Burma: Painted and Described*, 1905. The Shwe Zigon remains one of the most important and frequented of Burmese pagodas; Kelly skilfully captured its atmosphere.

133

analyse the undoubted charm each possesses. When to all this is added the effect of gilding in one case, and the subduing influence of age and weather in another, combined with an infinite variety of environment, the pagoda can never become monotonous, particularly when seen as principal object in a landscape of tropical richness, whose beauties are reflected in one of the noblest rivers in the world, and bathed in an atmosphere which lends an enchantment to the whole.

R. Talbot Kelly, *Burma: Painted and Described*, 1905; reprinted London: Adam and Charles Black, 1912, pp. 250–2.

24
Bangkok and Its Temples

GEOFFREY GORER

Geoffrey Gorer read anthropology at Cambridge, but initially decided to pursue a career in creative writing. However his first book, *Africa Dances* (1934), written after a trip of three months in West Africa, attracted the attention of Margaret Mead, who persuaded him to take up anthropological research. He did fieldwork with the Lepchas of Sikkim in the Himalayas, about whom he published a book in 1938. Like his contemporaries Mead, Bateson, and Benedict, he developed a strong interest in psychology and the interface between the individual and his or her culture; he went on to produce several studies of American, Russian, French, and English character. *Bali and Angkor* is a more light-hearted travel book, though not without some serious opinions. Unlike many of his predecessors in the genre, Gorer is self-consciously anti-romantic. By turns witty and irritating, not to say impertinent, Gorer's opinionated account is no doubt as revealing of its author, and the period in which he was writing, as it is of the sights he records.

BANGKOK has only been the capital of the country since 1782. It is on the banks of the Menam, a river which is continuously silting up, and creating more and more land at its estuary; Ayudha, the earlier capital, was formerly a seaport, and is now some hours' journey from the coast; and since the foundation of Bangkok the sea has receded even further. In the modern part of the town there are some fine roads, with European buildings, but most of the communications are still canals and waterways; owing to the presence of water in both cases Europeans have dubbed Bangkok the Venice of the East; guileless monarchs have believed them and have tried to make the parallel nearer by erecting at enormous cost and in the face of untold difficulties mock-Venetian palaces and buildings. The Throne-room, or House of Parliament, is built of Carrara marble, imported at great expense; half-way through its construction the subsoil started to give way, and the building now floats on air-filled concrete pontoons. It is in a sort of Renaissance style, vaguely reminiscent of Santa Maria della Salute, with dome and all; it doesn't, however, look quite so silly as the small-scale Palace of the Doges built as the residence for some prince.

It is very difficult to take Bangkok quite seriously; it is the most hokum place I have ever seen, never having been to California. It is the triumph of the 'imitation' school; nothing is what it looks like; if it's not parodying European buildings it is parodying Khmer ones; failing anything else it will parody itself.

The Siamese have considerable technical skill, but absolutely no taste. The Siamese artistic canons are 'Make it as life-like as possible, twice as big, and four times as expensive.' Siamese temples are like a rather naïve person's idea of heaven—say St. John of the Apocalpyse; but everything is fake, the gold, the precious stones, the jewels, the flowers. The best comment on this theatrical effect is the remark in a guide-book that 'the farther away (the Wat Arun) is seen, the

135

better it looks'. Yes, indeed. You can't be too far away from these buildings to get the best effect.

The Siamese have also a passion for record-breaking, as far as Buddhas are concerned. In the centre of the town is a gilt Buddha skyscraper, twice as high as a church. In Wat Po is the World's Biggest Buddha, a reclining statue made of bricks covered with cement and gilded; it is about a hundred and sixty feet long and nearly forty feet high; it is enclosed in a room and looks for all the world like Alice in the Rabbit's house, after she had drunk the second bottle. One feels the Buddha would be much more comfortable if there was a chimney he could put his leg up.

Sometimes the records are broken by accumulation. I think Wat Po holds the record with something over four hundred Buddhas in and around the building; there are, however, a number of runners-up.

Siamese in London must feel most at home at Madame Tussaud's. The art which that lady and her descendants have mastered so successfully is the real aim of Siamese sculptors; unfortunately the climate is unsuitable for waxworks. They go as near as they can, however; and there can be few sights more disconcerting than the Wat Sudat, where Buddha in gilt is shown preaching to a congregation of eighty disciples seated on the pews in front of him like any other congregation; the said disciples being made out of painted plaster, coloured completely naturally, life-size and dressed in real clothes. I presume that during services the living mingle with the stuffed; it gives opportunities for endless imbroglios.

The tableau vivant—as vivant as possible—is a constantly recurring motif in Siamese temples. The finest collection is in the Wat Po; first of all there is a group of the Buddha preaching to five hermits; next a Buddha, about twice life-size, seated on a coiled cobra, the animal's head rising behind the figure with the hood spread out like a sunshade. Finally, there is a Buddha, four yards high, seated under a tree made of rubber and metal; before him a white monkey and a white elephant, hardly larger than life but just as real, offer him honeycomb and water. This group is extremely impressive, but rather dusty. (Incidentally sacred white elephants and monkeys—the latter true albinos—are kept near the Parliament House. The elephants have titles—as who might say Baron Jumbo; only the king rides on them, and then only on ceremonial occasions.)

Undoubtedly the high spot of Bangkok fakes is the Pu Khao Tong, or Golden Mountain, an artificial hill of brick of respectable dimensions. This artificial hill is covered with artificial caves and grottoes, which are adorned with artificial stalactites and artificial hermits; a few real trees here and there, introduced to give it the appearance of 'a real mountain', appear quite unconvincing. This super-hokum houses a portion of the bones of the Buddha, discovered in 1898.

The principle of Siamese architecture is the same as Cambodian, but with knobs on—lots of knobs. Wherever a bit of decoration or twirly-whirly can be fixed with some possibility of its staying put it is stuck on. The hedgehog is the model at which all Siamese architects aim in their skyline. The Siamese also employ two types of tower, vaguely reminiscent of Angkor; *phra prang*, or tall rounded towers, rather phallic in shape, and chedi, a variant of the *stûpa* or bell-tower, but stylised into a steep pyramid with a very long thin spike on top. The *phra prang* sometimes reach enormous height—in Wat Arun the tallest is nearly two hundred feet high, made of brick-covered plaster in which thousands of bits of glazed tile have been inserted; the *chedi*, on the other hand, are usually fairly small, and simply litter up what free ground there is inside the temple precincts.

Most exterior walls are white-washed; they are the only plain surfaces in the buildings. Roofs and gables are decorated with polychromatic tiles in various design; and all windows, doorways, vestibules, and so on are covered with glass mosaic to look like gold and jewels, carved woodwork, and wood inlaid with mother-of-pearl. This last type of decoration is extraordinarily well executed; if application could make a work of art these doorways and shutters should be masterpieces; but at their best they are never more than quaint and amusing. In contrast with the tawdriness of the rest of the decoration these fairly sombre panels stand out as the summit of restraint; when isolated they are very fidgety.

Byzantine mosaics show that richness of materials does not necessarily produce vulgarity. There is probably as much gold in the cathedral of Monreale, for example, as in any Siamese building of equivalent size; this cathedral is, I think, one of the loveliest buildings, as far as decoration goes, in the world. With the Byzantines, indeed, the richness adds to the general effect, for we feel that the precious materials are used, not for their value, but for their decorative qualities. In Siam all the fake gold and jewels are used merely to give an appearance of opulence. I have never been much of an admirer of the more precious metals and stones; they are usually too small to have any significance. Until I went to Siam, though, I never realised how appallingly ugly they would be if they weren't so tiny; for the gold leaf, and the glass rubies and emeralds and sapphires were exactly like the real thing, except in size; and the general effect was indescribably garish. Even the treasures of the Spanish cathedrals, and heaven knows they are mostly hideous enough, pale in comparison.

The Siamese love of richness reaches its culmination—and its nadir—in the Wat Phra Keo, the Temple of the Emerald Buddha. This is the holiest shrine of Siam, and stands inside the grounds of the palace. The blue-tiled building is decorated outside with flowers and patterns of gold and sapphire; huge gold monsters guard the doors; golden bells hang from the eaves. The interior is gold, upon gold, upon gold, except for a few indifferently painted panels in the walls. The sacred image itself is cut out of a solid piece of jasper about eighteen inches high, and is of considerable antiquity; it is the Luck and Palladium of the kingdom. It is impossible to gain any idea of the workmanship, for it is raised on a gold altar some thirty feet high; and it has three changes of clothing, according to the season, made of real gold and precious stones. From the ceiling and from the floor rises and descends more gold in every direction and shape; life-sized gold figures, holding many-tiered gold parasols; artificial shrubs made of silver and gold, gold flags, gold lamps, gold flower vases, and heaven knows what besides; and not a single thing, which, were it made in base metal, one would willingly have about the house. Outside is a small farmyard of life-size sculptured animals, holy cows and lions from a giant baby's Noah's Ark.

The Palace is in the same style, only rather more so. The two most striking ornaments are a model of the Albert Memorial in solid silver, and a model of Angkor Wat in solid concrete. There is also a very fine collection of white elephants in bronze. In the European style there are a number of portraits of crowned heads executed in oils; they are, however, I think surpassed by the life-size bronze statue of H. M. King Chulalongkorn in field-marshal's uniform, which more than justifies Rajadmnoen Avenue being dubbed the Siamese Champs Elysées, or even Siegesallée.

The prettiest things about the palace are the dwarf trees tortured by topiary into fantastic shapes; and the Chinese statues, which, here and in most of the temples, serve as guardians to the gateways. Most of these statues are of wood, but a few are decorated with plaster and porcelain; they represent demons, godlets, and occasionally European or Siamese soldiers; they are above life-size, and roughly carved, most of them rather grotesque; they have, however, a strength and dignity of conception quite alien to the surrounding work. They were used as ballast in the Chinese boats which came empty to Bangkok to trade.

Some of the most peculiar statues are a group of little lead figures in the courtyard of Wat Po. They are arranged in pairs, in the most extraordinary contortions; according to some they represent methods of jiu-jitsu; others say that they are diagrams to show how to stop the major arteries. They might be anything. Nearby, if my memory does not fail, is a model bear's den, which is very efficacious against sterility.

These temples form the background for most of the Siamese festivities, of which there are a great number. At one temple on the far side of the river a fair was being held in connection with some festivity or other. Besides the usual stalls, mostly presided over by Chinese, there were a number of entertainments. It is perhaps not fair to judge either Siamese music or dancing from the performances seen there; the costumes were slightly fantastic, with very complicated head-dresses; they followed the Siamese mania of trying to appear worth a million tikal, by being smothered in imitation jewels. The dancing seemed very similar to the Cambodian, the music rather more complicated, with no recognisable melodic line. The Siamese sing with a very ugly nasal tone, the voice produced as it were from the palate, with the throat practically closed. The most intriguing performance was a play acted entirely by boys; I was told that the dialogue was extremely indecent, but unfortunately I was not able to understand it, and the interpreter was bashful.

The pleasantest thing about Bangkok are the klongs, or water markets. The western or poorer bank of the Menam is riddled with canals, with small groups of huts interspersed with fields and orchards along their banks. Early every morning markets are held at different parts of the canals, the goods being piled in the boats which act the dual rôle of conveyance and stall; the marketers arrive in boats and canoes of a variety of shapes and sizes, going from market to market as they do the day's shopping. Against the background of trees the continuous movement is very pretty to watch.

Geoffrey Gorer, *Bali and Angkor: A 1930s Pleasure Trip Looking at Life and Death*, London: Michael Joseph, 1936; reprinted Singapore: Oxford University Press, 1986, pp. 160–9.

25

The Temples of Bali

MIGUEL COVARRUBIAS

The Mexican artist Miguel Covarrubias (1904–57) and his wife
Rose took up residence in Bali for nine months in 1930. During
that time, he compiled what immediately became and has
remained ever since the classic book on Bali. Fluidly written and
beautifully illustrated, both with his paintings and line drawings
and Rose's photographs, it describes Bali as the perfect, artistic, and
harmonious society. In his particular romantic vision, Covarrubias
cleverly synthesized all the images of Bali already created by other
European writers; and if on closer inspection this concealed various
contradictions in Balinese society, the great richness of ethnographic materials which he wove into his account have retained
their value. No other foreign writer (until the most recent ethnographers) described Balinese architecture anything like as informat-
ively as Covarrubias.

T HE temple is certainly the most important institution
on the island and the clearest illustration of the spirit of
the Balinese religion. There are temples everywhere,
from the modest family shrines in every household, to the
extravagant temples of the princes and great town temples;
large or small, plain or richly carved temples found in the
ricefields, in the cemeteries, in the markets, on the beaches,
in caves, among the tangle of gnarled roots of old *waringins*,
on deserted hill tops and even on the barren rocks along the
coastline.

When we discovered that the Balinese did not seem to
mind in the least our going in and out of the temples, we
started visiting them systematically, looking for unusual
statues or reliefs, and although from the beginning we
received the impression that there were not two temples
exactly alike, we became aware that there were features common to all; unlike the forbidding, sombre temples of other
Oriental countries, the Balinese temple is a gay, open-air

affair; one, two, or three open courtyards surrounded by a low wall, each court leading into the next through more or less elaborate stone gates, and with a number of empty sheds, pavilions, and shrines in varied styles, the majority covered with thatch, some with only one roof, others with as many as eleven superimposed roofs like pagodas.

There were no soot-blackened rooms filled with incense smoke for mysterious rites performed in front of great idols; as a matter of fact, there were no idols at all worshipped in any of the hundreds of Balinese temples we visited. In many there were ancient statues from former times, together with many shapeless stones kept as amulets by the community, which, because of their antiquity or because they were found in extraordinary circumstances, came to be regarded as gifts of the gods, or as their name (*peturun*) indicates, as heirlooms from their ancestors. The gods are invisible and impalpable and in all Bali there is not an image of a Hindu deity worshipped for the sake of its representation. Most often not even the priests in charge were aware of the names of the divinities represented.

Our interest in temples grew when we tried to understand the rules that dictated their intriguing design, but the first attempts left us only more confused than before. Explanations by the *pemangkus*, the temple-keepers, did not agree and the discrepancies were often greater than the points of agreement. With Spies I started into a more systematic search; we went into a temple, sought the *pemangku*, and drew a plan in which the names and purposes of each unit were indicated. Repetitions started to appear in many plans, and when we had gathered many ground plans of various sorts of temples we traced the common features in them. From those that appeared most frequently I set myself to the task of reconstructing one 'ideal' Balinese temple.

Most typical was the temple with two courtyards, the outer court called *djaban*, 'outside', and the other the *dalam*, the 'inside'. Entrance into the first court was gained through the *tjandí bentar*, the 'split monument' or split gate (A. See

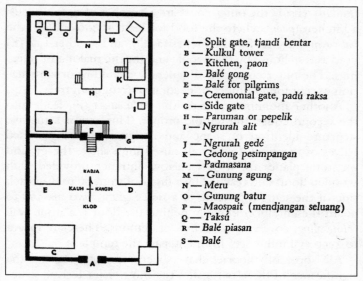

A — Split gate, *tjandí bentar*
B — *Kulkul* tower
C — Kitchen, *paon*
D — *Balé gong*
E — *Balé* for pilgrims
F — Ceremonial gate, *padú raksa*
G — Side gate
H — Paruman or *pepelik*
I — Ngrurah alit

J — Ngrurah gedé
K — Gedong pesimpangan
L — Padmasana
M — Gunung agung
N — Meru
O — Gunung batur
P — Maospait (*mendjangan seluang*)
Q — Taksú
R — *Balé piasan*
S — *Balé*

Ground plan of a typical Balinese temple

plan), which was like the two halves of a solid tower cut clean through the middle, each half pushed apart to give access into the temple. That the *tjandí bentar* represented the two halves of a unit was obvious; in most of them each side was elaborately carved, often with the design also cut in two, as in a temple near Mengwi where half of a monstrous face adorned each side of the gate. Furthermore, the two inner sides were invariably left smooth, clean surfaces that shone by contrast with the elaborately carved rest of the temple. This we decided was an inviolable law until we found one *tjandí bentar* in Pura Bangkung, in Sukasada, North Bali, with its inner sides carved. This exception, however, is not important, given the anarchy that prevails in North Balinese temples, and since there is no rule in Bali without its exception.

In the right-hand corner of the first courtyard, or outside the gate, is the high tower (B) where hang the village drums (*kulkul*). Inside the outer court are a number of simple sheds: a kitchen (*paon*) where the food for feasts is cooked (C), the *balé* gong, a shed for the orchestra (D), and another *balé* (E) used as rest-house by the people and for the making of offerings. The outer courtyard is generally devoid of ornamentation except for a number of decorative frangipani trees.

Another monumental gate, the *padú raksa* (F), leads into the second court, the temple proper. This gate is a massive structure identical in shape and design with the reunited halves of the *tjandí bentar*, but raised high above the ground on stone platforms, with a narrow entrance provided with wooden doors and reached by a flight of stone steps. On each side of the stairs is a statue of a fierce giant, two *raksasas* to guard the entrance. Directly behind the door is a stone wall (*aling aling*) covered with reliefs of demons. These are meant to keep evil influences from entering the temple.

All sorts of theories have been advanced as to the significance of these two gates, the most characteristic structures in the temples. It has been said that the *tjandí bentar* represents the two halves of the mountain Mahameru, which was split by Pasupati (Siva) in order to place each half in Bali, one as the Gunung Agung and the other as the Batur. A scholarly Balinese told me that it represents the two halves of a complete thing, the male at the right, the female at the left; or it is perhaps symbolical of the splitting of the material world to permit the entrance into the mystery with the physical body. Dr Goris suggests as the origin of these gates the remainders of the old *tjandís*, the burial towers of the former kings, a logical explanation because of the cult of deified kings linked to the ancestor-worship and, further, because of the identical shape of the Balinese temple gates and the old *tjandís*, a shape of temple gates which dates back to the most ancient of Javanese temples. The *tjandí* form appears throughout Balinese ritual as the symbol for the universe: a pyramid of receding platforms—the foundation of the earth and the mountains—the intermediate space between heaven and earth, and the stratified heavens, represented by the pagoda–like roofs (*tumpang*), or by gradually decreasing stone mouldings.

The first courtyard is only an antechamber for the preparation of feasts and for other social purposes. It is in the inner court that are erected the altars and shrines that serve as rest-houses for the gods during their visits to this earth. The principle of orientation—the relation of the mountains to the sea, high and low, right and left—that constitutes the ever present Balinese Rose of the Winds (*nawa sanggah*), rules the orientation and distribution of the temple units. The principal altars and shrines are arranged in two rows on the honoured sides of the court: *kadja*, upward to the mountain, and *kangin*, to the right of this direction.

First in importance is the *gedong pesimpangan* (K), built in the middle of the *kangin* side, a masonry building closed by wooden doors dedicated to the local deity, the ancestor-founder of the community, often named after the village, as, for instance, in *desa* Dedap he is called Ratú Dalam Dedapan. Inside there is often a stone phallus (*lingga*) and, since the building can be locked, there the relics and heirlooms of the temple are also kept: ancient statues of stone, wood, or gold, old bronzes, and so forth.

Most impressive are the *merus*, high pagodas of wood resting on stone platforms, always with an odd number of super-imposed receding roofs (from three to eleven) made of thick layers of *idjuk*, the everlasting and costly fibre of the sugar palm. These roofs are arranged along an open shaft through which the gods are supposed to descend into the *meru*. The temple of Besakih, the greatest in all Bali, on the slopes of the Gunung Agung, consists practically of *merus*, and other important temples have three, five, seven, or nine *merus*, but our typical temple has one, built in the principal place, the centre of the *kadja* side of the courtyard. The *meru* is supposed to represent the great cosmic mountain *Mahameru* and is the seat of the high Hindu gods. A curious feature of *merus* is the miniature iron implements buried under the building, together with little gold and silver roast chickens, lotus flowers, crabs, shrimps, and so forth. Again, where the rafters of the uppermost roof meet, there is a vertical beam of sandalwood with a hole in which is deposited a small covered Chinese bowl of porcelain containing nine precious stones or nine *pripíh*, plates of various metals inscribed with magic words.

Never missing are two shrines for the great mountains: one for the Gunung Agung (M) and other for the Batur (O) (or for the Batukau in the villages in its neighbourhood). They resemble little *merus* of one roof, also made of *idjuk* and ending in tall phallic points. Of great importance is the *padmasana* (L), the stone throne for the sun-god Surya, which stands invariably in the uppermost right-hand corner of the temple, with its back directed always towards the Gunung Agung. The form of the *padmasana* is again the representation of the cosmos. On a wide platform shaped like the mythical turtle *bedawang*, with two stone serpents coiled around its body, rest three receding platforms, the mountains, the whole surmounted by a stone chair with a high back.

Other shrines that are never missing are the little houses for *Ngrurah Alit* (I) and *Ngrurah Gedé* (J), the 'secretaries' of the gods, who watch that the proper offerings are made, and the stone niche for the *Taksú* (Q), the interpreter of the deities. It is the *Taksú* who enters the bodies of mediums when in a trance and speaks through them to make known the decisions of the gods to the people. There is still one more shrine, the *Maospait* (P), dedicated to the totemic gods of the settlers from Madjapahit, the 'original deer' (*medjangan seluang*). This can be recognized by a small sculpture of a deer's head or by the stylization of antlers carved in wood.

There are, besides, other pavilions; one in the middle of the temple which serves as a communal seat for the gods, the *pepelik*, or *paruman* (H), and the *balé piasan* (R, S), simple sheds for offerings.

This lengthy description is still far from complete and is limited to the main features of a would-be average temple, but unfortunately such typical temples could hardly be found in Bali. Despite the rules, practically every temple has curious contradictory individual features; besides, such is the variety of types of temples and so great the local differences, that only for the purpose of a general understanding of the spirit of Balinese temples can this 'typical' temple be of use. To note down all the variants of Balinese temples would require a great volume.

Besides the family shrines, every Balinese 'complete' community, a *desa*, should have at least the three reglementary temples: first a 'naval' temple, *pura puséh*, the old temple of the original community from which the village sprang; a second, *pura desa*, the town temple for official celebrations of the entire village, which, in case it has a *balé agung*, the old-fashioned assembly hall of the village Elders, receives the name of *pura balé agung*; and third, a *pura dalam*, the temple of the dead, built out in the cemetery, dedicated to the deities of death and cremation. It often happens that the *pura puséh*, despite its being the most important centre of worship, is located in another village or even in another district, because it was from there that came the settlers of the later village. In some places the *pura puséh* and the *pura desa* are combined into one, with only a wall separating the two departments. There are still the private temples of the princes; the royal temples (*pura panataran*), and the *pura dadia*, the private temple of origin of the family, the connecting link between the scattered branches of a common stock. Other important temples are the *pura bedugul*, the rice temple of each agricultural guild; the *pura pamaksan*, little temples of each village ward (*bandjar*), from which the *pura puséh* evolves; hill temples (*pura bukit*), sea temples on the beaches (*pura segara*), temples for the deities of seed and markets (*pura melanting*), bathing-temples, temples in lakes, caves, springs, trees, and so forth.

Except for the old *pemangku*, the keeper and officiating priest of the temple, who can be seen there occasionally sweeping the yard, the temples are ordinarily deserted because the Balinese go into them only for public gatherings,

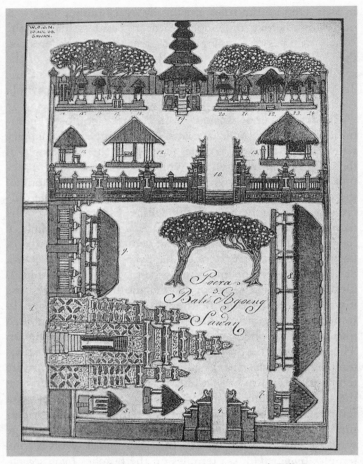

Plan of a village temple (*pura bale agung*) in Sawan, north Bali. From
W. O J. Nieuwenkamp, *Bouwkunst van Bali*, The Hague: H. P. Leopold,
1926.

festivals, and meetings. *Pemangkus* are simple people of the
common class with old-fashioned manners, polite, good-
natured, and with a charming modesty, who live near the
temple and perform all of its duties, from sweeping it to

invoking and impersonating the deities. The haughty Brahmanic priests, the *pedandas*, refer to them contemptuously as *djero sapúh*, 'sweepers', but the *pemangkus* are the really active priests of the people's ritual and alone officiate at temple feasts, when the *pedandas* do not take an active part. Furthermore there are villages where the *pedandas* are even barred from the temple.

The office of the *pemangku* is often hereditary, but he may also be chosen by some mystic while inspired by the spirits. He dresses in all-white clothes with a characteristic coat with tight sleeves and wears his head-cloth in the old-style high crest. *Pemangkus* lead a normal routine life without great religious restrictions, attending to their personal affairs until the date for the feast of the temple approaches, when they will become the centre of all activity.

Miguel Covarrubias, *Island of Bali*, New York: Alfred A. Knopf, 1937, pp. 263–71.

Villages

26
Meegyoungyai and Nyaung-U, on the Banks of the Irrawaddy

R. TALBOT KELLY

In this passage, Kelly provides a dramatic eye-witness account of a distinctive aspect of South-East Asian architecture—the ever-present danger of fire to timber buildings. Historical records tell us of several instances in the more densely populated cities such as Aceh, Makasar, and Ayutthaya, where fire caused the loss of hundreds or even thousands of houses. As Kelly remarks, however, loss of life is relatively rare in these circumstances, and houses can be easily rebuilt, which goes some way to explain the apparent apathy of the villagers on this occasion. Kelly seems to have had a particular enthusiasm for fires. Later in the book he lyrically describes the beauty of forest fires at night; in fact he almost got stuck in one while travelling in north-east Burma.

LEAVING early in the morning, a short run brought us to Meegyoungyai, where it had been arranged for coolies, bullock gharries, and ponies to be waiting to transport us to the forest; and, our stores and kits having been landed, we found ourselves at about 4 P.M. comfortably installed in the dâk bungalow for the night. I noticed, by the way, that all the coolie work in connection with the landing of the cargo from the steamer was performed by women and girls (the men preferring to look on and smoke), and it was surprising what enormous weights even young girls were able to carry on their heads.

This village and dâk being typical, I may as well describe them here.

The village is built on the banks of the river, prettily situated among the groves of trees which overhang the pools below. On its other three sides is a high stockade of thorns, overgrown with yellow convolvulus and other creepers. At each side are gates, which are shut at night and placed under the charge of a guard, no one being allowed to pass after dark. Within the huge compound so formed are groves of toddy palms, mango, and tamarind, amongst which are the houses of the Burmans. These are usually built of bamboo, though many have their principal timbers of eng wood, all being raised from the ground on piles four to six feet in height as a safeguard against floods, snakes, and malaria. The floors are usually of split bamboo, the thatch of elephant grass, or 'thekke'; bamboo mats, called 'tayan', prettily plaited and often in coloured patterns, serve as walls, but as the side nearest the street is usually open the whole interior arrangements and domestic occupations are exposed to view. About the houses are the occupants, brightly picturesque, while the little boys and girls run naked. Pigeons and poultry, geese and dogs are everywhere, inside and underneath the houses, and the hot air is full of sweet nastiness from the Burmese kitchens. Generally speaking, the houses are more or less in line, forming streets, which are now busy with returning bullock gharries and driven cattle coming home for the night, as it is not safe for cattle to be left outside after sunset.

All villages in Burma are stockaded, usually by a thorn zariba, or, in the case of hill villages, by chevaux-de-frise. On each side is a gate made of heavy planks of teak, which run on wheels, and are by law closed at nightfall as a protection against both wild animals and dacoits. The villagers are compelled to keep guard at night, when no stranger is allowed to enter the village. Keeping guard is called 'kin', the guard himself 'kinthamah', and by the gate is usually erected a little booth, which serves as his sentry-box and is called 'kin-teaine'. These stockades, overgrown as they usually are by many kinds of flowering creepers, have a very pretty effect.

The dâk bungalow lies outside the town, among a number of ruined pagodas, and stands in a stockade of its own. It is built much in the same manner as the Burmese huts, but is mainly composed of wood and stands higher. A flight of steps leads to the verandah, which is about 10 feet above the ground. This verandah forms the general living room, out of which are two bedrooms, each with a bathroom attached. The kitchen, stables, and servants' quarters are built in the compound outside. These dâks are built by the Government for the use of travellers, and have usually a Durwan or Kansammah in charge, and are supplied with such utensils as are absolutely necessary for comfort.

The view from the bungalow, looking across the Irrawaddy valley towards the distant Arracan Yomas ('Yoma' means literally 'backbone'), was exceedingly beautiful, green to the farthest distance with its first spring foliage.

The name Meegyoungyai, I was informed, meant alligator water, a title sufficiently appropriate, though I was later given another explanation, which I believe to be more correct, and which is certainly quaint enough to repeat. Long ago, says the legend, a huge alligator carried away a cow belonging to a poor farmer, who, in great distress, appealed to the forest 'Nats' for assistance, which was readily forthcoming. One of these, assuming the form of a monkey, went down to the river bank and began to disport himself in the trees which overhung the pool in which the alligator was lying. Attracted by his antics and chattering, the alligator slowly came out of the water on to the bank, the better to watch him, but said nothing. Pretending to have just discovered the alligator's presence the monkey poured forth a torrent of derision and abuse upon him, but still the alligator remained silent. After a time the monkey suddenly exclaimed: 'Why, it is not an alligator at all, it cannot even laugh.' 'Yes, I can,' exclaimed the now exasperated saurian, and opening his wide jaws for that purpose, out jumped the cow, which ran away up the bank into the forest, and was restored by the Nat to its owner. From that day the place has been called 'Meegyoungyai' or 'laughing alligator', the word Meegyoung meaning alligator, and the terminal syllable, ye or yai, meaning 'water or laughter', a very slight difference of intonation being the only possible difference between the two interpretations.

At one time Meegyoungyai must have been a town of some importance, a large number of pagodas still remaining, while far beyond the limits of the present village may be found traces of larger theins, shrines, and monastic buildings, so ruinous as to be hardly distinguishable among the undergrowth. One of these 'kyaungs' is still occupied, and I was greatly struck by a pretty ceremony which takes place daily.

The sun had just set, and while preparing for our evening meal, the sound of a deep-toned gong stole through the warm air; before its reverberations had ceased, first one and then another was sounded, until perhaps twenty or more gongs of different pitches, but all with that purity of tone distinctive of the Burmese bronzes, combined in one swelling and melodious evensong. I inquired as to its meaning, and was informed that this was the usual 'pyashikoh,' the habits of the monastery being as follows. At first break of dawn all the priests, novices, and pupils assemble for prayer, after which the boys are occupied with their lessons. Meals are taken at 7 and 11.30 A.M., the priests being forbidden to touch food from 12 noon until after morning prayers the next day, the pupils, however, having their meals as usual. The day's work being finished, priests and pupils assemble in their different kyaungs, and to the sound of the first gong the lessons learned during the day are repeated. A second gong is the signal for general prayer; the third, in which all the gongs in the different monasteries are struck together, is the final amen, and after this silence. . . .

153

* * *

Nyaung-U is a pretty village lying among toddy-palms and tamarinds, and though its narrow roads are usually a cloud of dust from passing gharries it has many attractions; the men

'Street in Nyaung-U', from R. Talbot Kelly, *Burma: Painted and Described*, 1905.

154

are very civil, the women shy but infinitely graceful and attractive in manner, while pretty children run about naked as they play with the dogs and goats.

This is a great centre for the manufacture of red and black lacquer work, quite the best in Burma being produced here. As, however, the chance of direct sale is limited to the wants of occasional steamboat passengers, the people are almost entirely dependent upon the dealers, who evidently do not treat them too liberally. In fact they are desperately poor, and, I am told, cannot even indulge in a full meal of rice, but are obliged to mix millet with it in order to eke out the meal. Yet in spite of this poverty, and many fruitless tramps over miles of dusty road to await the arrival of a steamer, only perhaps to be disappointed of a sale, they are a cheerful community, who try to beautify their lives and their surroundings.

The houses are, as usual, built largely of bamboo, the matting, of which the walls are composed, being plaited in bold designs, of two or three colours. In front of many are stands of flowers in pots of various kinds, some plain earthenware, others glazed in bright colours. The plants are usually lilies, which, though generally dusty, gleam brightly in the sunlight against the dark background of the gloomy interiors. Surrounding the house is often trellis-work supporting bougainvillaea, wisteria, and other flowering creepers, and the footpaths, such as they are, are often shaded by vines.

Except for the shops in which lacquer work is displayed there is not much colour in the articles for sale, food-stuffs and utensils being the principal items; but on the other hand incidents are plentiful, and, like their more prosperous brethren in more favoured spots, the people are brightly clothed, nor do the women neglect to place a flower in their hair.

I was very much attracted by the people here, and one day asked the myook if he could procure me two pretty girls as models for a picture which I had in hand. Next day they arrived, and were quite the *ugliest* girls I had seen in Burma; so do our ideas of beauty vary! However, as they wore very beautiful clothes, and were neat little things, I was quite pleased to paint them. As models, however, they were hopeless, for the moment they were posed and I began to paint, all their native grace fled and they became rigid as automata. I was hopeless until it occurred to me to pose them *together*, and while pretending to paint one (who immediately became petrified), I was in reality painting the other, who, thinking I was not looking at her, assumed naturally beautiful positions!

Being the daughters of a merchant in the town they were far too high class to accept money, so I gave them each a bundle of cigars and took their photographs as a reward.

A dramatic episode terminated my visit to Pagan. Macfarlane had gone on a tour of inspection, leaving me in sole occupation of his bungalow. Sitting on the verandah after dinner I noticed a fire in the distance, glowing among the palm-trees, and, welcoming any variety in the monotony of a lonely evening, I strolled down to the village to see what was happening.

During my ten minutes' walk to the seat of the fire, which was evidently extending, I met hurrying groups of excited people carrying away their beds and furniture to the river bank for safety, and as I neared the spot I found it was evidently a big blaze. Though terribly sorry for the sufferers, I have never seen anything finer as a display, ten or twelve houses being alight, the blaze shining on gilded pagodas and through the dark palm groves, while the heat was such that I could not approach without screening my face with my hands. The fire was spreading quickly, and seemed likely to burn the whole place down; and the flames, leaping across the street or dropping like molten metal from the eaves, spread in all directions. No one appeared to be doing anything, the police contenting themselves with patrolling the place with bayonets fixed. I felt really indignant at the apathy displayed, and through an interpreter I got some men together and started to grapple with the situation. The fire was progressing at the rate of a house every five minutes, so, telling the people to remove their belongings, we began to demolish the houses some little way down the street as an interceptor. No one seemed to dispute my authority, and it was almost amusing the way in which the crowd seemed to enjoy the demolition of another's property!

Meanwhile palms and other trees had caught fire, and the flames threatened the handsome group of pagodas and *kyaungs* which was the pride of the village. Fortunately the wind changed before they were seriously endangered, and the demolished buildings effectually arrested the progress of flames in the other direction, but not before twenty-five homes had been completely destroyed. It was certainly a great catastrophe, though the people took it for the most part with apathetic indifference. One poor woman alone became quite crazy and stood, crying and shouting, until she was almost caught by the fire, before some one dragged her away from her burning domicile.

I was much amused by one man who was comfortably seated on his doorstep smoking a cheroot, and entirely indifferent to the excitement which surrounded him. His house, however, was one which had to be sacrificed, and his disgusted expression, as we began to pull the place down and his neighbours to remove his goods, was truly comical. It was not so much anger or distress at the destruction of his home, but simple annoyance at being so rudely disturbed in the enjoyment of his smoke!

Many of the women were engaged in bringing water from the river, which they did in small chatties, strolling quietly to and from the scene of the fire, then waiting, chattering, until it would occur to somebody to take the pot from off their head and pour the water on the flames! An absolutely futile operation, but it kept them occupied and out of the way.

I was engaged in this way until after midnight, and in spite of my sympathy with the sufferers hugely enjoyed the fillip of this exciting experience. I had certain doubts, however, as to the legality of my action in ordering the destruction of so much property, but was relieved to find afterwards that Mr. Dunn, the local representative of authority, had been engaged in precisely similar operations on the other side of the conflagration.

The following morning before leaving I visited the scene of the fire, where, over an acre or more of still smoking timbers and hot ashes, strewn with innumerable water-pots and cooking utensils apparently none the worse for their firing, roamed dozens of these homeless people searching among the débris for lost treasures. No one, I heard, was burnt, and those whose homes had been destroyed had all been accommodated by their neighbours, and even before I had left, life was again going on as happily and placidly as if nothing had occurred.

R. Talbot Kelly, *Burma: Painted and Described*, 1905, reprinted London: Adam and Charles Black, 1912, pp. 41–7, 179–84.

27
Choquan, a Vietnamese Village

JOHN THOMSON

After his travels in Siam and Cambodia, and a year back in Edinburgh, Thomson (see also Passage 7) returned to Singapore in 1867. From there he set out again on a three- month photographic journey through Vietnam (Annam and Cochin-China). This part of his travels occupies only a rather slim chapter of his book, however. Thomson stayed with a French merchant and went on walks, on one of which he came across the Vietnamese village here described. It was situated a short distance outside Saigon, in between the city and its native quarter, Cholon, about three miles away.

THE village of Choquan stands about half way between Saigon and Cholon. On the right of the pathway by which it is reached there is a well-grown bamboo hedge, and on the left, in the centre of a ricefield, a deep pool in which buffaloes delight to wallow, plastering their hides with mud to prevent the attacks of the moschettos. Upon approaching Choquan there is nothing to be seen of the village, save the fruit-trees that cluster round the houses; and at the time of my visit, orange and pumeloe-trees (*Citrus decumana*) were in full fruit, bending down over the enclosures with the burden of their crops. The village, in so far as I could make out, is entered through a narrow lane between two walls of prickly cactus; this lane led to a labyrinth of other lanes, so I was puzzled to know which to take to find Choquan. But I had passed through the heart of the hamlet several times without being aware of it, as the scattered houses were each shut in by high hedges of cactus or bamboo. The natives love privacy; every prickle in the hedges that encompass their dwelling is, as it were, a token that the family within would rather be alone. If one be not satisfied with this, the outer doorway has only to be opened, when one or two ill-conditioned pariah dogs will show their fangs, and use them too. Groups of naked children roll about in the dust in the lanes, or loll in the shade smoking, inflating their chubby cheeks with the fumes of the cigarette and blowing them out again through mouth and nostrils with that air of intense satisfaction which belongs usually to maturer years. Men, too, block up the way squatting or (as the hedge is not an inviting object to lean against) lying down in the dust to have a talk, or else—as there are no 'Swans', 'Wheat Sheaves', or 'Royal Oaks', one of which always seems to be the next house we come to in our village streets at home—they betake themselves to their own abodes, bar the outer gate, get into the verandah, into seats, or upon matted benches furnished with wooden pillows, and then, in a recumbent position, with tea, cigarette, sam-shu* and betel-nut within reach, resume the topic of discussion, the interest in which has carried them so far through the listless day.

Now let us enter one of these dwellings. The two men (for

*A Chinese rice spirit.

what I relate I have actually witnessed), now prostrated with their conversational efforts, are landowners in the village, and their estates measure about an acre apiece. The pair of pleasant-faced unwashed little girls who fan their masters are domestic slaves. The lady of the house sits smoking and dandling her child in a dark corner of the interior. The edifice itself is well built, and the floor stands upon brick pillars about three feet above ground. An ornamental framework of carved wood supports the tiled roof, and the interior is partitioned off into apartments for the decent accommodation of the family. In front there are verandahs on each side of the doorway, and above the lattice is a board inscribed with the owner's name or title, while suspended from the doorposts are additional boards bearing texts from the Chinese classics. If the owner be a man of wealth, the entire front of his house is carved into open work, which with the addition of paint and gilding presents an imposing aspect, and serves to screen the defects within, where the family are kept lively by the vermin that revel in the darkness and dirt. The fetid air of the interior deters one from a prolonged inspection. Let us notice, however, the unique arrangement of a boudoir where an old woman is seated on a table sewing, and an elderly gentleman reclines on a neatly-covered couch. A few chairs of Chinese make are ranged round the apartment. On one of them stands a rice-pot filled with oranges, a bowl of rice, a cup of sam-shu, and one or two disused idols. On another we may see sundry articles of horse harness, and above it a Roman Catholic picture in red and yellow. Beneath the chair are a bag of fruits and a lot of agricultural implements. Chinese and European pictures are hung about the walls; and one or two mirrors, which give most hideous contortions of the human face, make up the adornments of the dwelling.

Now for a breath of pure air, and I will take you to another quarter of Choquan, where a sorcerer resides. His house is situated in a retired part of the village, and is surrounded by a thick cactus hedge. There is only one way by which this curious retreat can be entered, and that is by ascending a tree which bends over the hedge, then walking along a branch, and dropping from it to the doorway of the hut. When we have got inside we find the doctor, soothsayer, and magician, bent over a volume. Strewn on a rough deal table before him are the herbs by means of which he works some of his potent spells. One herb there is in frequent demand, and is a love-philter; and this, when used by some ardent but disappointed swain, must be reduced to a powder, and applied to the end of a cigarette which he presents to the unsuspecting but fickle fair one. When the first few whiffs of the enchanted vapour have been puffed through her nostrils, she loses her heart to its assailant, and is conquered.

John Thomson, *The Straits of Malacca, Siam and Indo-China*, London: Sampson Low, Marston, Low and Searle, 1875; reprinted Singapore: Oxford University Press, 1993, pp. 171–4.

28
East Coast Malay Fishing Villages in the Monsoon Season

HUGH CLIFFORD

Sir Hugh Clifford began his career in Malaya in 1883 at the age of seventeen, as an administrator in Perak and later in Pahang. In 1895 he led an expedition against rebel chiefs in Kelantan and Trengganu, who had been raiding in Pahang. This adventure provided material for several short stories, including the one from which this brief but evocative extract is taken. It appeared in the first of his several collected volumes, published in 1897. Among British imperialists, Clifford stands out as an exceptionally sensitive and romantic one, who formed a strong attachment to Malaya and its peoples, and developed a very detailed knowledge of them. His wider opportunities for travel in Malaya gave him in some ways a broader experience than his fellow author Frank Swettenham, and he proved still more skilful at rendering this experience in short stories. He continued to miss Malaya intensely after he had left it for other postings, including West Africa and Ceylon, and many of his stories were written in these other places. Although this extract lacks architectural detail, it conveys with great economy the atmosphere of a typical east coast Malay fishing village.

WHEN they have at last been fairly beaten by the monsoon, the fisher-folk betake themselves to the scattered coastal villages, which serve to break the monotonous line of jungle and shivering casuarina trees that fringe the sandy beach and the rock headlands of the shore. Here, under the coconut palms, amid chips from boats that are being repaired and others that still lie upon the stocks, surrounded by nets, sails, masts and empty craft lying high and dry upon the beach out of reach of the tide, the fishermen spend their months of captivity.

Their women live here all the year around, labouring incessantly in drying and salting the fish which have been taken by the men, or pounding prawns into *blachan*, that evil-smelling condiment which has been named 'Malaysian caviar'. It needs all the violence of the fresh, strong monsoon winds to purge these villages of the rank odours which cling to them at the end of the fishing season; and when all has been done, the saltiness of the sea air, the brackish water of the wells, and the faint stale smells emitted by the nets and fishing tackle still tell unmistakeable tales of the one trade in which every member of these communities is more or less engaged.

The winds blow strong, and the rains fall heavily. The frogs in the marshes behind the village fill the night air with the croakings of a thousand throats, and the little bull-frogs sound their deep see-saw note during all the hours of darkness. The sun is often hidden by the heavy cloud-banks, and a subdued melancholy falls upon the moist and steaming land.

The people, whom the monsoon has robbed of their occupation, lounge away the hours, building boats and mending nets casually, without haste or concentrated effort. Four months must elapse before they can again put to sea, so there is no cause for hurry. They are frankly bored by the life they have to lead between fishing season and fishing season, but they are a healthy-minded and withal a law-abiding people, who do little evil even when their hands are idle.

Then the monsoon ends, and they put out to sea once more, stretching to their paddles, shouting in chorus as they dance across the waves to the fishing grounds. During this season numerous ugly and unclean steamboats tramp up the coast, calling at all the principal ports for the cargoes of dried fish that find a ready market in Singapore, and thus the fisher-folk have no difficulty in disposing of their catch.

Hugh Clifford, *In Court and Kampung*, London: G. Richards, 1897; reprinted Singapore: Graham Brash, 1989, pp. 106–7.

29
Villages of the Melanau, Kanowit, and Bidayuh of Sarawak

SPENSER ST JOHN

During an excursion up the Rejang River, St John (see also Passage 19) received hospitality from Melanau and Kanowit peoples, while on his exploration of the left hand branch of the Sarawak River, he stayed with the Bidayuh (Land Dayak). He noticed many interesting features of their villages, including the building of longhouses on very tall piles for defensive purposes, accounts of house-building sacrifices, swinging (a custom here apparently for entertainment only, but having widespread ritual significance in India and South-East Asia), and the distinctive circular 'head-house' or bachelors' house of the Bidayuh.

A T the entrance of the Rejang is a small town of Milla-
naus, a people differing greatly from the Malays in
manners and customs; some converted to Islamism
are clothed like other Mahomedans, while those who still
delight in pork dress like Dayaks, to which race they
undoubtedly belong. Their houses are built on lofty posts, or
rather whole trunks of trees are used for the purpose, to
defend themselves against the Seribas.

It is stated that at the erection of the largest house, a deep
hole was dug to receive the first post, which was then suspended over it; a slave girl was placed in the excavation, and
at a signal the lashings were cut, and the enormous timber
descended, crushing the girl to death. It was a sacrifice to the
spirits. I once saw a more quiet imitation of the same ceremony. The chief of the Quop Dayaks was about to erect a
flag-staff near his house: the excavation was made, and the
timber secured, but a chicken only was thrown in and
crushed by the descending flag-staff. . . .

In front of the houses were erected swings for the amusement of the young lads and the little children. One about
forty feet in height was fastened to strong poles arranged as a
triangle, and kept firm in their position by ropes like the
shrouds of a ship. From the top hung a strong cane rope, with
a large ring or hoop at the end. About thirty feet on one side
was erected a sloping stage as a starting-point. Mounting on
this, one of the boys with a string drew the hoop towards
him, and making a spring into it, away he went. Other lads
were ready, who successively sprung upon the ring or seized
the rope, until there were five or six in a cluster, shouting,
laughing, yelling and swinging. For the younger children
smaller ones were erected, as it required courage and skill to
play on the larger. . . .

* * *

Anchored opposite the entrance of the Kanowit, where it
was intended to build a fort to stop the exit of the fleets of
Dayak boats that used to descend this river to attack the

'Town of Kenowit, Rejang River', where St John stayed on his journey. Note the very tall piles of the Kenowit longhouses, for defense against attack. From Henry Ling Roth, *The Natives of Sarawak and British North Borneo*, Vol II, London: Truslove and Hudson, 1896.

people of the Sago countries. Leaving the force thus engaged, I went and took up my residence in the village of the Kanowit Dayaks, built opposite the entrance of that stream. The Rejang is here about 600 or 700 yards broad.

The village consisted of two long houses, one measuring 200 feet, the other 475. They were built on posts about forty feet in height and some eighteen inches in diameter. The reason they give for making their posts so thick is this: that when the Kayans attack a village they drag one of their long tamuis or war boats ashore, and, turning it over, use it as a monstrous shield. About fifty bear it on their heads till they arrive at the ill-made palisades that surround the hamlets, which they have little difficulty in demolishing; they then get under the house, and endeavour to cut away the posts, being well protected from the villagers above by their extemporized shield. If the posts are thin, the assailants quickly gain the victory; if very thick, it gives the garrison time to defeat them by allowing heavy beams and stones to fall upon the boat, and even to bring their little brass war pieces to bear upon it; the Kayans will fly if they suffer a slight loss....

* * *

In our evening walk we were much struck with the remarkable beauty of this place;* the two lofty and almost perpendicular mountains rise abruptly on either side of the river, leaving but a strip of land on the water's edge. One called Sibayat towers above the village on the left bank; the other, Si Bigi, is on the opposite side; the river, now running through limestone, sparkles clear at their feet, undermining the rocks on either side, and forming fantastic little caves, crowned above with noble overhanging trees. Abrupt turns, short reaches, and pebbly beds added to the beauty of the scene, and, just as the last rays of the sun were gilding the summits of the twin peaks, we sat down on the huge trunk of a fallen tree, which the floods of the rainy season had swept down

*San Pro, a Bidayuh village.

from the interior, and half buried in the sand and pebbles. There we remained till the shades of evening had completely closed in around us, speculating on the probable future of the country, and the words almost rose simultaneously to our lips—were we missionaries, we would fix our houses here. With my own idea of what a missionary should do, there could be no better spot than San Pro to commence operations. The village was not large, but it is better completely to gain over twenty families, than exhaust one's energies merely skimming over the surface of a dozen tribes, leaving no permanent impression. We fixed on the best locality for a house, a trim garden, a diminutive church, and a school. It is a soil that would repay culture.

We were not fortunate in the time of our visit, as most of the people were away preparing their farms. We took up our residence in the head-house, which, however, was destitute of the usual ornaments. It was quite new. All head-houses have the same appearance, being built on high posts above the ground, and in a circular form, with a sharp conical roof. The windows are, in fact, a large portion of the roof, being raised up, like the lid of a desk, during fine weather, and supported by props; but when rain or night comes on, they are removed, and the whole appearance is snug in the extreme, particularly when a bright fire is lit in the centre, and throws a fitful glow on all the surrounding objects. Around the room are rough divans, on which the men usually sit or sleep, but that night, there being a cold wind and a drizzling rain, a good fire was kept up, and the people crowded near. I awoke at about two, and put my head out of my curtains to look at a night-scene: a dozen of the old men were there collected close over the fire, smoking the tobacco we had given them, and discoursing in a low tone about us. The flames occasionally shot up brilliantly and showed me the curious group, and then, as they faded away, nothing but the outlines of the half-naked old men could be seen cowering over the embers, as a ruder blast or a heavier shower brought the cold wind upon them.

Spenser St John, *Life in the Forests of the Far East: Travels in Sabah and Sarawak in the 1860s*, London: Smith, Elder & Co., 1862; reprinted Singapore: Oxford University Press, 1986, Vol. I, pp. 35, 36–7, 38–9, 128–30.

30
'The Village of a Chief'

VIOLET CLIFTON

Violet Clifton, who travelled with her husband through Indonesia in 1912, was a great deal more adventurous than most travellers of that time, who rarely went further than Java. Clifton, on the contrary, declared: 'I cannot bear to say anything of Ceylon, Singapore, or even of Java, places that were but prefaces to the real journey'—a journey which took them to some of the most remote parts of the archipelago. They first visited Sumatra, Nias, and Mentawai, while on a second trip in 1921, they explored widely in Sulawesi, Ternate, Sumbawa, Lombok, and Bali. Her book, first published as *Islands of Queen Wilhelmina* in 1927, is full of poetic and colourful images, as well as insightful comment on the rare sights she encountered. It shows her to have been a perceptive and open-minded traveller, who relished all the cultural differences she encountered. Here, she describes a visit to the South Nias village of Hiliganowö.

O N the last day in South Nias we visited Kanôlôô, the Chief of the village of Hiliganowô....
 Near the village were sweet water baths, shut in by high walls. The women's bathing place lay apart from the men's and was guarded by inviolate law, for death was deemed the proper punishment to him who should intrude on women bathing.* Calling out loudly a warning of our approach, our host led me to this sanctuary. I went in among the women who were drawing water and cooling themselves

---

*A heavy fine is now imposed by the Chiefs.

in the running stream that passed through their bathing place. The walls guarding it and the stones paving it were overgrown with ferns, its roof was the firmament.

By the sea were low stone seats, whereon sat young Nias men looking out lazily over the waters. Only Gauguin could paint them with their strange charm.

From the foot of the hills started a long flight of rude steps leading steeply to the double walls and the gates of the village. A path ran up a further part of the hill under the palms, but we chose the six hundred steps, for near them we could see rough memorials of the dead, wooden shrines hung with rags, and dishes, and odd treasures, left there to symbolise the thoughts of the living for the dead.

Up the six hundred steps through the gates, on to the flagged street, past the thatched shrine of the ancestor gods, into the house of Kanôlôô, we went.

Into the great central room of the Chief's house we climbed, going up a ladder which led from under the building into this wide upper hall, which was most beautiful. The walls were of polished wood hung about with tusks of boars and the horns of deer, of which the antlers had but six tines at most. Big Chinese plates were suspended from the raftered ceiling, some being enclosed in wicker baskets. Others hung revealed, their colours blending with the blue and old rose painted bowls which also came from China. These bowls were used for the washing of the hands of guests after food.

There were no windows, but a kind of wide lattice ran round one side of the hall. Below the lattice was the large curved wooden seat of the Chief and of his sons, the seat being raised above the floor by long, shallow steps.

The fireplace was very handsome. It stood on carved legs of wood, raised from the ground, and its sides were supported by wooden pillars. It came far out into the room; in its centre stood a brazier wherein was the fire. The tall image of a god was near. Beyond stood the peeping women of the house, watching us with dark eyes, their small heads shaved

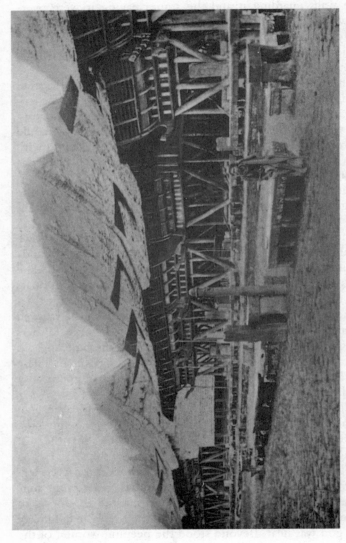

The Chief's house at Hiliganow ö, South Nias. From by Violet Clifton, *Islands of Indonesia*, London: Constable & Co., 1927.

closely, save where, in the centre of the head, a knot of hair was allowed to grow.

Kanôlôô had his warriors. He offered to show us their method of war dance and of fighting. Then he left us to clothe himself in his warrior dress.

When we had arrived in the morning he had been wearing a coloured jacket of stiff material and a pleated loin cloth; round the thick dark hair that fell on to his neck he had wound a coloured cloth.

When he reappeared in his martial dress it seemed we lived on another star or in another age. He shone with gold. A band of the yellow metal crowned his head, and from it rose flowers of gold, rudely formed, but pleasing. Heavy circles of gold were on his wrists, on his neck were ornaments of leaf gold. His jacket was of thick woven stuff, striped red, blue, white and yellow, and below it he wore balls of coloured wools to make the garment stand well out. A brilliant loin cloth fell below this jacket. Most remarkable of all was his sword sheathed in gold, with a handle shaped like a monkey's head with eyes of rubies, and enriched with tigers' teeth. He was amazing and splendid, and as dignified as in his simple clothing, but not more so. He then called on his men, and we pressed against the open squares in the room of our reception, to see them gathering below.

Like a play from Shakespeare, they prefaced their dancing with a speech. They assured us that they meant no harm, that all would end in peace, and then the war dance began.

The warriors came towards each other from either end of the village, advancing by two steps and retiring by one with each third movement. Slow progress, you may imagine! The men wore metal helmet caps, protecting only their heads, but not their faces. Their projecting jackets, which on working days are of roughest coconut fibre, had now been replaced by coats of crocodile skin. They carried spears, and cried out, 'Ha, ha!' and sang shrilly as they advanced, their wooden shields before them. When the opposing bodies met at last, they rushed together, stamping and spearing and clashing their shields.

When all was over Kanôlôô gave us some helmets and jackets, and we gave him silk in exchange, with which he would pay the Chinese for plates, or tiger teeth, or a little alcohol, if he dared to break Dutch laws. The Niasers of the South never drink to excess as do the Northerners, who make their own strong spirit from the fruit of a certain palm.

I felt sad at leaving the island, and through our German host I told the Chief of my regrets. 'Your heart is hairy,' was his unexpected answer; and I learned that, when the heart is hairy, it is in pain.

Among the people of Nias the heart is the centre of thought, understanding and feeling. It 'hurts' when a man is jealous, it 'grows big' when he loves, and 'broad' when he is patient and foreseeing. When he is insulted it is shaken, and it censures him in his hours of remorse, but when he is utterly discomforted or surprised it 'dies' within him. Finally, when his body is dead and cradled in his coffin among the trees, the 'Mōkōmōkō' rises up and leaves the body in the jungle, and goes on its mysterious way. The mōkōmōkō is the soul of the heart, the part that lives when the man is dead, whilst his spirit enters into his son. For 'flesh' the people of Nias have no word in their language.

Kanôlôô and most of his men are now gathered to their ancestors, for a great sickness smote the village soon after we left Nias, but when I think of Hiliganowô without him, the whole world seems to have lost a grace.

Violet Clifton, *Islands of Indonesia*, London: Constable & Co., 1927, reprinted Kuala Lumpur: Oxford University Press, 1991, pp. 97–101.

31

Villages and Megaliths of South Nias

F. M. SCHNITGER

Friedrich Martin Schnitger was a German archaeologist who holds the distinction of having written the first doctoral dissertation on Sumatran archaeology. He came out to Palembang (South Sumatra) in 1935 and excavated in a variety of sites. He also started Sumatra's first museum, acting as its Conservator. Very little was known of Sumatran archaeology at this time, and indeed many lacunae remain today. Schnitger did more than anyone else to draw together what was known into a systematic account. Although his writing is somewhat impressionistic, and his diffusionist theories are by now outdated, there remains much of value in his account. In some cases, his record is all that we have of things that have since been badly damaged or destroyed; he also made comparative ethnographic observations of traditional practices, at a time before drastic cultural change was to break and obscure many possible connections between the ancient and the contemporary. In 1938, Schnitger journeyed to the island of Nias (off the west coast of Sumatra), where he found a living megalithic culture to compare with ancient ones such as Pasemah which he had investigated. His descriptions of the remarkable villages of South Nias remain most vivid and evocative.

FOR a few weeks we camped at Lahoesa Idano Tai, in the southeast part of Nias, whence we made trips to various monuments in the vicinity. These consist of long rows of megaliths, which formerly stood in front of the houses. The villages, however, have long been deserted, the houses have disappeared and only these stone monuments are left in the desolate wilderness. There are still a few villages with monuments, but these are much smaller and cruder than the ones I have already mentioned.

Pure megaliths of magnificent design and execution are found in the South of Nias. These monuments, however, differ from those at Lahoesa. It must also be mentioned that nearly all the villages of Nias lie high and isolated on the hills, this being an urgent necessity, because war is being waged continually. For the scientific explorer these hills are a source of grief, especially when they have to be climbed in the heat of a burning midday sun!

The monuments of Lahoesa give a good impression of the plan of an old Nias village green. It consists of a rectangle, 16.50 × 40 m, the axis running NW-SE. The two extremities terminate in a stone terrace. On the northwest side stands a great, square column (*behoe*), crowned with the figure of a bird. On the terrace there is also a round, mushroom-shaped stone (*niogadji*), a smaller stone of the same form, upstanding pillars, plain or decorated, and benches with animal heads (*osaosa*).

A *behoe* serves to make the name of a native chief immortal and may only be erected after a head has been cut off. The severed head is laid on the figure of the bird. For a woman's marriage a *niogadji* is made and she dances upon it. An *osa* with one head commemorates a man, with three heads a woman. All these monuments serve as the final resting place for the founder's soul. They are found by the hundred on the village square and the people of Nias know exactly to whom each belongs.

In order to avoid repetition we must pause for a moment on the subject of *behoe*, *niogadji* and *osaosa*.

Behoes are square pillars or huge, rough, unhewn slabs of stone, placed in rows along the village green or at both extremities. Sometimes they are ornamented with figures of rosettes, breasts, a necklace or other jewel. Often they have a flight of steps on three sides. In Tetegewo is a *behoe* with a large knife. On top there is usually a bird which, however, can not always be plainly distinguished. Sometimes one recognizes a chicken and again a rhinoceros bird. The latter is sometimes portrayed without a horn but may be identified by its long downturned bill. Other specimens have a short, snubnosed bill with a horn. We saw a large, unusually well-formed head of a rhinoceros bird (40 cm long), with horns on the head and large ornaments in the ears. The portrayal is of course not true to life. For instance, the beak is too long in proportion to the horn. The sides of the beak are convex instead of concave, the ears are on top of the head instead of at the sides.

At Tjoedroebaho is still another specimen with horns on the beak. Four-footed birds are also not uncommon. Sometimes the wings are spread and the back has a flat surface to hold a severed head. But often, too, the wings are folded. On rare occasions the *behoe* has not one, but three birds.

The rhinoceros bird is called in Nias *gogowaja* or *lailoewo*. He is sacred to the creators of the earth and to all who create anything at the present time, especially goldsmiths. The main reason for placing him on the *behoe* is to guard the dead, but he is also supposed to attract the soul or the shadow of gold in some magic way, so as to enrich his master. For the same purpose the natives of Nias place massive stone money chests in front of their houses. The *behoe*, indeed, may only be erected after the village chief has had his golden ornaments melted and fashioned into new forms.

As the pillar (*behoe*) is the typical monument for a man, so the round, mushroom-shaped stone (*niogadji*) is dedicated to a woman. Very often the *behoe* and the *niogadji* stand side by side. As a rule the *niogadji* has a height of about one metre, but there are of course larger or smaller specimens. The smallest I saw has a diameter of 63 cm, the largest a diameter of 207 cm (Sisarahili). The base consists of a short pillar, which changes into an ogive-shaped section with a flat upper surface. The ogive is often beautifully decorated. The simplest form of decoration consists of grooves, sometimes edged by a band of rosettes, squares or loops. Two specimens at Tetegewo have triangles and rosettes, another spear-shaped ornaments. The most remarkable, however, is a *niogadji* with alternate triangles and spirals, among which two lizards are portrayed. *Niogadjis* with triangles on the upper border are found at Tjoedroebaho and with circles at Toehegewo.

One naturally wonders what is the real purpose of these ogive decorations, for unless one bends down they are practically invisible. It is possible that they were not made to please the eye but in order to attract some magic power.

These stones nearly always stand on the ground or on a foundation, occasionally on a pillar about 80 cm high. Quite often they are surrounded by stones of an equal height, or built into a terrace (Tjoedroebaho), an inexplicable fact.

As we have said before, the wives of prominent village chiefs perform dances on these stones. In this connection it may be mentioned that most of the *niogadjis* produce a musical sound when struck with the flat of the hand. It is quite possible that formerly the dancer produced this sound with her feet or that she was accompanied by the clapping of hands on the stone. During our explorations, whenever there were children in the vicinity they always began to strike the stones and to accompany each other. The effect is very pleasing, since every stone has a different tone ...

One twilight evening we came to the village of Hilisimaitano.* We mounted a flight of steps with artistic carvings and lovely volutes. And suddenly there lay before us a large village with rows of houses on both sides of a broad, paved street. The blue twilight dimmed the outlines of the high roofs, from which curled faint clouds of smoke. Men with broad, round straw hats on their heads and a spear over the shoulder were returning from the fields. Children brought water in hollow bamboos. A lone dog barked, then all was still. The evening wrapped Hilisimaitano in an atmosphere of deep rest, like a miracle from ages primeval. . . .

We stepped into the broad, central road. To the right and left stone monuments are placed in long rows before the houses,—simple benches and ornamented obelisks, round tables with a motif of leaves, a chair with a crocodile on the back. These stones serve to commemorate the dead and are often made during the lifetime of the person concerned.

Under the house of the aristocrat Samago we noticed a coffin, three metres long, with the head of a deer. Horns and

*In South Nias.

176

beard were made of gilded tin and fastened to the head with iron wire. The sculpturing was not yet completed, as the founder had just had the stone brought a month before from Botohilitano, 18 km away. Hundreds of people had dragged it over the hills, and Samago had been compelled to give great feasts and to pay dearly. But he did both with pleasure, for now his name would be immortal, the heartfelt wish of every man in Nias.

On the southeast coast, at Hiliganowo, stands a similar coffin, with a tiger head. It is richly painted and was erected only last year. It contains the remains of a certain Sihoewa. The dead man can no longer enjoy the lovely view over sea and waving palms but perhaps in his sleep he hears the sound of the breakers and the deep voices of the evening wind. . . .

These stone coffins in animal form were a tremendous surprise, especially because of their relation to the sarcophagi of Samosir. Their construction is entirely modern, the idea behind it, however, is very old. The prototypes must be sought in similar *wooden* coffins, found to this day on the Batoe Islands, and which were also found twenty five years ago in the Hinako Islands. The stone coffins of Samosir must also have been preceded by wooden chests, such as are still found here and there in the Pakpak Lands.

The second surprise was the village of Bawomataloewo, which lies high and inaccessible on a hill. After climbing hundreds of steps one turns around to look over miles and miles of mountains, valleys and gardens of Nias. Far in the distance Lagoedri Bay lies gleaming in the morning sun.

The chief's house in this village is one of the finest bits of architecture ever made by a primitive people. In front stand the round, stone tables and obelisks of the forefathers. The roof ascends steep and high. The gable is adorned with three dragon heads.

We mount a short flight of steps and walk through a forest of pillars, so large that a man can not span them. Like immense pylons of an Egyptian dream temple they rise, row on row, dark and deeply impressive. We mount a dark flight of stairs, enter a door and stand then in a large, dusky chamber, in the heart of a gigantic castle. In the warm ashes of the hearth dogs lie sleeping.... From the ceiling hang drums, one of which is cannon-shaped and 3 m in length. Whole rows of pigs' jaws, cunning hooks in the shape of birds, flat baskets with plates, etc. adorn the wall. In the centre arises a pillar which unfolds into a flower, cleverly carved and of wondrous beauty. The walls are of dark-stained wood, in which have been made all sorts of figures, even an entire ship with its crew and a shoal of fish. And if we look carefully we even see doorknob ornaments of a grace and delicacy almost unbelievable.

At the rear of the room hangs the figure of a pendant ape, with a bronze ring in its mouth. On festive occasions it is the custom to hang a whole pig on this ring.

Against the walls sit people with magnificent Mongolian features. The pale brown of their skin harmonizes wonderfully with the dark brown of the wall. They are the silent witnesses of a world of beauty which is doomed to vanish, of a people and its culture whose dying fills us Westerlings with pity and reverent silence....

We open a door and look down a flight of steps, where children are playing. They turn around and look up.... Through a crack in the ceiling a beam of golden light falls on their upturned brown faces. The impression is of something primeval, a picture by Rembrandt....

F. M. Schnitger, *Forgotten Kingdoms in Sumatra*, Leiden: E. J. Brill, 1939; reprinted Kuala Lumpur; Oxford University Press, 1989, pp. 150–61.

32
Villages in Lampung, South Sumatra

HENRY O. FORBES

Henry Forbes was a Scottish naturalist of considerable talent who, following the example of Alfred Russell Wallace, set out in 1878 on an intrepid five-year journey through the Indonesian archipelago, gathering extensive collections of plants, butterflies, beetles, and birds. He did not, however, trace Wallace's footsteps exactly, but took a different route, producing quite new descriptions of the Tanimbar Islands and Timor. His text describes with enthusiasm his encounters with the wildlife of the islands, but he was also an open-minded and observant recorder of ethnographic information. His descriptions of local cultures and their achievements in domestic architecture are much more detailed than those of many of his contemporaries, and his judgements more sensitive. He also gives us accounts, both lyrical and geological, of the wild and varied landscapes through which he passed—landscapes by now much altered.

The early part of his journey took him to West Java and thence to South Sumatra, where he travelled up the west coast, on the borders between Lampung and Bengkulu Regencies, then north into Palembang Regency. On the way he stayed in a number of interesting villages, of which two are described here. Having had an unpleasant experience the previous day, when he and his party accidentally floundered into a swamp 'swarming with enormous leeches', the hospitality extended to him in Kenali village was particularly welcome. Finding, however, that this place was too distant from Mount Besagi where he wished to pursue his collecting, he reluctantly moved on to another settlement nearer its foot. In Palembang, he stayed in another old and interesting village, Padjar-bulan, where in the *balai* or council-house he came upon an unusual carving.

A T dark we entered the village of Batu-brah, and I found ready for me, as the news of my coming had preceded me, a royal—compared with my late experiences—sleeping apartment in the Balai, with a table groaning under a load of fruits.

In the morning I was agreeably surprised by finding myself in a village of a character quite different from any that I had yet visited in Sumatra. The houses were high, large, and substantially built of planks raised for five or six feet on immense pillars formed of the largest trees of the forest, with pyramidal roofs, surrounded by an elegant ramshorn-like ornament universally used in the district, cut out of pumice blocks or of tree-fern roots, with a piece of mirror or a bright stone let into it to glitter in the sun. I did not camp here, but continued to Kenali, the capital of the marga, a large and very old village some miles eastward. Both sides of the road were fully cultivated with coffee, rice but principally tobacco, for which this region of Sumatra is famed. Indian corn is also grown in considerable quantity, along with European and sweet potatoes and cabbages of excellent quality.

On our way we crossed a small tributary of the Semangka, which, at a little distance below the ford, narrowing from a river of thirty yards to one of a yard or a yard and a-half wide, dashed itself into a frothy torrent down a narrow rocky gorge in a series of falls for about 100 feet into the main river. The falls reminded me of those of the Clyde at Stonebyres; they are more picturesque, but less imposing from the difficulty of viewing them from below where the cascade plunges into the main river. The road from Batu-brah to Kenali runs along a high plateau of about 3000 feet above the sea, extending between the Barisan range and the volcanoes of Besagi and Sekindjau, and is composed of mingled clay and a sandy pumice-stone tufa which, mixed with the black humus from the forests of centuries, has given its great fertility to the soil of this region.

The village, situated on a high bluff looking down on the river, is one of the oldest in the district, and is certainly one of the finest, cleanest, and most elegantly arranged that I had visited. One of its most noticeable features was its decorative art. The massive pillars, as well as the super-imposed beams and framework of the dwellings, were entirely covered with rich, intricate, and really beautiful carvings in an extremely

Drawing of the south Sumatran village of Kenali, from Henry Forbes, *A Naturalist's Wanderings* . . ., New York: Harper, 1885.

hard black wood, which, after one hundred and fifty years by their data, appeared perfectly fresh and sound. The supporting beams, which rested on the pillars, projected some feet beyond the corners, and were ornamented with carved terminals, somewhat like the figure-head of a ship. A broad stairway of wood, sometimes with rails elaborately carved, led up to the doors. The windows were constructed of solid blocks of wood cut into oval or straight apertures, which could be closed by a correspondingly cut and rotating piece of wood in the inside. The divisions between the apertures were ornamented on the outside with different colours or inlaid with elegant designs in mother-of-pearl. The sides of most of the houses were made of panels of wood let into a grooved framework and accurately fitted, with the aid of very few tools, and often without a single nail. The Balai, always the best looked-after building in a village, was covered everywhere with rich carvings....

The houses of the Kisam people were of a pattern of their own. They were mostly of bamboo wickerwork fitted into a framework of wood, and slated with little boards of cedrilla wood. Each house had built out from it a chamber on the same level with it under a slightly lower roof, which was used as a lounging place for the owner and a sleeping room for visitors. The door was reached—as the houses stood on tall piles—by a slanting tree-trunk, in which a series of notches only large enough to admit the toes served as steps, and up which a booted traveller found it no easy matter to ascend. The space below the house was blocked with chopped-up wood, whose primary use was, doubtless, as a protection against the entrance of thieves or attack from below by enemies, as it is apparent how easy it would be to thrust a spear or other instrument through the bamboo floor into the bodies of the sleepers resting on it. The beneath of a man's house is considered almost as sacred as its interior, and their laws attached supreme penalties to the crime of being found at night there. The house framework in most of the villages was elaborately carved in intricate patterns executed with the most patient care. In Padjar-bulan, a very old village which I passed through, the decorative carving far exceeded in profusion and excellence that in any of the others, especially in its Balai, where I was greatly interested in finding what I may call a veritable coat of arms, carved out of an immense block of wood and erected in the central position, where one would expect an object with the significance of a coat of arms to be placed. From what I could learn it had such a significance in the estimation of the chief of the village; for he told me that only such villages as could claim origin from some distant village could erect such a carving in their Balai. I am not, however, master enough of the terms of blazonry current in the College of Arms to describe it in fitting language. The shield had double supporters; on each side a tiger rampant bearing on its back a snake defiant, upheld the shield, in whose centre the most prominent quartering was a floral ornament, which might be a sunflower shading two deer, one on each side—the dexter greater than the sinister. Above the floral ornament was a central and to me unintelligible halfmoon-like blazoning, but on either side of it was an 'ulai lidai' (Chorus of bystanders: 'Undoubtedly an ulai lidai'), but of what it was the similitude among created things, beyond suggesting faintly the lineaments of a scorpion, I was not pursuivant enough to recognise; on the sinister of the two, however, was a man 'tandacking' (dancing). Below the tips of the conjoined tails of the supporting tigers were two ornate triangles, the upper balanced on the apex of the lower, which might with truth be described as the supporter of the whole, but whether these bear any reference to the mystic signs recognised by the Worshipful Lodges is a question that I must leave for the Chief Mason to settle as best he can with the Chief Herald. I feel inclined, however, to assert that it was as good an escutcheon, and as well and honourably emblazoned, as any that ever emanated from the College; and who dare say that it is less ancient? The sight of that emblazoned board and its carved surroundings, hid away in a small little-known hamlet in the Kisam hills among a half-savage and pagan people, astonished me not a little, and added respect to my farewell salutation to its chief.

Herry O. Forbes, *A Naturalist's Wanderings in the Eastern Archipelago*, New York: Harper, 1885; reprinted Singapore: Oxford University Press, 1989, pp. 167–8, 179–81.

33
'Life in a *Dessa*'

HARRIET PONDER

Harriet Ponder (Passage 6) showed a detailed interest in all manner of aspects of life in Java, both Dutch and Javanese. Here, we enter with her into a typical Javanese village [*dessa*], of which she gives a colourful impression. Ponder was also impressed by Dutch industry and cultivation, and the major advances they had brought about in electricity, transport and communications, about all of which she wrote in her previous book, *Java Pageant*.[1] She viewed Java as the 'model colony', and had a rather rosily simplistic view, at this late date, of a subject people among whom independence movements were already stirring, as being 'gentle, good-natured, tractable, and as contented as any in the world'. Still, although she occasionally falls into the trap of describing the Javanese as 'simple' and 'childlike', there is a freshness about her account that still makes agreeable reading.

T HE *kampongs* have a life of their own; and in them, as in the central town or village of the *dessa*, all duties for the common weal are shared by the members of the community. The *Kepala* of the *kampong* is a mere subordinate member of the central *dessa* council, but in his own *kampong*

[1]Harriet Ponder, *Java Pageant: Impressions of the 1930s*, London: Seeley Service, 1934.

he rules supreme; usually without much difficulty, for local pride in each *kampong* is strong, and they vie with each other in the perfection of their close trimmed banks, their bridges and fences, and their paths, swept as meticulously as your drawing-room floor.

For the most part these *kampongs* are charming, especially in cool mountain regions, where in each little garden there is a proud display of flowers and vegetables, and orange or *pommelo* trees fill the air with the lovely scent of their blossom, or stand laden with golden fruit. There are always waving palms and bananas and clumps of bamboo, none the less ornamental because it is grown for strictly practical purposes; and often *palisades* of burnished green *sirih* or other climbing plants. The houses will be of split bamboo *bilik*; and nowadays almost if not quite all are roofed with the pretty red-brown tiles which are one of a thousand and one other minor native industries. A wise Dutch regulation has ordained of late years that the formerly much used palm leaf *atap* roofing, which gave dangerously hospitable harbourage to rats, must be abolished, as a precaution against plague.

Other simple and admirable hygienic regulations ordered by the Dutch, and transmitted through the *dessa* council to the heads of the *kampongs*, are rigorously enforced by each of them among their little groups of subjects. In every small compound you will see all rubbish neatly gathered and burned, bedding being aired in the sunshine, and walls freshly whitewashed at regular intervals. The people of the *kampongs* usually pay their head man's salary, or part of it, in kind. And in maize growing districts the long rows of tall bamboo drying-racks laden with the cobs thus paid in are a sight well worth seeing.

Every *kampong* has a more or less elaborate entrance gate and porch built of bamboo. Often these are most decorative, for this is a matter in which the community take special pride. Usually the large double gates, often eight feet or more high, made of *bilik*, are closed at night; and many of the entrances are provided with a covered platform and a *kentongan* where the hours of darkness are struck by a watchman. This same platform is also used to accommodate a *gamelan* orchestra on public festive occasions. In a particularly prosperous *kampong* there may be a fine avenue leading to the gate, and the approach may be beautified with hedges of alamanda or acalypha, or by walls covered with a veil of maidenhair fern. There is no need to teach these simple people the 'community spirit'. It is part of their natural make up; and despite their long hours of labour in the fields, nothing is too much trouble that will enhance the beauty of their 'home town', and incidentally give them an opportunity to crow over the inferior attractions of their *neighbours' kampong*.

No *kampong* is complete without its communal laundry and bathing place, made in the bed of some convenient stream, and fenced round with the indispensable bamboo. These are the women's clubs. Here, all and every morning, happy groups of women and children are busy, washing themselves, their babies, and the many coloured garments of their families, beating soapy *sarongs* on flat stones as they stand ankle or knee deep in the warm, soft, gently flowing stream, in a glorious mix up of splashing water, mud, ducks, soapsuds, laughter, and gossip. While higher up the stream, other women are washing rice for dinner, in bamboo baskets under the bamboo pipe that brings them their unfailing supply of running water.

Among the many communal customs of the *kampongs*, one which concerns theft might be recommended to other communities, for it is remarkably productive of honesty. If the property of any stranger visiting the *kampong* should be stolen, the whole community is held to share the responsibility, and every member of the population must contribute to the cost of replacing it. Hospitality to travellers is one of the accepted rules of Javanese native life, and no one is ever refused shelter for the night. That he should be robbed while the guest of the *kampong*, therefore, brings shame to everyone living in it.

Consideration for weary travellers is also shown in the custom, in many *dessas*, of keeping an earthenware jar filled daily with fresh water in a bamboo basket fixed on a post by the roadside. One of these is often to be seen at the point where the path to a *kampong* joins the road. The jar in its deftly woven split bamboo cover looks at first glance temptingly like a giant bottle of Chianti!

The *kampong* dweller, simple fellow though he may be, is not so unsophisticated that wireless is unknown to him, and in the most remote hamlets you will probably see several aerials made of slender, immensely tall bamboos, rearing their heads high above the thick foliage that hides the small houses. Their erection presents no difficulty, thanks to the genuine community feeling that prevails.

No sooner does Si Soswosipotro or Ah Woeng or some other village worthy announce his purchase of this latest kind of white man's magic, and his desire to appease the spirits that serve it with a tall pole, as advised by the Chinese who sold it to him, than all the male youth of the *kampong* not otherwise occupied at the moment will turn out to give a hand, well knowing that they will share as a matter of course in all the fun it may provide in the future.

Native houses in country *kampongs* are of extremely simple design. They rarely have any windows; and the one large room is carpeted with grass mats and crowded with furniture. Conservative though he is in the matter of house design, the Javanese, when he can afford it, is a convert to European furnishings at their very worst. Wardrobes and 'whatnots', china cabinets, occasional tables, and Nottingham lace curtains are his delight. He does not feel his home complete without an immense iron double bed for the heads of the family, the rest being quite content to sleep on the floor, for the Javanese have the happy knack of being able to sleep anyhow and anywhere. Even the hospitable instinct that is one of his most ancient traditions is given a European flavour when a card on which the words SALAMAT DATANG (Welcome) are printed, in large letters, is framed and glazed in the latest Dutch style and hung just inside the door.

Javanese taste in music, however, remains unchanged; and the vague indeterminate rhythms of the *gamelan* to be heard as you pass by any *kampong*, through all the countless *dessas* of Java, have probably changed little, if at all, through many hundreds of years. They are almost as indispensable to native life as light and air and food. These village *gamelans* usually consist only of the giant xylophone already mentioned: made of two long converging bamboos supporting the 'notes' of metal, wood, or split bamboo, called *saron* in the former case, and *gambang* in the latter, and of various drums and gongs. The full *gamelan*, which is an orchestra of about twenty-four players, is rare in Java outside the two royal palaces, though it is common in Bali.

In the old days, when every village was an independent fortress, Java shared with many other parts of tropical Asia the admirably practical custom of planting a dense grove of bamboo round each *kampong*, as the best of all defences against surprise attack, and a supply of all-purpose building material. The peaceful modern Javanese has happily no longer need of it to protect him from treacherous neighbours, but he still finds it as necessary as ever for a thousand peaceful purposes. To the casual passer-by the appearance of any *kampong* in a country *dessa* to-day, half hidden among its feathery bamboos, probably differs but little from what he would have seen if he had passed that way a thousand years ago.

H. W. Ponder, *Javanese Panorama*, London: Seeley, Service & Co., 1942; reprinted Kuala Lumpur: Oxford University Press, 1990, pp. 82–5.

Domestic Architecture

34
A Lao House at Kiang Hai in 1881

CARL BOCK

The Norwegian explorer Carl Alfred Bock was born in 1849. He studied Natural Sciences in London, and in 1878, embarked on a fauna-collecting expedition to West Sumatra. Unfortunately his steamer sank on the way home and half of his specimens were lost in the Red Sea. Undeterred, he set out the following year on a five-month expedition to the interior of south-eastern Borneo. His resulting book, *The Headhunters of Borneo*, made him famous in Europe, though it must be considered far more reliable on botanical and ornithological matters than it is on ethnographic ones. Bock's uncritical enthusiasm for danger and excitement led him to overseason his narrative with sensational accounts of headhunting, supposedly cannibal natives, and fierce orang utans; though his anecdotal, humorous style proved highly popular with his European audience. Another expedition followed to Siam and Laos, of which his second book *Temples and Elephants* provides an equally entertaining record. His account is full of acute observations on the appearances, manners, and customs of his hosts and other tribal peoples he encountered. Subsequently, Bock became recognized in Norway and Sweden as an authority on 'the East', and pursued a diplomatic career which took him in 1886 to Shanghai, and later to Lisbon. The following passage is extracted from Bock's lively and personal account of his stay in a Lao house in the countryside north of Chieng Mai.

PRESENTLY I went into the village, and called upon the Chow Hluang, who said the only accommodation he had for me was a small Sala, which, being out of repair, I declined. I then went, with the letter of introduction which the Chow Operat had given me, to his son-in-law, the Chow Radjasee, who very kindly offered me hospitality in his own house.

My host and hostess, who warmly shook hands with me, seemed friendly disposed, and were greatly delighted when I presented them with sixteen yards of blue silk cloth, interwoven with gold thread, and it was not long before they returned the compliment with the usual gift of rice and eggs, fruits and fowls.

My host was a man of about forty-five years of age, who, after being eighteen years in the priesthood, had married, two years previously, the Chow Operat's daughter, a very plain woman with a terrible squint, but a very good heart withal. They lived in a good-sized house, built in the ordinary style of teak and bamboo, where they did everything to make me comfortable.

As I have not yet fully described a Lao house, I give here a picture of the residence of the Chow Radjasee, not because it is of the most elaborate design, but because it will serve as a type of Lao architecture and domestic arrangements. There are no fine houses or palaces in the country; the houses of prince and peasant are the same in general plan and in mode of construction, the only difference being in the size and in the quality of material and workmanship. A few bits of extra carving on the gables, and the fact that it is constructed throughout of teak, may distinguish a prince's house from that of any ordinary person; but, beyond a difference in size, that is all. The roof of the house is usually of thatch, which is cheap and easily replaced. The better houses are sometimes roofed with 'tiles' made of teak, which are of course more durable, but do not keep the rain out any better than a well-repaired thatch.

The houses are never more than one story high, and always built on posts, with the floor at an elevation of from five to eight feet above the ground. In this space under the floor the elephant-howdahs or oxen-packsaddles are piled; while the fowls and ducks congregate here, and even the cattle themselves are very commonly sheltered for the night.

Going up some three or four rude steps in front of the house, one comes to a platform or balcony, running right round the house. The flooring is commonly made of split bamboo, laid across the main rafters supported by the posts on which the house is erected; but in the case of the wealthier classes the flooring is sometimes made entirely of teak. These balconies are always very slippery, and, what is worse, are often out of repair. I have a painful recollection of the dilapidated state into which this part of the house is often allowed to fall, for while staying at Kiang Hai I had several narrow escapes of falling, and one evening my foot slipped into one of the holes, and I sprained my ankle so severely that my kind host, though he could not mend my foot, did his best to prevent a repetition of the accident by setting his slaves to work next day to lay down a new bamboo flooring.

At one end of this platform is invariably erected a small covered shelf, or shed, called *han nam*, made of a few boards raised on posts, with a thatch-roof over the top. Here stand several large unglazed water-jars, which are daily filled with water for ordinary domestic purposes. By the side of these water-vessels lies a spoon, made of the half of a cocoanut-shell, with a wooden handle, with which, in dirty weather, any person entering the house ladles out some water from the jar, and pours it over his feet, to cleanse them.

Every morning and evening, the prince and princess would go out in turn on this platform to have a bath; it was too far for them to walk three or four minutes to the river. Their ablutions consisted merely in pouring water over themselves from the big waterjars with a large spoon or cup. Sometimes the lady would finish up by having a huge silver basin brought, containing a mixture of tamarind-water and lime-juice, with which she would wash her hair. I took the liberty of making the accompanying sketch of the princess during this operation.

This entrance-platform is generally ornamented by pots of orchids or other flowering plants.

The floor of the house proper is raised about a foot above this platform, the entrance to the room or rooms being through a passage with a covered apartment on each side, one for domestics and slaves, the other for members of the family. Each of these apartments is divided by walls of planks or plaited bamboo into two separate rooms, one used as a sleeping-chamber, and the other as a general living-room. The room appropriated to the members of the family is often subdivided again, either by a wall or a series of posts, into two sections, the innermost of which is raised above the level of the rest, and set apart for purely private purposes, or for the reception of 'distinguished visitors'.

Behind the servants' room is the kitchen, which generally extends along the whole length of the back of the house. On the kitchen-floor is a mound of earth or clay, several inches high, which serves as a fireplace, hemmed in all round with boards, and with a tripod in the centre, formed of three stones, on which the fire and oven are placed.

The house is surrounded by a garden, enclosed with a tall bamboo fence, spiked at the top. The entrance to this compound is guarded by a sliding door, made of teak, fitted at the bottom with a wheel which enables it to be easily opened and closed. It is always fastened at dark, to keep out thieves, both biped and quadruped; for tigers are numerous in some parts, and very aggressive. As an additional guard several pariah dogs are kept, but, though they bark at the slightest alarm, they seldom bite, for they are very timid, and easily frightened away with a stick or stone, and are not nearly such good watch-dogs as the trained dogs from Yunnan, which the better classes of Laosians keep, and which it is dangerous for a stranger to approach.

In the gardens are grown, in wild confusion, cocoa-palms, betelnut-palms, capsicums, and a few 'vegetables'.

Carl Bock, *Temples and Elephants: Travels in Siam in 1881–1882*, London: Sampson Low, Marston, Searle, & Rivington, 1884; reprinted Kuala Lumpur: Oxford University Press, 1986, pp. 303–7.

35
'A Laos Cabin'

JONATHAN WILSON

Wilson was co-founder, with Dr Daniel McGilvray, of the Laos Presbyterian Mission. Despite a generally favourable assessment of the Lao people of northern Thailand, and their habitations, described here, he had the common missionary's perception of his potential converts as living in 'darkness' and 'fear', and needing to be set free by Christianity. His observation of the Lao house is unusually detailed, and many features common in South-East Asian architecture are noted in it. For example, he notes the tremendous versatility of bamboo as a readily available building material, and the design of the house as a platform entirely enclosed by roof, without walls. He notes the convenience of being able to spit betel juice through the gaps in the split bamboo flooring, and the fact that the house is jointed together without the use of any nails. Also mentioned is the necessity to protect the house and its occupants with appropriate rituals and charms; the placing of cloths in the joints where the tops of the house posts meet the beams is a practice followed not only in north Thailand but also among the Malays, Acehnese, and Bugis.

THE Laos captives near Petchaburee live in houses whose roofs have a circular appearance. The gables are enclosed with thatch, so arranged as to form a continuous roof with that of the house. This roof reaches so low as to shut out all view of the house itself from the passer-by. These people have come from the north, where both cold and storms are more severe than where they now live. In Cheung Mai, the eaves of the roofs and the ends projecting beyond the gables are sometimes caught with such force by the whirling storm that the roof is carried away. The whole of this house seems to be resting upon those short posts which fork at the top. In most of the houses of the Cheung Mai peasantry these short posts serve to support only the flooring. Strong beams or sills are laid upon them. Bamboo poles are laid across these sills about a foot apart and tied with

A Lao house in north Thailand, from John Thomson, *The Straits of Malacca . . .* , London: Sampson Low, Marston, Low, and Searle, 1875.

ratan. Over these is spread the bamboo flooring. This is made from the trunk of a large-sized bamboo. It is cut into the proper lengths, and these are gashed lengthwise all over their surface by repeated strokes of the knife or axe. By this process the sticks become quite pliable. They are then slit open by passing the knife through one side of them from end to end. The broken and jagged edges of the inner side of the joints are smoothed off, and we have bamboo boards a foot or more wide. This flooring bends under the pressure of the feet, and when dry makes a creaking noise which is not very pleasant. When riddled by a small black beetle that burrows in its fibres, it becomes unsafe to tread upon, and sometimes one breaks through it. But by putting it, when green, into water, and keeping it submerged until it passes through the process of fermentation, it is, in a great measure, free from the ravages of this beetle. The many chinks in this bamboo floor offer convenient passage for the streams of red saliva that flow from the mouths of its betel-chewing inmates.

The walls and roofs of these huts are supported by posts set in the ground some two feet of their length and reaching to the plates. The ridge of the roof also rests upon posts of the necessary length. The posts for the walls are arranged accord-ing to a long-observed custom. They must be in sets of threes or fives, etc.; odd numbers bring luck. The spaces between each of these sets of posts have specific names. Religious superstition takes under its guidance almost every part of the work, and when the house is done it still directs as to the day and the manner of moving in to take possession. No doors or windows are found in the eastern wall. The family sleep with their heads toward the east. Part of the main building—generally the end facing south—is reserved for an open court. The east end of this court has a wall continuous with that of the house. Along this wall is a shelf upon which are placed flowers and other offerings in worship of Buddha and the good spirits. In this outer court, if the family are religiously inclined, the priests, by invitation, occasionally conduct a merit-making service for the prosperity of the household. In cases of sickness like services are held here. Preventives of sickness or other calamity are often seen resting on the top of the posts under the plate that receives the rafters. These consist of small pieces of cloth on which are written certain symbolic characters, the cloths themselves having become charms, potent against the intrusion of evil spirits, through the incantations of what our American Indians would call 'medicine-men'.

[T]he common Cheung Mai house has a platform from eight to twelve feet wide, raised within a few inches as high as the floor of the main building. This platform extend[s] from near the centre of the house at its southern end, beyond its south-western corner, to give passage-way to the kitchen. At the west end of this platform stands a covered settle for the earthen water-pots which hold water for drinking and cooking. The outer posts of this platform rise high enough to support a railing, and a board on top of this railing gives room for earthen flower-pots and for boxes of earth in which are growing, for family use, onions, red pepper, garlic, etc. The floor of the platform serves in daytime for drying betel-nuts and fruit. At night, after the heat of the day, it furnishes a place for rest under the cooling sky. The stairs are placed at the end of this platform. Such a house may be built entirely of bamboo except the grass thatch required for the roof. Neither hammer nor nail is needed for its construction. The different parts are held together by thongs of split bamboo or ratan. These houses are built at small cost. Very many of them are kept neat and tidy. And they have their conveniences. The writer had occasion to pay a native peasant a considerable sum of money. This man, after counting the rupees and testing their genuineness, one by one, by poising it on the tip of his finger and tapping it gently with another rupee, tied the money up in a piece of rag, and, rising, dropped it from the top into the hollow of one of the posts that supported the wall behind him. This post gave him a perfect concealment for his treasure. It was *his* 'safe', answering the same purpose to him that the iron one, with its intricate locks, does to the banker, except that in the case of the Oriental a stray spark would soon set his house and his 'safe' ablaze together. Still, he could linger near for the few moments it would take the flame to lick up his house and very soon after he would have his silver rupees, melted, it might possibly be, into a common mass.

There is no time—nor is it necessary—to speak of the trees that throw around and over the houses of the native peasantry their cool and protecting shade. Many of these houses are hidden away among the trees, some of which, for size, vie with those of the forest. Among the most beautiful of these trees are clumps of bamboo, from which material has been obtained for the building or repair of the very houses which they now envelop in their shade.

Jonathan Wilson, *Siam and Laos, As Seen by Our American Missionaries*, Philadelphia: Presbyterian Board of Publication, 1884, pp. 497–502.

36
Lunch at the Headman's House in Naning

J. R. LOGAN

James Richardson Logan was one of the earliest British travellers in the western Malay States to gain a first hand acquaintance with Malay people. Between 1847 and 1859, he was founder editor of the *Journal of the Indian Archipelago and Eastern Asia*, to which he contributed many pieces based on his own experiences, as well as collecting contributions from other British enthusiasts in Malaya. The journal was a precursor to the later *Journal of the Straits Branch of the Royal Asiatic Society* (renamed the *Journal of the Malay Branch of the Royal Asiatic Society*), which continues to be published today. Logan was a pioneer of ethnographic description of Malay culture. His account of a visit to a Malay headman's house, inland of

Malacca, shows a remarkable attention to detail and provides us with one of the earliest English descriptions of Malay domestic architecture.

A BDULRAHMAN'S house lay in one of the plantations on the right side of the road, and as it is a fair specimen of the style of the better class of houses in Naning, I will briefly describe it:- The body of the house is about 40 feet square and, like all Malay cottages, rests on posts, so that the floor is some feet above the ground. It is divided by a partition into a large and a small room. A few steps lead down from the former into a broad verandah or gallery, which runs along the whole front of the house, and at one end extends about 24 feet beyond it. The sides and partition of the house are of panelled wood work. The ends of the verandah are of similar wood work, with a curiously carved narrow window, or rather a row of slits, in each. In front and at the back of the projecting end, a wooden parapet about 2½ feet in height forms the only obstruction to the free ingress of air and light. On the wall of the verandah are hung some deer's horns and skulls, the trophies of the householder's forest craft. Fine mats are spread on a portion of the floor, and others lie at one end in readiness for any unusual influx of visitors, for the verandah forms at once the visiting, eating, and sleeping place for guests. The large room into which we ascend from the verandah, is only used as a reception room on feasts and other great occasions, and ordinarily forms a convenient store-room for the less valuable household stuff, such as baskets of different kinds, mats, &c. Around a wooden post in the middle are hung an abundance of spears, swords, and other weapons of several sorts, for the Malayan armoury displays a motley and curious assortment of weapons. A number of baskets of paddy, which had been newly brought in from the field and were not yet cleaned for the granary, were placed on the floor. The smaller room was my host's bed chamber, the only place in the whole kampong sacred to privacy. At one end was a curtained bed, and on the other were stuck or suspended some fire-arms and a great variety of krises, swords and knives. . . .

To complete the picture of the kampong, I must notice the kitchen, an attap fabric a few paces in the rear of the house, but connected with it by a covered platform of split nibong, —and the granary, a light and neat structure raised some feet from the ground, well-roofed, and having its sides of narrow bambu placed about an inch separate, so as to allow a free passage to the air. The paddy is not heaped on the floor, but stored in cylindrical receptacles about 2½ feet high and 3 to 4 feet broad, made by bending back upon itself a broad strip of the thick bark of the *Coopong Tree* an instance of that adaptation, by the simplest processes, of materials ready from the hand of nature, into neat and useful articles, which so frequently strikes and pleases the observer in a Malayan country. A number of fowls and a few goats were scattered about the kampong attending to the one business of their lives. Between the cocoanuts there are some dark-leaved coffee bushes which yield a crop of berries, scanty but sufficient for the use of the house. A well trodden path leads to an open well on the margin of the paddy flat. Some pieces of wood placed on the lower side serve as the bathing place of the whole family male and female, and it is one of the peculiarities of Náning that these bathing places are entirely open and uncovered and in bathing the sarong is not taken off.

The owner of all these possessions, and of the paddy fields in front, welcomed us at his gate, and struck me by his abrupt and homely manner, so different from that of the Malays in the town. . . . An ample repast of boiled rice, fish, &c., was soon spread on the mats, and I now learned from Mahomed [Logan's guide on the expedition] that our host had left his house in Malacca the preceding evening, and walked 18 miles during the night to have breakfast ready for us at an early hour. The Malay coolies who had been employed in carrying my baggage sat down with my host and Mahomed. A separate array of dishes was prepared for me at a little distance upon another mat, and I was invited to occupy the only chair that the house afforded. As the chair was ricketty, and table there was none, I preferred following the custom of my neighbours.

J. R. Logan, 'Five Days in Naning, with a Walk to the Foot of Gunong Datu in Rambau', *Journal of the Indian Archipelago and Eastern Asia*, 3 (1849): 26–9.

37
Malay Houses in Perak in the 1870s

J. F. A. McNAIR

J. F. A. (Fred) McNair was an Indian Army officer who lived for over twenty years in the Straits Settlements. He was Colonial Engineer (head of the Public Works Department) from 1867. He played a key role in the British intervention in the Malay States, since from 1875–6 he served as Chief Commissioner, heading the liason team of the civil government with the military forces engaged in the Perak War. A large part of his book, *Perak and the Malays*, is a justification of this British intervention, but it also reflects his considerable knowledge of the Malay way of life at that time. His descriptions of Malay architecture, reproduced here, are augmented with his first hand account of his stay at the house of Inche Maida, Princess of Perak, and her husband Nakoda Trong, who accommodated the British and their troops during their expedition in Perak.

S ITUATED as it is, with the river flowing before it, the appearance of a Malay village amongst its palms and other fruit trees is exceedingly picturesque, the graceful aspect of the waving trees, with their beautiful columnar trunks, and feathery fronds, shading the quaint bamboo palm-thatched structures, being pleasing in the extreme. There is but little attention paid to order; but the houses are placed here and there according to the taste and convenience of the owner, who readily plants cocoa-nut trees around, though he has to wait about seven years for their fruiting. When there are so many houses that a double row occupies the river-bank, a line of communication exists between them that does not deserve the title of road, for the Malay never thinks of constructing anything of this kind, but leaves as much as possible to Dame Nature. In this case the houses are built, and as the people walk to and fro the path comes of itself.

Below the houses ... posts are driven into the soil, and upon these small sheds are erected, which serve as bathing-places, and are extensively used by both men and women, and it is upon the palm-thatch of these places that the sarong is thrown as a sign of occupation. In fact, it is a rare thing to go up or down a river without seeing someone bathing, for the Malays of both sexes are very fond of the water; but great care has to be taken on account of the alligators, which are in places exceedingly numerous. After a bath the all-important sarong frequently occupies the place of a towel; and amongst the better classes cosmetiques are used to rub the body, which at other times, if not sufficiently lithe and pliable at the joints, is made to undergo a kind of shampooing or kneading, the joints being folded, the limbs stretched and pulled, and the knuckles carefully cracked; but this is generally when the Malay is ailing, or suffering from 'wind in the joints'.

The residence of the Malay is invariably built upon posts, some of which are close to and over the water, though there are no floating bamboo raft-houses as in Siam. The floor is from four to six feet above the ground; in fact, in the jungle, houses may be found built upon the natural posts formed by the growing trees, the floor, which is reached by a ladder, being fifteen, twenty, or even thirty feet from the ground. This is for protection from wild beasts, cases having been known of that formidable cat, the tiger, entering a hut and bearing its occupant away.

The Malay who desires to have a comfortable home literally builds two houses or huts—one at the back of the other—separately roofed, but with a way of communication to join them and form one shelter. The front house is the place for general reception; while the back, which is shut off by a doorway and curtain, is the exclusive home of the women and children. Again, behind this, there is a kind of shed or lead-to, in which the ordinary domestic arrangements, such as cooking and preparing food, are carried on.

The ground-floor, if it may be so called—that is to say the space between the supporting posts—is the general receptacle of all the dirt and refuse of the family; and so wanting in sanitary arrangements, and so idle is the Malay peasant, that sooner than construct drains, or clear away this rubbish, he will allow it to lie and fester, so that it very frequently brings on ailments which a due attention to cleanliness would have warded off.

Palm and bamboo are the chief village building materials, though in the Settlements good houses are constructed of bricks, for which there is plenty of excellent clay, while lime made from the limestone coral that abounds is easily procurable. It is mostly prepared by the Chinese, who build up a kiln of alternate layers of coral and timber, and after the requisite burning, a ready sale is found.

The uprights of a house and its sides having been constructed of bamboo or palm by the Malay of a campong, he makes the flooring either of bamboo, or, what is preferable, the nibong palm, which can readily be split into laths. This flooring is elastic, and not unpleasant to bare feet; and upon it the people, who sit upon the floor, are in the habit of spreading mats, which form their seats by day and beds by night. The sides of a house of the lower class are either made of the bark of trees or of split reeds; but in the better-class houses the walls are of far more elaborate work, being sometimes composed of planks which are laboriously cut from the serayah tree, though more often of a kind of mat which is in very general use. These mats are called *kadjangs*, and are made of the leaves of a kind of palm, carefully dried in the sun, and then literally stitched together with the universal rattan; for the Malay is most apt in the way in which he utilises the abundant materials that nature has placed to his hand.

Windows are not forgotten, and these are placed at a height suitable to the convenience of a gazer seated upon the floor; and in the better-class houses they are provided with a mat shutter, and a great deal of tasty work is visible in their framing. But, just as in our own land, there are very careless builders; and in some of the poorer houses, the supports being held together with rattans instead of nails, these former work loose, and at last the whole house goes over bodily right out of the perpendicular.

In such a case it might be supposed that, with abundant materials in the jungle, the Malay would at once proceed to rebuild. He does nothing of the kind; but evidently content with feeling that the slip has tightened the rattan lashings of his home, he accommodates himself to the new circumstances, and to the want of the horizontal in his dwelling, and goes on perfectly happy in the feeling that he is after all not called upon to take the trouble to rebuild his hut. In fact, there seems to be a belief that it is unlucky to pull down the old dilapidated dwelling, which stands till it falls; and the Malay strongly reminds one, in his home arrangements, of the Irish cotter, who could not get at the roof of his house to mend it when it was wet, while when it was dry it did not need repair.

The universal roofing of a Perak house is *attap* stretched over bamboo rafters and ridge-poles. This attap is the dried leaf of the nipah-palm, doubled over a small stick of bamboo or nibong. The pieces of attap for roofing are generally about four feet in length, and are bound on to the rafters with rattans; series overlapping series, and forming a splendid rain-proof thatch. Like all thatches, however, the attap will show tender places in time; when the Malays, instead of re-covering the whole roof, ingeniously introduce new leaves in the bad spots; for when driven to take measures, they are adepts at saving themselves trouble. Where extra protection seems to be needed, it is not uncommon for palm-leaves to be laid along the ridge of a roof over the pale, the leaflets being tightly plaited in and out; these efforts to obtain a waterproof roof being very necessary in a land where at times the rains are exceedingly heavy.

The attap makes a very cool and pleasant roofing material, and is used extensively by the Europeans of the Settlements, in place of slates or tiles for their dwellings; the former having to be brought from England at great cost and risk of breakage, while the latter are not easily procurable of good quality; those of Malacca however are the best. The objections to the attap-thatch are its inflammability and want of lasting qualities, since it has to be renewed every three or four years. It is still however used over the European barracks, and for the roofs of many of the residences in the Settlement....

The Malay, when put to the test, and compelled by necessity to work for his own benefit, is by no means slow in protecting himself from the elements. After a weary heating walk through the jungle, and securing his return journey by blazing or marking the trees with his parang, he does not think of lying down upon the ground to rest, but rapidly fits up a few posts, and a floor upon them, a yard above the level, places a palm-leaf roof over the structure, and then protects his loins from the wind as he lies down, by means of a few palm-leaves.

But it is in the building of a chief's house that the best efforts are put forth; and very picturesque are some of the efforts in this way, with their neat thatching, matted windows, and elegantly-woven sides, gracefully shadowed by the beautiful growth of palms; though there are irreverent Englishmen found ready to make comparisons between these jungle palaces and the barns of their native land.

A house of this kind will be decorated by the sides being formed of matting composed of split reeds, woven into a neat check pattern, red and white; while other parts are of strips

The residence of the Princess of Perak at Kuala Kangsar, used as headquarters by British forces during their intervention in the Perak War. From J. F. A. McNair, *Perak and the Malays*, London: Tinsley, 1878.

of bamboo neatly interlaced. An elegant lattice-work is often introduced with admirable effect, and various little efforts are made to embellish a building that is thoroughly in keeping with the jungle scene. Such a place will be protected by surrounding it with a stout fence of split bamboo; the best example of this being at the home of the Muntri of Laroot, at Bukit Gantang, which is perhaps one of the best-built places in Perak. At times these fences are so strong that they will throw off a musket-ball; and those not acquainted with the country, who have come across these *pagars*, as they are called, have taken them for the stockades used by the Malays in time of war. Sometimes these fences are merely placed round the base of a house itself, thus enclosing the open part between the posts through which an enemy could otherwise make his way. A necessary precaution; for it is said that at times, where revenge is sought, a Malay will wait till his enemy is at rest, and then, having obtained a knowledge of where he sleeps, will go beneath the house and pass his kris between the palm-strip flooring into the recumbent body— the mat which forms the unfortunate person's only bed being no protection against the keenly-pointed blade.

The residence of the Princess of Perak at Qualla Kungsa [Kuala Kangsar] gives—as will be seen in the illustration, from a photograph taken by the author during the Governor's progress—a very full idea of a Malay noble's residence. The house to the left is really the kitchen, while that on the right is, as far as its principal apartments is concerned, fitted up with a bed which occupies about two-thirds of the room, greatly resembling in the matter of size the Bed of Ware. This house, with the whole of the campong adjoining, was placed by Inche Maida at the disposal of the British during the disturbances, and formed the head-quarters of the general commanding and the commissioner with the contingent of troops from India.

J. F. A. McNair, *Perak and the Malays*, London: Tinsley, 1878; reprinted Kuala Lumpur: Oxford University Press, 1972, pp. 160–9.

38

Some Habitations of the *Orang Asli* of the Malay Peninsula

WALTER WILLIAM SKEAT AND CHARLES OTTO BLAGDEN

During the 1890s, W. W. Skeat was an administrator in the Selangor Government Service, where he developed an interest in Malay culture, as well as that of the indigenous *orang asli* groups of that region. In 1898 he was appointed District Magistrate for Larut in the State of Perak. His companion author, Charles Blagden, was a notable linguist who worked not only on Malay but also in Burma on the Mon-Khmer languages. He had served for a time in the Straits Settlements civil service, later becoming a professor at the School of Oriental and African Studies in London. Skeat planned and led the Cambridge University Expedition to the north-eastern Malay States and Upper Perak (1899–1900), a region at that time controlled by Siam. This enabled him to augment his data, especially on Negrito groups in the northern states. He fell seriously ill on this expedition, being told after his return to England that he should on no account return to Malaya. This led to his being invalided out of the Service in 1900, and having to decline an offer to become political adviser to the Sultan of Trengganu. *Pagan Races of the Malay Peninsula* was largely written by Skeat, Blagden contributing a sizeable appendix of linguistic data. Except for one work[1] dwelling largely on physical anthropology, which appeared just a year earlier, this was the first systematic attempt to describe *orang asli* cultures. Some of these groups are nomadic foragers and collectors of jungle produce for trade, while others are shifting cultivators; their houses range from the simplest of weather-screens and jungle shelters to more solid longhouses of the Semang. From Skeat's Chapter on 'Habitations', extracts are here presented on the Semang of Perak, Kedah, and Kelantan, the 'Perak Sakai' (Semai, or possibly Temiar), and finally, the indigenous Orang Seletar of Singapore, whom Skeat describes as entirely boat-dwelling. The Orang Seletar continued their marine-oriented way of life (though with houses on shore as well as boats) on

[1]Rudolf Martin, *Die Inlandstämme der Malayischen Halbinsel*, Jena: Verlag von Gustav Fischer, 1905.

Singapore's north coast into the late 1980s, when they were displaced by the building of the Seletar Dam. They were then either dispersed into public housing, or chose to move across the strait to Johor, where they claimed traditional protection from the Sultan.

The Rock shelter.

Kedah Semang.—The Semang are almost ineradicably nomadic, have no fixed habitations, and rove about like the beasts of the forest. The wilder ones seldom stay more (they informed me) than three days in one place. Rock-shelters are also commonly used by them.

Pangan.—At Ban tun, in the province of Patalung on the north-western shore of the Inland Sea (Singora), I visited one of these small rock-shelters which had been inhabited, up to the night of our arrival, by nine Pangans, who had only deserted it on hearing our approach. It was formed by a large overhanging rock under the brow of a very steep and lofty hill. Its size was very small, measuring only from about 9 to 12 feet (2.7 m. to 3.6 m.) in length by 6 to 8 feet (1.8 m. to 2.4 m.) in width, and from about 4 to 5 feet (1.2 m. to 1.5 m.) in height. Its position on a shoulder of the hill was very well chosen, as the ground fell away precipitously in front of it, and the only way to reach it was to go round by the back of the overhanging rock itself. The mouth of the cave was, moreover, further concealed and protected by a thicket of thorny bamboo, which grew at the more precipitous end. Altogether it was as difficult a spot to find without a guide as any which could have been selected. The sole article of furniture was one of the rough bamboo sleeping-stages, or 'barbicans', which are to be seen in most Semang encampments, and which are made by lashing half a dozen thick bamboo poles together. This particular bed, however, could not have accommodated more than one or two persons at most, and the other members of the family had evidently been sleeping on beds of heaped-up leaves, which were still quite green and fresh on our arrival. There were also the ashes of four separate fires, one at least of which had been extinguished by water; and there were fragments of the ribs of a small tortoise on which they had been feeding, as well as a half-smoked (native) cigarette, an indication that they had probably had some traffic, either direct or through the medium of 'tamer' fellow-tribesmen, with the Malays or Siamese of the locality.

Tree-shelters.

Perak Semang.—Another obvious kind of 'natural shelter' is that afforded by the branches of trees, the scanty protection thus obtained being speedily improved by the building of a weather-screen, out of which is easily and naturally developed the tree-built hut. The exact purpose served by those arboreal dwellings has been much disputed, but the most reasonable explanation—and I think undoubtedly the correct one—is that they are built for protection from wild beasts. In most cases the proximity of wild beasts is certainly their *raison d'être*. We are told, for instance, in so many words, that some of the Semang 'in the thicker parts of the forest, *where the elephants, tigers, and other wild animals are most abundant*, make their temporary dwellings upon the cliffs and branches of large trees'. The simplest form of the tree-shelter consists of a screen of leaves fixed across the branches of the tree a little above the fork to serve as a roof. Usually, however, side-screens are added, for comfort's sake.

I am told by Mr Wray that he once visited a Semang house in the Piah valley, in Upper Perak. It measured about 50 feet (15.2 m. × 6 m.) in length by 20 feet in width, and was built on posts of such a height that the floor was 15 feet (4·5 m.) above the ground. There were three ladders on one side of the house to give access to it, and it appeared to have been inhabited by at least three families. Underneath it Mr Wray found the bones of the wild pig, deer, and 'sĕladang' (*Bos gaurus*, the wild bull or 'bison'), as well as the horn of one of these latter animals.

Pangan.—The Pangan tree-huts observed by Messrs Ridley and Kelsall on the banks of the Ulu Tahan river in Pahang (in 1891) were 'small roofed platforms, raised about 15 or 20 feet (4.5 m. to 6 m.) from the ground', and were reached (as Mr Ridley tells me) by a ladder formed of sticks lashed across two neighbouring trees.

Ground-screens of Leaves.

Semang and Pangan.—Yet another kind of shelter used by the Semang is the palm-leaf ground-screen, which is intended simply as a protection against rain and wind. It is constructed by planting three or four stout sticks or poles in a row in the ground at an angle of about 60° to 75°, and lashing palm-leaves across them so closely that the rain cannot penetrate. Shelters of this type are also largely used by the Malays for temporary purposes, especially in the eastern states of the Peninsula.

Pangan.—The next stage would appear to be that of the round or bee-hive hut. In the interior of Kelantan (near Kampong Buntal in Ulu Aring), Mr Laidlaw and I visited several of these curious habitations. One that we photographed was a hemispherical leaf-shelter, very slenderly constructed, the materials employed being leaves of the 'bĕrtam' palm (*Eugeissona*) and a Rattan or *Calamus* called 'Rotan Dudok'. The bases of the leaf-stalks were firmly planted in the ground, the upper ends of the leaves bending naturally over so as to protect about one-half of the hut-floor from the rain. The leaves planted round the circumference of the semicircle at the back of the shelter were of full length, but a slight fence of shorter leaves, about 2 feet (60 cm.) high, completed the circumference. At the back of the hut was the usual big *abattis* or *chevaux-de-frise* of felled trees, which is very generally formed by these people for protection against wild beasts.

A slightly different type of hut was seen on the banks of the Tahan river by Mr Ridley in 1891. The huts themselves consisted of a bee-hive-shaped structure of palm-leaves about 4 feet (1.2 m.) high, the bases of the leaves planted in the ground and their upper parts interwoven together. So far the structure was similar to those already described, but these particular huts 'were completely filled with palm-leaves, in the midst of which could be seen the depression caused by the occupant when he curled himself up in them' either for rest or warmth. 'There were altogether seven of these 'nests' on the river-bank', and the occupants, who were, I think, undoubtedly Pangan, had only just left them before his and his companion's arrival.

Communal Shelters.

Semang of Kedah.—From an ordinary round hut which will shelter one or two small families the transition to an elongated shelter which will hold a greater number is not very difficult. The Semang shelter at Siong in Kedah accommodated all the members of the tribe who were living in the neighbourhood, and contained no fewer than eleven (?) sleeping-places arranged in two long rows; it may therefore be described as being of the 'barrack' or 'long-house' type. The upright timbers of this shelter consisted of young saplings planted in two opposite rows, across them being lashed the leaves of the 'chĕnchảm', a low-growing palm not unlike the well-known 'bĕrtam' palm (*Eugeissona tristis*) in appearance, but which was declared by the Semang to be a different tree. The uprights of the shelter were called 'pengkong', and the leaves lashed across them 'hapoi'. There were, besides, two central posts or pillars ('jĕhu'), each about a third of the distance from either end of the shelter, and a dozen poles placed, as props or 'wind-braces', in various positions and at various angles, in order to strengthen the structure and keep it from being blown over in a high wind. In front of the shelter at the upper end was a big opening which served as the main entrance, but there were in addition several in Kedah, where, side by side with the long 'communal' shelter in which the tribe lived, stood a tiny granary in which their scanty stores of rice were preserved. This little granary stood on six thin posts, the floor being raised about 4–5 ft. (1.2 m. to 1.5 m.) from the ground, for the purpose of protecting its contents from small marauders. It measured about 4 ft. in length by about 3 ft. (1.2 m. × .91 m.) in width, and was little more in fact than a large box on posts. Its walls were made of tree-bark, and the roof was thatched with the leaf of the 'bĕrtam' palm, and it was entered by a tiny doorway to which access was afforded by a long inclined pole. From the stage in which these tiny huts were used solely for the purposes of storage, to one in which they could be used as dwellings, the transition would be as easy and as natural as possible.

On the other hand, it must here be remarked that although in this way they may sometimes come to dwelling—in Malayan fashion—in a hut with raised flooring, the Semang nevertheless appear to retain a strong predilection for building their huts either altogether aloft in trees, or else upon the level of the ground itself....

Huts and Houses.

Perak Sakai.—The Sakai in commencing to build their huts with rather more reference to Malay models still retain the communal idea. One of these Sakai communal houses, described by Hale, was built on a slope, close to the summit of a lofty hill. The thatching of the roof (with leaves of the bĕrtam palm) was a clumsy imitation of Malayan methods. The floor of the house, which was raised above the ground, rested upon nine posts, eight of inconsiderable and one of very great diameter, which was, in fact, the trunk of a large tree. Every other part of the house was entirely built of bamboo. The walls consisted of long screens of sheet-thatch, which were suspended loosely at their upper ends under the eaves, so that the lower ends could be pushed open outwards. The house in question was more than an hour's climb from water. It was surrounded by a clearing of about two acres in extent, where tapioca, maize, sugar-cane, and tobacco were grown. The house contained sixteen inhabitants, divided into six distinct family units, each of which had its own hearth. In the case of a man having two wives, each wife had her own hearth, marked out by means of a low partition of split bamboos. There was a door in the end-wall, and also an outlet in the slope of the roof.

On the other hand, the Sakai huts observed in Ulu Kinta by De Morgan are described as being built very far apart from each other, and situated in the midst of immense plantations of tapioca, 'sorgho' (?) and maize, from which it may possibly be deduced that they were on rather less strictly communal principles. De Morgan was invited to enter the Penghulu's hut, which was, like those at S. Raya, built at a height of about 1.50 m. from the ground. It was very small, but very clean. Blowpipes, arrows, and a spear hung from the roof, and it contained many betel-leaf-wallets, necklaces, nets, lines, and a small but highly decorated piece of bamboo, the use of which was for carrying the worms used in rod-fishing.

In another place, De la Croix, in describing the Sakai village of Kampong Chabang, in the upper reaches of S. Kerbu (a tributary of the Plus river in Perak, which is a few miles further north than Ulu Kinta), remarks that the village consisted of a dozen huts, erected in the midst of a clearing, on the banks of the river. The chief's hut (the largest) was built upon piles, and measured ten metres in length by five metres in breadth. The flooring, consisting of flattened tree-bark, was raised about a metre above the ground. Both the walls and the roof with its double slope were constructed alike of broad strips of bark, which afforded an excellent shelter from the floods of rain that fell in the wet season. A notched tree-trunk served as house-ladder for giving access to the interior of the building.

In the middle of the only room was placed a hearth consisting of a thick layer of clay deposited in a (square) wooden frame. This was the hearth ('dapor') of Malay houses. A few pots and receptacles of various kinds containing provisions were hung upon the walls. The remaining huts were all of the same type, except two or three whose side-walls were made of matwork, in imitation of the Malays.

Pahang Sakai.—A graphic description of the mountain hut of a Sakai by Mr L. Wray is interesting from the fact that the locality referred to is in the far interior of Pahang.

Mr Wray wrote that the house (in the Tahan valley) in which he passed the night was a large and well-built one, and seemed to be occupied by two families. It was at an elevation of about 4000 feet (1225 m.), and being perched on the top of a cleared hill fully exposed to the winds, he found it very cold.

Hanging up in the house were strings of the lower jaws of monkeys, musangs, and other animals, and in another house he saw bunches of hornbill skulls. These were kept hanging up in the smoke as trophies, in the same way as the Dayaks keep human heads in their houses. Another custom which seemed to point to a connection between the two races was that they kept large fires burning in the centre of their houses during the night, and that it was only during the first part of the night that they slept, after that they sat up round the fire and talked till morning. . . .

ORANG LAUT OR SEA-JAKUN.

Orang Laut, Sletar.—The Sletar tribe of the Orang Laut, though confining their wanderings to a limit of some 30 m. sq. (7500 hectares), might still be considered highly nomadic. In boats (or 'sampans') barely sufficient to float their load, they would skirt the mangroves, collecting their food from the shores and forests as they proceeded, exhausting one spot and then searching for another. To one accustomed to the comforts and wants of civilisation, their life appeared to be one of extreme hardship. Huddled up in a small boat hardly measuring 20 ft. (6 m.) in length, they yet found in it all the domestic comfort they were in want of; at one end was the fire-place, in the middle the few utensils of which they might be in possession, and at the other end beneath a network awning (or 'kajang'), not exceeding six feet in length, was the sleeping apartment of a family numbering as many as five or six, together with a cat and dog; under this awning they took shelter from the dews and rains of the night, and from the heat of the day. Even the Malays in pointing out these confined quarters exclaimed 'how miserable', though of any misery the objects of their commiseration were not aware. In these same quarters they found all their wants supplied; their children would sport on the shore at low water in search of shell-fish; and during high water they might be seen climbing the mangrove branches, and dashing from thence into the water, with all the life and energy of children of a colder clime, at once affording a proof that even they were not without their joys.

Walter William Skeat and Charles Otto Blagden, *Pagan Races of the Malay Peninsula*, London: Macmillan, 1906; reprinted London: Frank Cass & Co., 1996, Vol. I, pp. 168–99.

39
The Ritual Selection of a House Site among the Malays

WALTER WILLIAM SKEAT

Skeat collected the materials for his *Malay Magic* during his period in the Selangor Government Service in the 1890s. This book, encyclopaedic in its contents, remains a major historical source on Malay folk religion. It provides much information on what Skeat termed the 'Malay theory of Animism', a world-view which conceives all of nature, including minerals, plants, and even man-made objects, as possessing a share of the vitality of the cosmos. A consequence of this world-view, confirmed by all other authors on the subject, is the perception that houses, too (as well as other objects such as boats, wooden chests, or *kris* [daggers]) have a vital force (known in Malay as *semangat*) which can harm the user if not properly managed. Annandale and Robinson, for example, write in their valuable accounts of the Patani Malays, 'All those peculiar nocturnal sounds that one hears, even in a European house, often without being able to assign them a cause, are believed in Patani, where the houses are far more noisy at night, to be expressions of the soul of the building.'[1] This 'soul' or vitality derives in part from the fact that the trees from which house timbers are made have their own *semangat*; throughout South-East Asia it has been common to perform some ritual to ask permission of a tree before felling it. Partly, the vitality of the house is also said to come into being as the building itself is assembled. It is not surprising, then, that for the Malays as for other South-East Asian peoples, house building was traditionally surrounded by ritual. One of Skeat's informants was a *Pawang* (ritual specialist in construction matters), Abdul Razzak of Klang in Selangor, who allowed him to copy his charm book, containing detailed instructions for house building. A much more recent work[2] offers proof that these traditions have not been entirely lost today.

T HE first operation in building is the selection of the site. This is determined by an elaborate code of rules which make the choice depend—firstly, upon the nature of the soil with respect to colour, taste, and smell; secondly, upon the formation of its surface; and, thirdly, upon its aspect:-

'The best soil, whether for a house, village, orchard, or town, is a greenish yellow, fragrant-scented, tart-tasting loam: such a soil will ensure abundance of gold and silver unto the third generation.

'The best site, whether for a house, village, orchard, or town, is level.

[1] Nelson Annandale and Herbert C. Robinson, *Fasciculi Malayenses: Anthropological and Zoological Results of an Expedition to Perak and the Siamese Malay States, 1901–1902*. London: Longmans, 1903, p.100.

[2] Phillip Gibbs, *Building a Malay House*, Kuala Lumpur: Oxford University Press, 1987.

'The best aspect (of the surface) is that of land which is low upon the north side and high upon the south side: such a site will bring absolute peacefulness.'

When you have found a site complying with more or less favourable conditions, in accordance with the code, you must next clear the ground of forest or undergrowth, lay down four sticks to form a rectangle in the centre thereof, and call upon the name of the lords of that spot (*i.e.* the presiding local deities or spirits). Now dig up the soil (enclosed by the four sticks), and taking a clod in your hand, call upon the lords of that spot as follows:-

'Ho, children of Měntri Guru,
Who dwell In the Four Corners of the World,
I crave this plot as a boon.'

(Here mention the purpose to which you wish to put it.)

'If it is good, show me a good omen,
If it is bad, show me a bad omen.'

Wrap the clod up in white cloth, and after fumigating it with incense, place it at night beneath your pillow, and when you retire to rest repeat the last two lines of the above charm as before and go to sleep. If your dream is good proceed with, if bad desist from, your operations. Supposing your dream to be 'good', you must (approximately) clear the site of the main building and peg out the four corners with dead sticks; then take a dead branch and heap it up lightly with earth (in the centre of the site?); set fire to it, and when the whole heap has been reduced to ashes, sweep it all up together and cover it over while you repeat the charm (which differs but little from that given above). Next morning uncover it early in the morning and God will show you the good and the bad.

The site being finally selected, you must proceed to choose a day for erecting the central house-post, by consulting first the schedule of lucky and unlucky months, and next the schedule of lucky and unlucky days of the week.

[The best time of day for the operation to take place is said to be always seven o'clock in the morning. Hence there seems to be no need to consult a schedule to discover it, though some magicians may do so.]

The propitious moment having been at last ascertained, the erection of the centre-post will be proceeded with. First, the hole for its reception must be dug (the operation being accompanied by the recital of a charm) and the post erected, the greatest precautions being taken to prevent the shadow of any of the workers from falling either upon the post itself or upon the hole dug to receive it, sickness and trouble being otherwise sure to follow....

'When the hole has been dug and before the centre-post is actually erected, some sort of sacrifice or offering has to be made. First you take a little brazilwood (*kayu sĕpang*), and a little ebony-wood (*kayu arang*), a little assafœtida (*inggu*), and a little scrap-iron (*tahi bĕsi*), and deposit them in the hole which you have dug. Then take a fowl, a goat, or a buffalo [according to the ascertained or reputed malignity of the locally presiding earth-demon (*puaka*)], and cut its throat according to Muhammadan custom, spilling its blood into the hole. Then cut off its head and feet, and deposit them within the hole to serve as a foundation for the centre-post to rest upon (*buat lapik tiang s'ri*). Put a ring on your little finger out of compliment to the earth-spirit (*akan mĕmbujok jĕmbalang itu*), repeat the charm and erect the post.'

Another form of the above ceremony was described to me by a magician as follows:-

'Deposit in the hole a little scrap-iron and tin-ore, a candle nut (*buah k'ras* or *buah gorek*), a broken hatchet head (*b'liong patah*), and a cent (in copper). Wait till everybody else has returned home, and, standing close to the hole, pick up three clods (*kĕpal*) of earth, hold them (*gĕnggam*) over the incense, turn 'right-about-face' and repeat the charm. Then take the three clods home (without once turning round to look behind you till you reach home), place them under your sleeping pillow and wait till nightfall, when you may have either a good or a bad dream. If the first night's dream be bad, throw away one of the clods and dream again. If the second night's dream be bad, repeat the process, and whenever you get a good dream deposit the clod or clods under the butt-end of the centre-post to serve as a foundation.'

A magician gave me this specimen of a charm used at this ceremony (of erecting the centre-post):-

> 'Ho, Raja Guru, Maharaja Guru,
> You are the sons of Batara Guru.
> I know the origin from which you spring,
> From the Flashing of Lightning's spurs;
> I know the origin from which you spring,
> From the Brightening of Daybreak.
> Ho, Spectre of the Earth, Brains of the Earth, Demon
>   of the Earth,
> Retire ye hence to the depths of the Ocean,
> To the peace of the primeval forest.
> Betwixt you and me
> Division was made by Adam.'

Another rule of importance in house-building is that which regulates the length of the threshold, as to which the instructions are as follows:-

'Measure off (on a piece of string) the stretch (fathom) of the arms of her who is to be mistress of the proposed house. Fold this string in three and cut off one third. Take the remainder, fold it in eight and cut off seven-eighths. Take the remaining eighth, see how many times it is contained in the length of the threshold, and check off the number (of these measurements) against the "category" (*bilangan*) of the "eight beasts" (*běnatang yang d'lapan*). This category runs as follows:- (1) The dragon (*naga*); (2) the dairy-cow (*sapi*); (3) the lion (*singa*); (4) the dog (*anjing*); (5) the draught-cow (*lěmbu*); (6) the ass (*kaldei*); (7) the elephant (*gajah*), and (8) the crow (*gagak*), all of which have certain ominous significations. If the last measurement coincides with one of the unlucky beasts in the category, such as the crow (which signifies the

death of the master of the house), the threshold is cut shorter
to make it fit in with one that is more auspicious.'

The names of the 'eight beasts', coupled with the events
which they are supposed to foreshadow, are often commemorated in rhyming stanzas.

Here is a specimen:-

I.—*The Dragon* (naga).

'A dragon of bulk, a monster dragon,
Is this dragon that turns round month by month.
Wherever you go you will be safe from stumbling-blocks,
And all who meet you will be your friends.'

II.—*The Dairy-Cow* (sapi).

'There is the smoke of a fire in the forest,
Where Inche 'Ali is burning lime;
They were milking the young dairy-cow,
And in the midst of the milking it sprawled and fell down
    dead.'

III.—*The Lion* (singa).

'A lion of courage, a lion of valour,
Is the lion gambolling at the end of the Point.
The luck of this house will be lasting,
Bringing you prosperity from year to year.'

IV.—*The Dog* (anjing).

'The wild dog, the jackal,
Barks at the deer from night to night;
Whatever you do will be a stumbling-block;
In this house men will stab one another.'

V.—*The Draught-Cow* (lĕmbu).

'The big cow from the middle of the clearing
Has gone to the Deep Forest to calve there.
Great good luck will be your portion,
Never will you cease to be prosperous.'

VI.—*The Ass* (kaldei).

'The ass within the Fort
Carries grass from morn to eve;
Whatever you pray for will not be granted,
Though big your capital, the half will be lost.'

VII.—*The Elephant* (gajah).

'The big riding elephant of the Sultan
Has its tusks covered with amalgam.
Good luck is your portion,
No harm or blemish will you suffer.'

VIII.—*The Crow* (gagak).

'A black crow soaring by night
Has perched on the house of the great Magic Prince;
Great indeed is the calamity which has happened:
Within the house its master lies dead.'

In close connection with the ceremonies for the selection of individual house sites are the forms by which the princes of Malay tradition selected sites for the towns which they founded. The following extract will perhaps convey some idea of their character:-

'One day Raja Marong Maha Podisat went into his outer audience hall, where all his ministers, warriors, and officers were in attendance, and commanded the four *Mantris* to equip an expedition with all the necessary officers and armed men, and with horses and elephants, arms and accoutrements. The four *Mantris* did as they were ordered, and when all was ready informed the Raja. The latter waited for a lucky day and an auspicious moment, and then desired his second son to set out. The Prince took leave after saluting his father and mother, and all the ministers, officers, and warriors who followed him performed obeisance before the Raja. They then set out in search of a place of settlement, directing their course between south and east, intending to select a place with good soil, and there to build a town with fort, moat, palace, and *balei*.* They amused themselves in every forest, wood, and thicket through which they passed, crossing numbers of hills and mountains, and stopping here and there to hunt wild beasts, or to fish if they happened to fall in with a pool or lake.

'After they had pursued their quest for some time they came to the tributary of a large river which flowed down to the sea. Farther on they came to a large sheet of water, in the midst of which were four islands. The Prince was much pleased with the appearance of the islands, and straightway took a silver arrow and fitted it to his bow named *Indra Sakti*, and said: 'O arrow of the bow *Indra Sakti*, fall thou on good soil in this group of islands; wherever thou mayest chance to fall, there will I make a palace in which to live.' He then drew his bow and discharged the arrow, which flew upwards with the rapidity of lightning, and with a humming sound like that made by a beetle as it flies round a flower, and went out of sight. Presently it came in sight again, and fell upon one of the islands, which on that account was called *Pulau Indra Sakti*. On that spot was erected a town with fort, palace, and *balei,* and all the people who were living scattered about in the vicinity were collected together and set to work on the various buildings.'

Even in the making of roads through the forest it would appear that sacrificial ceremonies are not invariably neglected. On one occasion I came upon a party of Malays in the Labu jungle who were engaged in making a bridle-track for the Selangor Government. A small bamboo censer, on which incense had been burning, had been erected in the middle of the trace; and I was informed that the necessary rites (for exorcising the demons from the trace) had just been successfully concluded.

Walter William Skeat, *Malay Magic*, London: Macmillan, 1900; reprinted Singapore: Oxford University Press, 1984, pp. 141–9.

*balei [*balai*]: an open-walled meeting house or council house.

40
The Furnishings of a Malay House

RICHARD O. WINSTEDT

Sir Richard Winstedt was a gifted scholar of Malay who served in
the Malayan Civil Service from 1902 to 1935; during the 1920s he
was Director of Education. He made extensive contributions to
Malay studies on many subjects, particularly language and history.
His prolific output was made possible through a rigorous discipline:
he used regularly to get up at 4.30 a.m. and work on his research
until 8.00 a.m. before going to work at his official job. His account
of the furnishings of a Malay house (abridged here) was one of the
papers written early in his career, with the encouragement of
Richard Wilkinson, then a senior civil servant. Its materials were
gathered during his early experiences as Inspector of Schools in
Perak, a job which, as Winstedt recalls in his memoirs, required
travel by an unpredictable mixture of river raft, ox-cart, pony-trap,
elephant, and bicycle. It is incredibly detailed (the original contains
also the Malay vocabulary for every item described), yet also
evocative and fluidly written, of interest not least because few
writers gave so much attention to the contents of a house as they
did to its exterior.

THE feature that strikes the casual observer on entering
a Malay house is the absence of what the European
conceives to be furniture; and should he be interested
further and discover that the words for chair and book-
rest are Arabic, the words for towel table and cupboard
Portuguese, the words for curtain bedstead and box Tamil,
then he will certainly imagine that there is no such thing as
native Malay furniture. This impression will be confirmed if
the house he has chosen for inspection be that of a school-
master or some such hybrid mind and reveal all the horrors
of crocheted antimacassars and bentwood Austrian chairs,
photos of the owner by a Chinese perpetrator and oleographs
of Queen Victoria or the Sultan of Turkey. Yet the Malay hut
has furniture as much its own as ours is, though, like ours,
built up of borrowings from many ancient sources.

Ascend the verandah, the part of the house proper to the mere male, his gatherings and his pursuits, and the visitor will find himself in a space empty, save for a few shelves or bamboo racks, for the plank or bamboo bed platform of an unmarried son at the further end, for the fisherman's net, the hunter's noose, and the bird-cage of rattan hanging from the roof; save, too, for the half-finished trap or basket that lies scattered on the floor to employ the indoor hours of men and boys. Look around at these things and at the household furniture and he is in the midst of a prehistoric civilisation. There is a fable telling how a fairy taught Malay women to copy the patterns of those remnants of nets and baskets which Sang Kelembai left behind when fear of the human race drove him away to the sky's edge. Here is every variety of article plaited of dried palm-leaf: mats spread over part of the floor; mats piled aside to be unrolled for the accommodation of visitors; a small prayer-mat of Arabic name but home workmanship; the plaited tobacco pouch or box, or the bag receptacle for betel utensils handy for daily use; plaited sacks stacked in a corner, full of rice from the clearing. They are sometimes plain, sometimes adorned with open-work, or the interweaving of strips dyed red black yellow, in both of which styles the craftsman's hand, subdued to what it works in, has evolved graceful geometrical designs.

The specimens of plaited palm-leaf work kept in the verandah are often little better than the coarse rough work of the aboriginal tribes, but in the inner room the women's apartment, there will be articles of more delicate material and intricate manipulation. Perak, Pahang, Patani, Kedah, Kelantan, all produce fine goods. And women store clothes in baskets (in Malacca of curious pyramidal shapes) adorned with raised fancy stitches called 'the jasmine bud', 'the roof-angle', and so on; decorated or debased by the frippery of later civilisations—the addition of coloured paper pasted upon them and the attachment of gold filigree chains or silver bosses. Even here however, in the ordinary way, articles of the most primitive kind will predominate. You may find the women plaiting a pattern like that of the bird-shaped receptacle for sweet rice which possibly dates from the days of belief in a bird-soul; or wrappers of coconut, plantain or palm-leaf wherein to boil rice, triangular, diamond, heptagonal, octagonal in shapes called 'the country's pride' 'the onion' 'the paddle handle', or pre-Muhammadan models of birds, buffaloes, stags, the crab, the horse, the durian, the dog. Water-gourds may be suspended from a beam in hanging palm-leaf holders. A kĕris may be stuck in a palm-leaf holder and pinned to the mosquito-net. For the central room of a Malay house is the place where sleep old married folk, men and women, with their children; sometimes on a raised platform, more often in cubicles formed by mosquito-nets and outer curtains, or merely by the mosquito-nets. The omnipresent baby hangs from the rafters in a cradle composed of three, five or seven layers of cloth, according to his degree; that is, after the young probationer has lain for the first seven days of his life on a mat in a rice-strewn tray, and before he descends to the indignity of a rattan basket cradle. In a loft that is lighted by a window or hole in the roof, the unmarried girls spend day and night above their parents' heads, safe from the invitation of admirers who might else slip love-tokens through the interspaces of the gridiron floor. On the walls of the room may be nailed, perhaps, a tiger's skull or a wild-goat's horns, or more probably, a pair or so of mouldering antlers, or ricketty pegs from which dangles the daily wear of the occupants; or the less prized daggers may hang there, while spears and an old gun stand in the corner. There may be a tall cupboard of Portuguese name and Chinese manufacture, wherein will be stored spare pillows, papers and the best crockery. There will be a wooden shelf or stand, on which, placed in plates or brass holders, will be natural or clay gourds and broad clay water-jars. A clay or brass brazier will be filled with charcoal and incense to accompany religious chantings. In old days the largest light in the house proceeded from resin torches stuck in a roughly carved wooden stand that was placed on the floor in the central room. Or shells fixed to wooden sticks and clay boats were used to hold oil. Later, probably, candles stuck in coconut shells, and eventually in brass sticks, were employed. Heavy brass lamps of Indian origin, suspended from the chains (that sometimes contain an interesting bird-shaped link), may still be collected in the form, apparently, of lotus cups, from the hollows of whose several petals wicks projected. Brass supplies a number of household utensils, some heavy and thick, such as lamps, bowls, basins; some thin and decorated with florid realistic representations of butterflies, deer, flowers and birds, of which sort trays and large lidded boxes offer example; yet a third kind, fretted with chisel or file, provides glass-stands braziers and betel-trays.

Women and children feed generally in the kitchen, male guests in the verandah, but female guests, and in the absence of guests the lordly male proprietor, feed in the central room, so that writing of its furniture we may conveniently deal with the utensils of a Malay meal in conjunction with that brass-work which has played so large a part in its service. Here we have layer upon layer of civilisations. The most primitive plate in the Malay world is a banana leaf; next a shallow coconut shell (whose existence of course premises some kind of settled cultivation); and then the wooden platter. The Chinese in the sixteenth century note that the king of Johor affected gold and silver eating utensils and other folk earthenware. Rare specimens of obsolete green celadon ware from Sawankalok in Siamese territory, survive among the old-world treasures of rajas under the name of 'the ware of a thousand cracks'. Cheap Chinese earthenware is common everywhere now, but examples of fine early work are extant in large flat dishes used for rice, and an enamelled Chinese curry-tray is occasionally found. Europe has long imported earthenware, ranging from old Dutch ware or fine old willow pattern to German coffee-cups with the legend *Sĕlamat minum*. The most primitive drinking cup is a half coconut shell carved or plain; then came a smaller silver bowl modelled upon it; then the European glass, for which a brass stand is provided. The most primitive jug, as we have seen, will be a dried gourd or a large polished coconut shell with a hole about three inches across at the top, and both are still in vogue even in palaces, where they will be tied up in a covering of yellow cloth, a string with a golden knob at the end being pulled to close the mouth of the covering: it is also customary to place a plate of silver or brass atop the mouth of the coconut shell, and to set thereon the small drinking bowl. . . .

Finally, there are tobacco and betel boxes, those appanages of the last course of a Malay meal. . . . Betel-nut scissors, shaped in the form of the head of a bird or dragon, whichever it be, and in the form of the magic steed, *kuda sĕmbrani*, exhibit some of the earliest iron work.

Malay life, even in palaces, is essentially simple, and this may serve to excuse transition from the refinements of the table (or rather the floor) to the mere utensils of the kitchen. Also the kitchen, if not in the back of the central room itself, is not far separated; moreover, it is as interesting as any part of the house, and though it is impossible absolutely to distinguish the most primitive utensils from later accretions, more perhaps than any other room it bears traces of ultimate civilisations. There are examples of bamboo work in a bamboo bellows, or rather blower; in· a cooking-pot for rice, constructed of a single joint of bamboo, the green cane resisting the fire long enough to cook one mess; in bamboo racks. There are specimens of bamboo and rattan weaving in hanging plate-holders, in stands for round bottomed cooking-pots, in fish creels, in baskets for fish or vegetables, in strainers, in rice sieves. There are utensils of dried coconut shell: ladles, bowls with rattan handles, spoons. There is some important carved wood-work: a parrot-shaped handle to sweet-rice spoons, spoons with rudely carved foliated handles, oval carved enscrolled blocks (such as are used also by Dyaks) for crushing salt and pepper, and last, but not least, cake-moulds, and a spurred coconut rasper. In the south of the Peninsula the coconut rasper is decorated with foliated carving like the pepper-block: in the far north, in Patani there is far wider scope in design, probably due to Cambodian influence, and coconut raspers are carved in the form of grotesque beasts, of human figures kneeling prostrate with the spur-scraper offered in uplifted hands; and there too cake-moulds bear the carved impress of buffaloes, elephants, cows, cocks, tortoises, axes, *kĕris*, horses even and pistols, while cake-moulds in the south have only conventional foliated designs. . . .

For cooking-vessels, there is the earthenware pot and steamer; and of later use a number of brass and iron vessels, a covered brass rice-pot, a large open brass pot for sweetmeat cookery, a large open iron stew pot, a huge iron cauldron, an open iron frying pan. The cooking place is an arrangement of stones on which the pots are placed; above it is a shelf on which firewood is laid to dry, and more wood is stacked beside the fireplace. There is a grindstone for curry-stuffs and a tiny stone mortar for pounding chillies and other edible pods. In the purlieus of the kitchen there will be large earthenware water-jars and some basins for washing and culinary purposes.

The rest of the house is devoted to middle-age and meals: the best bed-room, in homes where there are daughters of marriageable age, to the apotheosis of youth. Here will be kept the finest furniture, the softest clothes, the best embroidery. The door will be curtained and its curtain adorned with the bo-leaf fringe or, alas for modern taste, hideous white crocheted work. There will be a stand just inside for the drinking vessels such as we have already described. Athwart the room, in the corner next the window and outer wall, will be a small day couch of one storey only, made of wood, with fretted skirting-board in front, or board pasted with coloured papers in floral scrolls. Thereon will be laid a mat of several thicknesses according to the house-owner's rank, edged with gold-threaded silk border and silver or embroidered corners; and at the head of the couch a large round pillow with embroidered or gold or silver 'faces' or ends [*bantal saraga*]. On this day couch will be found the best betel utensils in the house. But the greatest care will have been lavished on the large bed-platform that runs lengthwise along the room against the inner partition; it will be storied according to rank, with fretted or paper-pasted front; it will be enclosed in a large mosquito-net adorned within and without along the top with the bo-leaf fringe embroidered, and often having silver leaves among the embroidery. Like the day couch and the stand for water vessels, it will have hung above it a ceiling-cloth to keep off the dust and debris of the palm-leaf roof. At the head, and extending the full width of the bed-platform, will be an oblong hollow pillow, made of white cloth stretched over a wooden frame, its ends adorned with embroidery or silver plates, and on this pillow will be laid a prized *kĕris* and two or three round pillows with decorated ends facing outwards. Above it all will tower the triangular pyramidal back to the dais, decorated with coloured paper, and sometimes exhibiting the tiered roof with upcurving crockets found in Buddhist *wats*, though the pyramidal shape is not, I believe, common in the south. Below the hollow oblong pillow are laid flat sleeping pillows, and then comes the bed proper, covered with a mattress, on which are laid two mats, one for bride and one for groom, with embroidered corners and of several thicknesses according to rank; one or more long Dutch-wife pillows stretch the length of the mats; perhaps a silk coverlet will be spread. There will be various household articles inside this mosquito-curtain; on the inner wall side of the bed, at the head, between the sleeping pillows and the *bantal saraga*, are kept squat, round-lidded boxes of Palembang brass or Palembang lacquer, receptacles for clothes and toilet necessaries; and there is a wooden clothes-rack, carved with upturned crockets, suspended from the mosquito-net or standing in the inner side of the bed.

Such in outline, tiresome skeleton outline as I have had to make it, are the articles of furniture in a Malay house. Not a tithe of them will be found in the ordinary house, for it is not a museum but a home, generally untidy, disordered, yet neat in the effect of dim backgrounds and recesses and dun natural colours.

Richard O. Winstedt, *The Circumstances of Malay Life*, Kuala Lumpur: J. Russell, 1909, p.. 19–31.

41
The *Pangah* or 'Head-house' of the Land Dayak

HUGH LOW

Sir Hugh Low, a talented botanist, was the son of a horticulturalist with a particular interest in orchid cultivation. His father dispatched Hugh on a journey in 1844, to collect plant and seed specimens in the Indonesian islands, especially Borneo, with a view to future commercial development in his nursery at Clapton. A good-looking young man with an attractive personality, Low became a friend of Rajah James Brooke soon after his arrival in Sarawak, and was influenced by his views on the enlightened government of native peoples. He made two major collecting expeditions up the right and left branches of the Sarawak River, collecting pitcher plants and orchids (including the magnificent *Vanda Lowii*, with 10-foot chains of flowers, each 3 inches across) and relishing the 'delightful solitude' of wild jungle landscapes. He also enjoyed staying with local Dayak tribes, first-hand acquaintance with whom soon removed many of his initial prejudices about them. Low kept a detailed diary during his first two and a half years in Sarawak. As well as his botanical work, he also made numerous detailed ethnographic descriptions of the people he met. His book *Sarawak* was based on this diary, and set a new standard in writing about Borneo peoples, as well as providing a wealth of new botanical and geographical information. In this passage he describes a most distinctive architectural feature of Bidayuh communities, the 'head-house' or bachelors' residence called *pangah*.

Low never really received the acknowledgement he deserved for his notable contributions to South-East Asian botany and agriculture, but his name lingers on in Borneo, attached as it is not only to the spectacular orchid which carries it, but also to the infamous Low's Gully on the peak of Mt. Kinabalu, of which he made a pioneering ascent in 1851 with the help of his Dusun guide, Lemaing.

I N the villages of all the tribes of Land Dyaks [Bidayuh] are found one, and sometimes more houses of an octagonal form, with their roofs ending in a point at the top. They always stand apart from the others; and instead of having a door at the side, these, which are never built with verandas, are entered by a trap-door at the bottom, in the flooring. These houses vary in size, according to the wants of the hamlet by which they are built; but are generally much larger than ordinary domiciles. The term by which they are distinguished is 'Pangah', 'Ramin', being the Dyak word for an ordinary house. The Pangah is built by the united efforts of the boys and unmarried men of the tribe, who, after having attained the age of puberty, are obliged to leave the houses of the village; and do not generally frequent them after they have attained the age of eight or nine years. A large fire-place, of similar construction to those of the ordinary residences, is placed in the centre of this hall, and around its sides are platforms similar to those used by the women in the other dwellings of the village.

The Pangah, being generally the best house in the place, is set apart for the use of strangers visiting the tribe; and in it all the councils of the old men are held, and all business connected with the welfare of the people is transacted. A large drum, formed of the skin of some animal, stretched upon the end of a hollow tree, is placed above the heads of the persons on the floor, for the purpose of apprising the village of any approaching danger. From the timbers which cross the house and support the slight flooring of the loft, where the young men keep their sleeping-mats and other things by day, usually depend the skulls collected during ages, by the tribe. But on account of the bloodless nature of their wars, these are seldom numerous; and frequently would not equal in number the heads in the possession of a single family of the Sea Dyaks [Iban].

Hugh Low, *Sarawak: Notes during a Residence in that Country with H. H. The Rajah Brooke*, London: Richard Bentley, 1848; reprinted Singapore: Oxford University Press, 1988, pp. 280–2.

42
The Construction of a Sarawak Longhouse

CHARLES HOSE

Charles Hose (1863–1929), 'one of the British Empire's true originals', went out to Sarawak in 1884 as an administrative cadet under the second Rajah, Charles Brooke. By 1891 he had become Resident (Second Class) of the Baram District. An excellent administrator, his work in this remote area gave him great scope also for the passionate pursuit of natural history and ethnography. He was another of those outstanding, eccentric colonial figures who seems from the beginning to have developed a genuine sympathy with Borneo peoples. A large man, memories have been passed down in upriver Baram longhouses of young men hurrying to reinforce the floorboards at the news of his impending arrival. His books contributed enormously to knowledge of Borneo cultures, replacing the garishly sensational images which had coloured much earlier literature written by the more ignorant. Hose seems to have been so good at his job in this isolated posting that the Rajah kept him there thirteen years, which delayed his promotion. He was eventually moved to the Third Division at Sibu, as Resident (First Class), at which point he married, taking early retirement three years later. Returning to England, he remained busy with writing and lecturing, working hard to establish a scholarly reputation. He made many and varied contributions in his career, from the collection of a large number of new animal and botanical species, to establishing that beri-beri was a deficiency disease and not an infectious one, to helping British Petroleum in the development of a large coastal oilfield. Among Borneo peoples he seems particularly to have admired the more hierarchical Kayan and Kenyah, finding the Iban 'truculent' and their individualism a little too unruly. His is one of the best accounts of life in a longhouse, which he had many occasions to observe. His detailed description of the techniques of construction is a special rarity. He must have had occasion to witness the building of longhouses, something most short-term travellers would not have the opportunity to see. Just as in most other parts of South-East Asia, construction here involves a great deal of ritual and the careful observation of omen birds (a Bornean speciality) to ensure a good result.

T HE most typical, and perhaps the most striking phenomenon in the whole of Borneo is the communal Long House. It is interesting, for it is found amongst most of the hill tribes of Burma and Assam and in the South Sea Islands of the Pacific, a fact which raises questions as to its origin. But whatever doubts may exist, one thing is certain, that it exists all over Borneo. All the tribes build these houses; and all except, of course, the Punans, build them of one type; but the size and proportions, the strength of the materials used, and the skill and care displayed in the work of construction show wide differences. The houses of the Kayans are perhaps better and more solidly built than any others and may be taken as the type. Each house is built to accommodate many families; an average house may contain some forty to fifty, making up with children some two or three hundred persons; while some of the larger houses are built for as many as a hundred and twenty families, or some five to six hundred persons. The house is always close to a river, and it usually lies along the bank at a distance of from twenty to fifty yards from the water, parallel to the course of the river.

Its roof is always a simple ridge extending the whole length of the building and is made of shingles of ironwood or some other durable kind. The framework of the roof is supported at a height of some twenty to thirty feet from the ground on massive piles of ironwood, and the floor is supported by the same piles at a level some seven or eight feet below the cross-beams of the roof. The floor consists of cross-beams mortised through the piles, and of very large planks of hard wood laid upon them parallel to the length of the house. The projecting eaves of the roof come down to a level midway between that of the roof-beams and that of the floor, and the interval of some four to five feet between the eaves and the floor remains open along the whole length of the front of the house, save for a low parapet which bounds the floor along its outer edge. This space serves to admit both light and air, and affords an easy view over the river to those sitting in the gallery.

The length of the house is in some cases as much as 400 yards, but the average length is probably about 200 yards. The width of the floor varies from about thirty to sixty feet; the whole space between roof and floor is divided into two parts by a longitudinal wall of vertical planks, which runs the whole length of the building. This wall lies not quite in the middle line, but a little to the river side of it. Of the two lengthwise divisions of the house, that which adjoins the river is thus somewhat narrower than the other in its whole length; it remains undivided. The other and wider part is divided by transverse walls at intervals of some twenty or thirty feet, so as to form a single row of spacious chambers of approximately equal size.

Each such chamber is the private apartment of one family; in it father, mother, daughters, and the younger sons sleep and eat. Within each chamber are usually several sleeping-places or alcoves more or less completely screened or walled off from the central space. The chamber contains a fire-place, generally merely a slab of clay in a wooden framework placed near the centre. The outside wall on this side of the house is carried up to meet the roof, except for a square section which works on a hinge and with a strut, something like a sun-blind. This serves as both window, ventilator, and chimney. This aperture can be easily closed, during heavy rain, by removing the prop and allowing the flap to fall into its original position.

The front part of the house is undivided, and forms a single long gallery serving as a common antechamber to all the private rooms. It is in a sense, though roofed and raised some twenty feet above the ground, the village street as well as a common living and reception hall. Along the outer border of the floor runs a low platform on which the inmates sit on mats. One part of this, usually that opposite the chief's apartment in the middle of the house, is formed of several large slabs of hardwood, sometimes raised above the floor on crudely carved wooden figures. These platforms are specially reserved for the reception of guests and for formal meetings. Between them there are smaller platforms, which are the sleeping quarters assigned to the bachelors and male visitors. At intervals of some thirty or forty feet throughout the gallery are fire-places similar to those in the private chambers; on some of these fire constantly smoulders. Over them and generally near the middle of the great gallery is hung a row of trophies obtained in war, together with a number of charms and objects used in various rites.

Alongside the inner wall of the gallery stand the large wooden mortars used by the women in husking the rice. Above these hang the winnowing trays and mats, and along this wall are various implements of common use—hats, paddles, fish-traps, and so forth.

The gallery is reached from the ground by several ladders, each of which consists of a notched beam sloping at an angle of about 75°, and furnished with a slender handrail. The more carefully made ladder is fashioned from a single log, but the wood is so cut as to leave a handrail projecting forwards a few inches on either side of the notched gully or trough in which the feet are placed. From the foot of each ladder a row of logs, laid end to end, forms a footway to the water's edge. In wet weather such a footway is a necessity, because pigs, fowls, and dogs, and in some cases goats, run freely beneath and around the house, and churn the surface of the ground into a thick layer of slippery mire. Here and there along the front of the house are open platforms raised to the level of the floor, on which the rice-grain is exposed to the sun to be dried before being husked.

Under the house, among the piles on which it is raised, such boats as are not in daily use are stored. Round about the house, and especially on the space between it and the brink of the river, are numerous rice-barns. Each of these, the storehouse of the grain harvested by one family, is a large wooden bin about ten feet square, raised on piles some seven feet from the ground. Just below the floor-level each pile passes through a large circular disc, which serves to keep out rats. In the clear space round the house there are generally a few fruit trees and tobacco plants, and between it and the river are usually some rudely carved wooden figures, around which rites and ceremonies are performed from time to time.

Kayan villages generally consist of several, in some cases as many as seven or eight, such houses of various lengths, grouped closely together. The favourite situation for such a village is a peninsula formed by a sharp bend of the river.

Of the houses built by the other peoples, those of the Kenyahs very closely resemble those of the Kayans. The Kenyah village frequently consists of a single Long House (and with the Ibans this is invariably the case), and it is in many cases perched on a high steep bank immediately above the river. Some of the Klemantans also build houses little if at all inferior to those of the Kayans, and very similar to them in general plan. But in this as in all other respects the Klemantans exhibit great diversities, some of their houses being built in a comparatively flimsy manner, light timber and even bamboos being used, and the roof being made of leaves. The houses of the Muruts are usually small and low, and of poorer construction.

The Iban house differs from that of the Kayan more than any of the others. The general plan is the same; but the place of the few massive piles is taken by a much larger number of slender piles which pass up to the roof through the gallery and chambers. Of the gallery only a narrow passage-way alongside the main partition-wall is kept clear of piles and other obstructions. The floor is of split bamboo covered with coarse mats. An open platform at the level of the floor runs along the whole length of the open side of the house. There are no rice-barns about the house, the rice being kept in bins in the roofs. The roof itself is low, giving little head space. The gallery of the house makes an impression of lack of space, very different from that made by the long, wide gallery of a Kayan or Kenyah house.

Although the more solidly built houses, such as those of the Kayans, would be habitable for many generations, few of them are inhabited for more than fifteen or twenty years, and some are used for much shorter periods only. Villages are constantly being broken up or removed, either because of accidents, such as fires or epidemics, or for superstitious reasons, but most commonly because the soil of the neighbourhood has been worked out....

The Long House, that most typical Kayan product, is built on piles, and the timbers that support it are usually floated down-river from an old house so as to be used in the construction of the new. The great planks of the floor, the main cross-beams, and the wooden shingles of the roof are also commonly used. If a house has been partially destroyed by fire, no part of the materials of the old house is used in the construction of the new; for it is felt in some indefinable way that the use of the old material would render the new house liable, by a perpetuation of ill-fortune, to the same fate. In such cases, or upon migration to a different river, the whole of the timbers for the house have to be procured, shaped, and erected—a laborious process. But when once the timber has been collected, the work goes on so rapidly that a whole Long House may be substantially completed within a fortnight.

The main supports of the structure are four rows of massive columns of ironwood. These are driven down into the soil to a depth of about four feet, and so arranged that a single row supports the front of the house, another the back, and a double row the middle. The intervals between the columns of each row are about twenty feet. To sink a pile in its required position, rattans are tied round it a little above its middle, and then passed over a tall tripod of stout poles. A number of men haul on to these, while others shove up the top end of the pile with their shoulders. The pile is thus suspended with its butt end resting so lightly on the ground that it can easily be guided into the hole prepared for its reception. Smaller accessory piles, to serve as additional supports, are also put under the main cross-beams of the floor. The columns of the double row in the middle line are about six feet taller than those of the front and back rows. For the support of the floor a massive squared transverse tie is mortised through each set of four columns at a height of some fifteen to twenty feet from the ground, and secured by a wooden pin through each extremity.

A squared roof-plate, still more massive than the floor-ties, is now laid upon the crowns of the columns of the front row, along its whole length, and a second one upon the back row. This is dowelled upon the columns (*i.e.* the top of the column is cut to form a pin which is let into the longitudinal beam); and the beams which make up the roof-plate are spliced, generally in such a way that the top of column serves as the pin of the splice. Each of these heavy beams is generally lifted into its place by tiers of men standing on poles lashed at different heights across the columns, their efforts being seconded by others pulling on rattans which run from the beam over the topmost cross-pole. The framework of the roof is then completed by laying stout roof-ties across the crowns of the double row of columns of the middle line, and lashing their extremities to stout purlins (longitudinal beams for the support of the rafters in the middle of their length), and by laying the ridge-timber upon a line of perpendicular struts. The ridge-timber and purlins, though less heavy than the roof-plates, consist also of stout squared timbers, spliced to form beams continuous throughout the whole length of the house. The rafters are laid at an angle of about forty degrees and at intervals of eighteen inches, they are lashed to the ridge-timber and to the purlins, and lipped on to the roof-plates, beyond which they project about four feet to form an eave. Strong flat strips or laths are laid along the rafters parallel to the length of the house at intervals of about sixteen inches. On these are laid the shingles or slats of ironwood in regular rows, just as roof-tiles are laid in this country. Each slat is a slab about $1 \times 30 \times 12$ inches, and is lashed by a strip of rattan, which pierces its upper end, to one of the laths.

The floor is built of stout longitudinal joists lying across the main floor-ties, and notched to grip the ties. Upon, and transversely to them, are laid a number of flat strips which immediately support the floor planks; these are kept in place by their own weight.

In a well-built house these planks are between thirty and forty feet in length, two or three feet in breadth. and three or four inches thick. They are made from tough strong timber, and are moved from house to house, some of them being, probably, hundreds of years old. A single tree is generally made to yield two such planks. After being felled it is split into halves longitudinally in the following way. A deep groove is cut along one side, into which wedges of hardwood are driven with heavy mallets. When the trunk is split, each half is fined down by cutting deep transverse grooves at an interval of from three to four feet, when the intervening masses of wood can be split off. In this way each half is whittled down until it is only some six inches thick. The plank is then trimmed down to the desired thickness by blows of the adze struck across the grain. The two ends are generally left untrimmed until the plank has been transported to the site of the house and has lain there for some time. This prevents its splitting during the journey to the house and during the period of seasoning.

When the floor has been laid it only remains to make (1) the main partition wall which separates the gallery from the rooms, and (2) the walls between the several rooms. These walls are made only some eight or nine feet in height. The wall of the gallery is made of vertical planks lashed to horizontal rails, the extremities of which are let into the columns of the front set of the two middle rows.

The work of construction is carried on by all the men of the house; the women and children lend what aid they can in the way of fetching and carrying, and in preparing strips of rattans for tying. The ownership of each section is arranged beforehand; the section of the chief being generally in the middle, and those of his near relatives on either side of it. Each man pays special attention to the construction of his own section, and carries out the lighter work of that part, such as laying the shingles, with the help of his own household. If the head of a household is a widow, her section is constructed by her male neighbours or relatives without payment.

Before beginning the building of a new house favourable omens must be obtained; and the Kayans would be much troubled if bad omens were observed during the building, especially during the first few days. At this time, therefore, children are told off to beat upon gongs so as to prevent the appearance or the hearing of bad omen-birds. Unfavourable omens combined with ill luck , such as death, bad dreams, or an attack by enemies during building (even if this were successfully repelled), would lead to the desertion of a partially built house and the choice of another site.

All the interior peoples construct their houses on principles similar to those described above, but with considerable diversity in detail. The greatest diversity of plan is exhibited by the houses of Ibans. An Iban community seldom remains in the same house more than three or four years; and, no doubt for this reason, their houses are built in a less solid style than those of most other tribes. The timbers used are lighter; the house is not raised so high above the ground, and the floor is usually made of split bamboo in place of the heavy planks used by Kayans and others.

Charles Hose, *Natural Man: A Record from Borneo*, London: Macmillan, 1926; reprinted Singapore: Oxford University Press, 1988, pp. 163–7.

43

Houses of Sumatra in the 1770s

WILLIAM MARSDEN

William Marsden followed his elder brother John to West Sumatra at the age of sixteen and spent eight years (1771–9) in Bencoolen, where John was in the service of the British East India Company. William was also taken on by the Company and, after he came of age, received an appointment as Secretary to the Government in Fort Marlborough. His duties kept him close to the Fort, but although he was not able to travel widely, he collected information from other British Residents who were familiar with other parts of the island, while concentrating his own attention upon the Rejang people of the immediately surrounding region. He augmented personal observation with information collected from the Chief of the Rejang, Linggang Alam. He writes factually and straightforwardly, eschewing the exaggerated travellers' tales with which, he notes, other authors of the day strove to impress their readers. *Sumatra* was first published in 1873 and was highly praised by Marsden's contemporaries. It provided the first detailed account of the island in English. Reprinted many times, Marsden's work set a standard for later Indonesian studies and has retained its reputation till today. Marsden went on to become First Secretary of the Admiralty and the distinguished author of many more books including a Dictionary and Grammar of Malay.

T HE *dusuns* or villages (for the small number of inhabitants assembled in each does not entitle them to the appellations of towns) are always situated on the banks of a river or lake, for the convenience of bathing, and of transporting goods. An eminence difficult of ascent is usually made choice of for security. The access to them is by footways, narrow and winding, of which there are seldom more than two; one to the country, and the other to the water; the latter in most places so steep, as to render it necessary to cut steps in the cliff or rock. The *dusuns* being surrounded with abundance of fruit trees, some of considerable height, as the *durian*, *coco*, and *betel-nut*, the neighbouring country, for a little space about, being in some degree cleared of wood for the rice and pepper plantations, these villages strike the eye at a distance as clumps merely, exhibiting no appearance of a town or any place of habitation. The rows of houses form commonly a quadrangle, with passages or lanes at intervals between the buildings, where, in the more considerable villages, live the lower class of inhabitants, and where also their *padi*-houses or granaries are erected. In the middle of the square stands the *balei* or town hall, a room about fifty to an hundred feet long, and twenty or thirty wide, without division, and open at the sides, excepting when on particular occasions it is hung with mats or chintz; but sheltered in a lateral direction by the deep overhanging roof.

In their buildings neither stone, brick, nor clay, are ever made use of, which is the case in most countries where timber abounds, and where the warmth of the climate renders the free admission of air, a matter rather to be desired, than guarded against: but in Sumatra the frequency of earthquakes is alone sufficient to have prevented the natives from adopting a substantial mode of building. The frames of the houses are of wood, the underplate resting on pillars of about six or eight feet in height, which have a sort of capital, but no base, and are wider at top than at bottom. The people appear to have no idea of architecture as a science, though much ingenuity is often shewn in the manner of working up their materials, and they have, the Malays at least, technical terms corresponding to all those employed by our house carpenters. Their conception of proportions is extremely rude, often leaving those parts of a frame which have the greatest bearing, with the weakest support, and lavishing strength upon inadequate pressure. For the floorings they lay whole *bamboos* (a well known species of large cane) of four or five inches diameter, close to each other, and fasten them at the ends to the timbers. Across these are laid laths of split bamboo, about an inch wide and of the length of the room, which are tied down with filaments of the *rattan*; and over these are usually spread mats of different kinds. This sort of flooring has an elasticity alarming to strangers when they first tread on it. The sides of the houses are generally closed in with *palupo*, which is the bamboo opened, and rendered flat by notching or splitting the circular joints on the outside, chipping away the corresponding divisions within, and laying it to dry in the sun, pressed down with weights. This is sometimes nailed on to the upright timbers or bamboos, but in the country parts, it is more commonly interwoven, or matted, in breadths of six inches, and a piece, or sheet, formed at once of the size required. In some places they use for the same purpose the *kulitkayu*, or coolicoy, as it is pronounced by the Europeans, who employ it on board ship, as dunnage, in pepper and other cargoes. This is a bark procured from some particular trees, of which the *bunut* and *ĭbu* are the most common. When they prepare to take it, the outer rind is first torn or cut away; the inner, which affords the material, is then marked out with a *prang*, *pateel*, or other tool, to the size required, which is usually three cubits by one; it is afterwards beaten for some time with a heavy stick, to loosen it from the stem, and beeing peeled off, is laid in the sun to dry, care being taken to prevent its warping. The thicker or thinner sorts of the same species of *kulitkayu*, owe their difference to their being taken nearer to, or farther from, the root. That which is used in building has nearly the texture and hardness of wood. The pliable and delicate bark of which clothing is made, is procured from a tree called *kalawi*, a bastard species of the bread-fruit.

The most general mode of covering houses is with the *atap*, which is the leaf of a species of palm called *nĭpah*. These, previous to their being laid on, are formed into sheets of about five feet long, and as deep as the length of the leaf will admit, which is doubled at one end over a slip or lath of bamboo; they are then disposed on the roof, so as that one sheet shall lap over the other, and are tied to the bamboos which serve for rafters. There are various other and more durable kinds of covering used. The *kulitkayu*, before described, is sometimes employed for this purpose; the *galumpei*—this is a thatch of narrow, split bamboos, six feet in length, placed in regular layers, each reaching within two feet of the extremity of that beneath it, by which a treble covering is formed: *īju*— this is a vegetable production, so nearly resembling horse-hair, as scarcely to be distinguished from it. It envelops the stem of that species of palm called *anau*, from which the best toddy or palm wine is procured, and is employed by the natives for a great variety of purposes. It is bound on as a thatch, in the manner we do straw, and not infrequently over the *galumpei*; in which case the roof is so durable as never to require renewal, the *īju* being of all vegetable substances the least prone to decay, and for this reason it is a common prac-tice to wrap a quantity of it round the ends of timbers or posts which are to be fixed in the ground. I saw a house about twenty miles up *Manna* River, belonging to *Dupati Bandar Agung*, the roof of which was of fifty years standing. The larger houses have three pitches in the roof; the middle one, under which the door is placed, being much lower than the other two. In smaller houses there are but two pitches which are always of unequal height, and the entrance is in the smaller, which covers a kind of hall, or cooking room.

There is another kind of houses, erected mostly for a tem-porary purpose, the roof of which is flat, and is covered in a very uncommon, simple, and ingenious manner. Large, straight bamboos are cut of a length sufficient to lie across the house, and being split exactly in two, and the joints knocked out, a first layer of them is disposed in close order, with the inner or hollow sides up; after which a second layer, with the outer or convex sides up, is placed upon the others in such manner, that each of the convex falls into the two contiguous concave pieces, covering their edges; the latter serving as gutters to carry off the water that falls upon the upper or convex layer.

The mode of ascent to the houses is by a piece of timber, or stout bamboo, cut in notches, which latter an European cannot avail himself of, especially as the precaution is seldom taken of binding them fast. These are the wonderful light scaling ladders, which the old Portuguese writers described to have been used by the people of Achin in their wars with their nation. It is probable that the apprehension of danger from the wild beasts, caused them to adopt and continue this rude expedient, in preference to more regular and commodious steps. The detached buildings in the country, near to their plantations, called *talāngs*, they raise to the height of ten or twelve feet from the ground, and make a practice of taking up their ladder at night, to secure themselves from the destructive ravages of the tigers. I have been assured, but do not pledge myself for the truth of the story, that an elephant, attempting to pass under one of these houses, which stand on four or six posts, stuck by the way; but disdaining to retreat, carried it, with the family it contained, on his back, to a considerable distance.

In the buildings of the *dusuns*, particularly where the most respectable families reside, the wood-work in front is carved, in the style of bas-relief, in a variety of uncouth ornaments and grotesque figures, not much unlike the Egyptian hieroglyphics, but certainly without any mystic or historical allusion.

The furniture of their houses, corresponding with their manner of living, is very simple, and consists of but few articles. Their bed is a mat, usually of fine texture, and manufactured for the purpose, with a number of pillows, worked at the ends, and adorned with a shining substance that resembles foil. A sort of canopy or valance, formed of various coloured cloths, hangs over head. Instead of tables, they have what resemble large wooden salvers, with feet, called *dulang*; round each of which three or four persons dispose themselves; and on these are laid the *talams* or brass waiters, which hold the cups that contain their curry, and plantain leaves, or matted vessels, filled with rice. Their mode of sitting is not cross-legged, as the inhabitants of Turkey and our tailors use, but either on the haunches, or on the left side, supported by the left hand, with the legs tucked in on the right side; leaving that hand at liberty, which they always, from motives of delicacy, scrupulously eat with; the left being reserved for less

245

cleanly offices. Neither knives, spoons, nor any substitutes for them, are employed; they take up the rice, and other victuals, between the thumb and fingers, and dexterously throw it into the mouth by the action of the thumb, dipping frequently their hands in water as they eat.

The have a little coarse china ware, imported by the eastern praws, which is held a matter of luxury. In cooking they employ a kind of iron vessel, well known in India by the name of *quallie* or tauch, resembling in shape the pans used in some of our manufactures, having the rim wide, and bottom narrow. These are likewise brought from the eastward. The *prīu* and balañga, species of earthen pipkins, are in more common use, being made in small quantities in different parts of the island, particularly in *Lampong*, where they give them a sort of glazing; but the greater number of them are imported from Bantam. The original Sumatran vessel for boiling rice, and which is still much used for that purpose, is the *bamboo*; that material of general utility, with which bountiful nature has supplied an indolent people. By the time the rice is dressed, the utensil is nearly destroyed by the fire, but resists the flame so long as there is moisture within. . . .

At the back of the range of high mountains by which the countries of *Indrapura* and *Anak-suñgei* are bounded, lies the district or valley of *Korinchi*, which, from its secluded situation, has hitherto been little known to Europeans. In the year 1800, Mr. Charles Campbell, whose name I have had frequent occasion to mention, was led to visit this spot, in the laudable pursuit of objects for the improvement of natural history, and from his correspondence I shall extract such parts as I have reason to hope will be gratifying to the reader. . . .

'The people dwell in hordes, many families being crowded together in one long building. That in which I lived gave shelter to twenty-five families. The front was one long, undivided verandah, where the unmarried men slept; the back part was partitioned into small cabins, each of which had a round hole, with a door to fit it, and through this the female inmates crept backwards and forwards, in the most awkward manner and ridiculous posture. This house was in length two hundred and thirty feet, and elevated from the ground. Those belonging to the chiefs were smaller, well constructed of timber and plank, and covered with shingles or thin plates of board bound on with rattans, about the size, and having much the appearance, of our slates. . . .'

In the Phil. Transact. for the year 1778, is a brief account of the *Batta* [Batak] country and the manners of its inhabitants, extracted from the private letters of Mr. Charles Miller, the Company's botanist, whose observations I have had repeated occasion to quote. . . .

'June 21st, 1772. We set out from *Pulo Punchong*, and went in boats to the quallo [kuala] (mouth or entrance) of *Pinang Suri* river, which is in the bay, about ten or twelve miles south-east of *Punchong*. Next morning we went up the river in sampans, and in about six hours arrived at a place called quallo *Lumut*. The whole of the land on both sides of the river is low, covered with wood, and uninhabited. In these woods I observed camphor trees, two species of oak, *maranti*, *rañgi*, and several other timber-trees. About a quarter of a mile from that place, on the opposite side of the river, is a *Batta kampong*, situated on the summit of a regular and very beautiful little hill, which rises in a pyramidical form, in the middle of a small meadow. The *raja* of this *kampong* being informed by the Malays that we were at their houses, came over to see us, and invited us to his house, where we were received with great ceremony, and saluted with about thirty guns. This *kampong* consists of about eight or ten houses, with their respective *padi*-houses. It is strongly fortified with a double fence of strong, rough camphor planks, driven deep into the earth, and about eight or nine feet high, so placed, that their points project considerably outward. These fences are about twelve feet asunder, and in the space between them the buffaloes are kept at night. Without-side these fences they plant a row of a prickly kind of *bamboo*, which forms an almost impenetrable hedge, from twelve to twenty feet thick. In the *sapiyau* or building in which the *raja* receives strangers, we saw a man's skull hanging up, which he told us was hung there as a trophy, it being the skull of an enemy they had taken prisoner, whose body (according to the custom of the *Battas*) they had eaten about two months before. . . .

They fortify their *kampongs* with large ramparts of earth, half way up which they plant brush-wood. There is a ditch without the rampart, and on each side of that a tall palisade of camphor timber. Beyond this is an impenetrable hedge of prickly bamboo, which, when of sufficient growth, acquires an extraordinary density, and perfectly conceals all appearance of a town. *Ranjaus*, of a length both for the body and the feet, are disposed without all these, and render the approaches hazardous to assailants who are almost naked. At each corner of the fortress, instead of a tower of watch-houses, they contrive to have a tall tree, which they ascend to reconnoitre or fire from. But they are not fond of remaining on the defensive in these fortified villages, and therefore, leaving a few to guard them, usually advance into the plains, and throw up temporary breastworks and entrenchments. . . .

The houses are built with frames of wood, with the sides of boards, and roof covered with *iju*. They usually consist of a single large room, which is entered by a trap-door in the middle. The number seldom exceeds twenty in one *kampong*; but opposite to each is a kind of open building, that serves for sitting in during the day, and as a sleeping-place for the unmarried men at night. These together form a sort of street. To each *kampong* there is also a *balei*,* where the inhabitants assemble for transacting public business, celebrating feasts, and the reception of strangers, whom they entertain with frankness and hospitality. At the end of this building is a place divided off, from whence the women see the spectacles of fencing and dancing; and below that is a kind of orchestra for music.

William Marsden, *The History of Sumatra*, London, 1783; reprinted Kuala Lumpur: Oxford University Press, 1966, pp. 55–60, 305, 370, 379, 381.

**balei [balai]: an open-walled meeting house.

44
The Houses of the Minangkabau

THOMAS STAMFORD RAFFLES

After the return of Java to the Dutch at the end of the Napoleonic
Wars, Sir Thomas Stamford Raffles went on to a much less palatable
job in the run-down British settlement at Bencoolen [Bengkulu],
West Sumatra, where he remained from 1818 to 1824. From a personal point of view, it was a tragic posting, since having already lost
his first wife and their small children in Java, he and his second wife
Sophia were here to suffer the loss of four of their five children from
malaria. Even here, Raffles used his huge energies to what advantage
he could in his efforts to promote British influence in the region,
notably by founding Singapore in 1819. He travelled widely through
Sumatra, being accompanied on some of these journeys, difficult and
hazardous though they were, by Sophia. Raffles was convinced that
the Malays, like the Javanese, had once had a great civilization,
though no one at this time knew of the existence of Srivijaya. His
journey to the Minangkabau highlands therefore proved particularly
exciting to him because of his discovery there of two stones bearing
Kawi inscriptions, as well as a Hindu statue. The seat of contemporary Minangkabau royalty at Pagarruyung, however, had just been
destroyed by zealots of the militant Islamic movement, the Padris. In
the letter that he wrote to his patron, the Duchess of Somerset,
Raffles expresses an optimistic hope that this royal house could soon,
under British protection, rise to prominence again, but this was never
to come about. His letter gives us good descriptions of Minangkabau
houses, which represent one of the most elegant of all the distinctive
architectural styles of Indonesia. He also noted other interesting
structures, which can still be seen in operation today in the highlands,
just as he describes them: a large wooden water-wheel and a buffalo-
operated mill for crushing sugar-cane. Sophia attracted great attention among the local people. She tells us that they crowded around
her by the hundreds in some of the houses they stayed, and insisted
on watching her eat and go to sleep, 'and during the night strange
dark faces were continually seen peeping through the curtain which
parted off her place of rest from the numerous inmates of the same
room'. The letter from which this extract is taken was published by
Sophia in her Memoir of her husband.

'ON entering the town of Solaya, we passed through the burial-ground, distinguished by a very large waringin-tree and several tombs built of wood, here termed *jiri*; these are peculiar, sometimes little more than a shed, but frequently with a raised flooring, and seats raised one above the other at each end, like the stern of a vessel. Several of these were observed outside of the town, and in the middle of the rice-fields; these, we were informed, had been raised in memory of persons who had died at a distance; they now served as a shelter for the children, when watching the birds, as the rice ripened, and as places of amusement for the younger branches of the family. The waringin, or banyan trees, reminded me very much of Java; they are here even larger than any I ever observed in that country. Nothing in the vegetable creation can well exceed the peaceful grandeur of these trees.

'The houses are for the most part extensive and well built; in length seldom less than sixty feet; the interior, one long hall, with several small chambers in the rear opening into it. In the front of each house are generally two *lombongs*, or granaries, on the same principle as those in Java, but much longer and more substantial: they were not less than thirty feet high, and capable of holding an immense quantity; many of them very highly ornamented, various flowers and figures being carved on the uprights and cross-beams; some of them coloured. The taste for ornament is not confined to the lombongs; the wood-work of most of the houses is carved, and coloured with red, white, and black. The ridge-poles of the houses, lombongs, &c. have a peculiar appearance, in being extremely concave, the ends or points of the crescent being very sharp. In the larger houses they give the appearance of two roofs, one crescent being, as it were, within another. The whole of the buildings are constructed in the most substantial manner, but entirely of wood and matting.

'In the evening, I was much amused by the return of the cattle from pasture. To every house there appeared attached several head of cattle; these came in, as the sun declined, of

Residence of Raja Mangkuto, near Bukittinggi in the Minangkabau highlands of Sumatra, after 1880. (Koninklijk Instituut voor Taal-, Land- en Volkenkunde).

their own accord, and were severally secured by the children and women, the cattle being quite as docile as those in Europe, in which respect they form a striking contrast to those on the coast, which are, for the most part, too wild to be approached.

'Being anxious to refresh myself in the river which passed at the back of the town, I enquired for a convenient place to bathe; my intention was no sooner intimated, than the women of the village flocked round me, and insisted on accompanying me to the place; but, however great their curiosity, my modesty did not allow me to gratify it, and I was content to disappoint myself as well as them....

'We had embarked at a quarter-past eight, it was now half-past one, when we landed at the foot of the hill on which Samawang is situated, and at the source of the Kuantau or Indragiri river, which issues from the lake of Sincara at this place. We had a very hot and fatiguing walk for above an hour in ascending the hill, but were amply repaid for our labour by the friendly and cordial reception we met with at the summit, where the head of the village, a venerable old man, quietly conducted us into his dwelling, and made every preparation for our comfort without subjecting us to exposure under the waringin tree, or any of the ridiculous and annoying ceremonies and delays to which we had in former instances been liable.

'The house in which we were now accommodated was in length about one hundred feet, and from thirty to forty in depth, built in a most substantial manner, and supported along the centre by three large wooden pillars, fit for the masts of a ship: indeed from the peculiar construction of the house, the gable end of which was raised in tiers like the stern of a vessel, they had very much this appearance. The floor was raised from the ground about ten feet, the lower part being inclosed and appropriated to cattle, &c. The principal entrance is about the centre, but there is a second door at one end. The interior consists of one large room or hall, the height proportioned to the other dimensions; three fireplaces equally distant from each other were placed on the front side, and at the back were several small chambers, in which we perceived the spinning-wheels and other articles belonging to the women. This may serve as a general description for the houses in this part of the country, which I have described thus particularly, because they differ essentially from those on the coast, and from what Mr Marsden has described as the usual dwellings of the Sumatrans.

'Notwithstanding the room in which we were now accommodated was so commodious, we suffered more from the heat at this place than elsewhere, on account of the greater number of people admitted, and the number of fires. That end of the hall which rose in tiers, like the stern of a ship, was set apart for Lady Raffles and me, and separated from the rest by mats. The number at one time accommodated in this caravansera did not fall short of a hundred and fifty persons.

Lady Sophia Raffles, *Memoir of the Life and Public Services of Sir Thomas Stamford Raffles*, London: John Murray, 1830; reprinted Singapore: Oxford University Press, 1991, pp. 351–2, 355–6.

45
The Houses of the Acehnese

C. SNOUCK HURGRONJE

C. Snouck Hurgronje, the famous Dutch Islamicist, was responsible for launching serious Western scholarship on South-East Asian Islam. He penetrated Dutch East Indies Muslim circles disguised as the skin-darkened Muslim scholar Abdul Gaffur, and also went to Mecca to observe the pilgrimage. From 1891–1908, he was principal adviser to the colonial government on Islamic and indigenous affairs, and from 1898 was particularly influential in advising the Dutch Governor of Aceh in North Sumatra. The Dutch were particularly concerned to contain the threat of radical Islam which had helped to fire fierce resistance to Dutch rule and cost the Dutch heavy losses in the bitter Aceh War, which started in 1873 and dragged on until 1912 (or, in the minds of some Acehnese, was never really terminated). Snouck's monumental two-volume ethnographic study, *Atjeh*, was first published in Dutch in 1893–4. It contains one of the most detailed early accounts of indigenous domestic architecture, complete with a fine set of measured drawings.

IT must be remembered that these [Acehnese] houses are composed of either three or five *rueuëngs* or divisions between the main rafters. In the first case the number of pillars supporting the main body of the house is 16, in the second 24. To form an idea of a house of three rueuëngs it is only necessary to cut off from that depicted ... all that lies to one side or the other of the central passage (*rambat*).

It has further to be noted that the back verandah (*sramòë likōt*) sometimes also serves as kitchen.... The gable-ends always face East and West, so that the main door and the steps leading up to it must have a northerly or southerly aspect.

Further additions are often made to the house on its East or West side, when the family is enlarged by the marriage of a daughter. These are as regards their floor-level (*aleuë*) tached on as annexes to the back verandah. Some new posts are set up along the side of the verandah to support an auxiliary roof, the inner edge of which projects from the edge of the main roof. Parents who are not wealthy enough to build for their daughters a separate house close by, retire, as far as their private life is concerned, into the temporary building we have just described (*anjōng*) and leave the inside room (*juròë*) to the young married couple.

We shall now make a survey of the Achehnese house and its belongings, not with the object of giving a full description of its subordinate parts, or a complete inventory of all its equipment, but to show the part played by the various portions of the house in the lives of its inmates.

Round about each dwelling is a court-yard, generally supplied with the necessary fruit-trees etc. and sometimes cultivated so as to deserve the name of a garden (*lampōïh*). Regular gardens, in which are planted sugarcane, betelnuts, cocoanuts etc., are sometimes to be found in this enclosure, sometimes in other parts of the gampōng. The courtyard is surrounded by a strong fence (*pageuë*) through which a door leads out on to the narrow gampōng-path (*jurōng*); this in its turn leads through the gampōng to the main road (*rèt*), which runs through rice-fields, gardens and uncultivated spaces, and unites one gampōng with another. The whole gampōng, like each courtyard, is surrounded with a fence.

A good fence is generally formed of two rows of *glundōng* or *keudundōng* trees or the like, set at a uniform distance apart, leaving a slight intervening space which is filled with *triëng*or thorny bamboo. The two rows are united firmly together by bamboos fastened horizontally from tree to tree as crosspieces. There are usually from three to five of these cross bamboos in the length of the fence.

Sometimes trees or bushes of other sorts which are themselves furnished with thorns, such as the *darèh*, are employed to fence in gardens, courtyards or gampōngs.

In many courtyards, as appears from what we have said above, more than a single dwelling house is to be found. As a rule each additional house is the habitation of one of the married daughters of the same family or in any case belongs to women descended from the same ancestress.

An indispensable item is the well (*mòn*), from which the women draw water for household use in buckets (*tima*) made of the spathe of the betel-palm (*seutuë'*), where they wash their clothes and utensils, bathe (so far as the uncleanly Achehnese deem it necessary to do so) and perform other needs. A gutter (*salōran*) carries off the water etc. to an earthenware conduit, which conducts both water and dung to a manure-heap (*adèn* or *jeu'a*) which is always very wet. Into this also falls by means of another gutter all the wet refuse that is thrown out from the back part of the house and kitchen. A screen (*pupalang*) shuts off those who are using the well from the gaze of the passers-by.

The space underneath the house (*yub mòh* or *yub rumòh*) serves as the receptacle of various articles. The *jeungki* or see-saw rice-pounder for husking rice; the *keupō'*, a space between four or six posts, separated off by a partition of plaited cocoanut leaves (*bleuët*) or similar material thrown round the posts, and in which the newly harvested rice is kept till threshed, and the threshing itself takes place; the *krōngs*, great tun-shaped barrels made of the bark of trees or plaited bamboo or rattan, wherein is kept the unhusked rice after threshing, which barrels are also sometimes placed in separate open buildings outside the house; the press (*peuneu-rah*) for extracting the oil from decayed cocoanuts (*pi u*), and a bamboo or wooden rack (*prataïh* or *panteuë*) on which lies the firewood cleft by the women; these are the principal inanimate objects to be met with in the *yub mòh*.

Should the space beneath the house happen to be flooded in the rainy season, the store of rice is of course removed indoors.

Dogs, goats, sheep, ducks and fowls are also housed in the *yub mòh*. The brooding hens are kept under a cage-shaped *seureukab*, the others at night in a *sriweuën* or *eumpung* (fowl-run), while the fighting-cocks are in the daytime fastened up here by strings to the posts, though at night these favourite animals are brought into the front verandah.

Cows and buffaloes are housed in separate stalls or *weuë*, while ponies are tied up here and there to trees. The Achehnese however seldom possess the latter animals; those who have them use them but little and treat them with scant care.

All the small live stock huddled together in the *yub mòh* naturally render the place somewhat the reverse of whole-some. To this it must be added that much of the refuse from the house is simply thrown in there instead of being con-veyed to the dung-heap by the gutter above referred to. Most contributions of this sort come through the *guha*, a hole pierced in the floor of the back verandah to receive odds and ends of refuse wet and dry, but which also serves as a latrine for children and invalids! Besides this, the floor of every inner room (*jurèè*) is furnished with a long open fissure over which the dead are laid to be washed, so as to let the water used in the ablution flow off easily.

Notwithstanding all this, the *yub mòh* is also used as a temporary resting-place for human beings. If there are children in the house, a large swinging cradle is hung here for their use. Here too the women set up their cloth on the loom and perform other household duties, for which purpose a certain portion is partitioned off by a screen (*pupalang*). At festivals some of the guests are entertained in the same place; and here it is customary to receive visits of condolence for a death. Some chiefs keep imprisoned in the *yub mòh* those who refuse to pay the fines imposed on them.

At the foot of the steps leading up to the house (*gaki reunye-un*) there always stands a great earthenware water-jar (*guchi*). Close to this is a hooked stick planted in the ground to hold a bucket (*seuneulat tima*) and a number of stones rather neatly arranged. Anyone who wishes to enter the house places his dusty or muddy feet on these stones and pours water over them from the bucket till they are clean.

Where there is a separate kitchen (*rumòh dapu*), a flight of steps leading down from this allows the inmates to quit the house from the back, but as a rule the steps in front are the only means of egress, so that the women must traverse the front verandah every time they go out of doors.

Some houses have a wooden platform surrounding the foot of the steps and protected by the penthouse roof which covers the latter. It is set against the side of the house and stands a little lower than the floor of the front verandah. This serves the inmates as an occasional place to sit and laze in and also for the pursuit of parasites in one another's hair, a practice as necessary and popular among the Achehnese as among the Javanese. Here too the little children play.

By the house door access is gained to the front verandah or as the Achehnese call it, the stair verandah (*sramòë reunyeun*), which is separated from the rest of the house by a partition in which are the doors of the inner chambers (*jurèë*) and the aperture leading into the central passage, filled generally either by a curtain or a door.

This is the portion of the Achehnese dwelling to which the uninitiated are admitted. Here guests are received, *kanduris* or religious feasts are given and business discussed. Part of the floor (*aleuë*) is covered with matting; on ceremonial occasions carpets (*plumadani* or *peureumadani*) are spread over this, and on top of these again each guest finds an ornamentally worked square sitting-mat (*tika duë*) placed ready for him. A sort of bench made of wood or bamboo called *prataïh* sometimes serves the master of the house as a bedstead during part of the night, when he finds the heat excessive within. Here too are to be found a number of objects which betray the calling or favourite sport of their owner, some on shelves or bamboo racks (*sandéng*) against the wall, some stuck in the crevices of the wall itself. There the fisherman hangs his nets (*jeuë* or *nyaréng*), the huntsman his snares (*taròn*), all alike their weapons; there too are kept certain kinds of birds such as the *leuë* (Mal. *tĕkukur*, a kind of small dove), which are much used for fighting-matches.

The passage (*rambat*) is at one side in a house of three sections, but in one of five it is right in the middle between the two bedrooms. It is entered by none but women, members of the household or the family, or men on very intimate terms of acquaintanceship, as it only gives access to the back verandah, the usual abode of the women, who there perform their daily household tasks.

Some provisions are stored in the *rambat*, as for instance a *guchi* or earthenware jar of decayed cocoanut (*pi u*) for making oil, and a jar of vinegar made from the juice of the arèn (*ië jö*) or the nipah. Here too stands the *tayeuën*, a smaller portable earthenware jar in which the mistress of the house or her maidservant fetches water from the well to fill the guchi which stands in the back verandah and contains the supply of water for household use.

Some short posts (*rang*) extending only from the roof to

the floor are furnished with small pieces of plank on which are hung the brass plates with stands of the same metal on which food is served to guests, the trays (*dalōng*) big enough to hold an idang* for four or five persons and the smaller ones (*krikay*) on which are dished the special viands for the most distinguished visitors. Either in the rambat or the sramòë likōt stands a chest (*peutòë*) containing the requisite china and earthenware.

Porcelain dishes (*pingan*) and plates or small dishes (*chipê*) are to be found in these chests almost everywhere in the lowland districts, but when there are no guests the simpler ware common in the Tunòng is here also used, viz. large earthenware or wooden plates called *chapah* and smaller ones known as *chuĕ'*.

The back verandah serves as it were as a sitting-room and as we have seen often answers the purpose of a kitchen as well. It contains a sitting mattress (*tilam duĕ'*) with a mat on it especially intended for the use of the master, when he comes here to eat his meals or to repose; while a low bench (*prataïh*) similarly covered with a mat serves as a resting-place for small children. Here are to be found, on shelves or racks fixed against the wall, plates, earthen cooking-pots (*blangòng*), circular earthen or brass saucepans (*kanèt*) in which rice is boiled, earthen frying-pans with handles (*sudu*) for frying fish etc., the curry-stone (*batèë neupéh*) for grinding spices etc., with the grater (*aneu'*) that appertains to it, and earthenware or brass lamps (*panyòt*) in the form of round dishes with four or seven mouths (*mata*) in each of which a wick is placed. Some of these lamps are suspended by cords from above (*panyòt gantung*), others rest on a stand (*panyòt dòng*). From the rafters and beams hang at intervals little nets called *salang*, neatly plaited of rattan, for holding dishes which contain food, so as to protect their contents to some extent from the attacks of various domestic animals.

Drinking vessels of brass (*mundam*) or earthenware (*peunu-*

---

*idang: a serving of rice accompanied by side dishes.

man) are to be found in all the different apartments. They have as covers brass drinking-cups which are inverted and replaced after use.

Cooking is performed in a very simple manner. Five stones arranged almost exactly in this form ∴ constitute two *teunungkèës* or primitive chafing-dishes in which wood fires are lit, one for the rice and the other for the vegetables (*gulè*). The use of iron chafing-dishes (*kran*) on three legs is a mark of a certain degree of luxury.

The holy of holies in the house is the one part of it that may be really called a room, the *jurèë*, to which access is had by a door leading out on to the back verandah. Here the married couple sleep, here takes place the first meeting of bride and bridegroom at the *mampleuë* and here the dead are washed. These rooms are seldom entered by any save the parents, children and servants.

The floor is as a rule entirely covered with matting. The roofing is hidden by a white cloth (*tirè dilangèt*) and the walls are in like manner covered with *tirè* or hangings. Round the topmost edge of the *tirè* runs a border formed of diamond-shaped pieces of cloth of various colours; these when stitched together form the pattern called in Acheh *chradi* or *mirahpati*. Such disguising of roof and walls is resorted to in the other parts of the house only on festive occasions. On a low bench or platform (*prataïh*) is placed a mattress (*tilam éh*) with a mat over it, and this couch is usually surrounded with a mosquitonet (*kleumbu*).

Besides this there is spread on the floor a sitting-mattress (*tilam duë'*) of considerable size, but intended only for the man's use, and thus provided with a sitting mat. On both mattresses are piles of cushions (*bantay susōn*) shaped like bolsters and adorned at either end with pretty and often costly trimming. A sitting mattress has about four, a sleeping mattress as many as fifteen cushions of this description.

The clothing and personal ornaments are kept in a chest which stands in the *jurèë*. Well-to-do people generally have for this purpose chests the front of which is formed of two

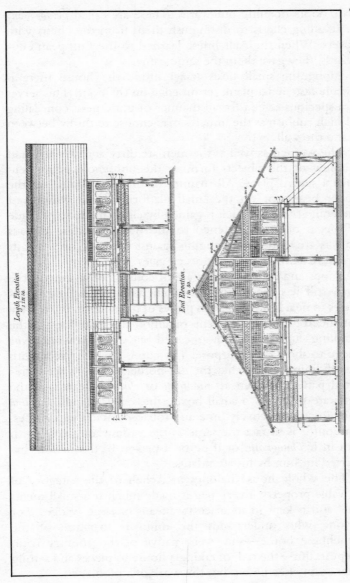

Front and side elevations of an Acehnese house. Note the rising floor levels, highest in the most important central room of the house (the *jurée*) where the householders sleep. From C. Snouck Hurgronje, *The Achehnese*, Leiden: Brill, 1906.

little doors opening out–wards. These are called *peutòë dòng* or standing chests to distinguish them from the chests with covers. When the Achehnese learned to use European cup-boards, they gave them the same name.

Along the small posts (*rang*) inside the house there is usually fastened a plank set on edge on the floor. This serves as a specious screen for all manner of untidiness, concealing all such rubbish as the inmates may choose to throw between it and the wall.

The women as well as the men are dirty and slovenly, and but few of the objects forming the household equipment have a settled place. All manner of things are piled on the upper beams or on the small platforms (*para*) which rest thereon, access to which is gained by climbing up steps made of pieces of plank fastened to the walls or posts. Various objects are to be seen hanging against the wall, or when its structure admits, stuck into its crevices (*lhat*).

Lamps and drinking–cups are of course not lacking in the *jurèë*, still less the requisites for chewing betel. The betel-leaves in neat little piles with pieces of betelnut on the top are contained in a little brass cup of almost the same form as the drinking-cups and like them called *baté* with the word *ranub* added to show their purpose. The cup is covered inside with a cloth lining, which, like the tirè-borders, exhibits the varie-gated pattern known as *mirahpati* or *chradi*. On top of the betel are placed two small boxes, the *krandam* and *cheuleupa* containing respectively lime and tobacco mixed with spices. The outfit is in fact the same as the pedestrian carries with him in his *bungkōïh*, or if he be a person of distinction, has carried for him by his attendants.

The whole house belongs in Acheh to the category of movable property. Every peg is made much too small for its hole and is kept in its place by means of large wedges. For anyone who understands the uniform structure of the Achehnese house—and every native of the country is an adept in this—the task of taking a house to pieces and setting it up again elsewhere is but the work of a moment.

So when an Achehnese sells his house, this means that the purchaser removes it to his own place of abode; a change of residence by the proprietor or rather the proprietress to another gampōng is quite a rare occurrence among the Achehnese.

Houses are transported in large numbers from the highlands to the lowlands, but seldom vice versâ, since the Tunòng possesses a greater abundance of building materials.

It is to be understood that even the most solidly built Achehnese house shakes if anyone pulls at the posts. Thieves and burglars begin by shaking the house to discover whether the inmates are sound enough asleep to admit of their carrying out their nefarious purposes. If they hear from the *jurèë* or the front verandah the cry 'who is that shaking the house?' they know that the time is unfavourable for their task.

Men who have forbidden intrigues with the wife or daughter of the house make known their presence in the same way, so that the object of their affections may come out to them if opportunity occurs.

The same course is adopted by the revengeful, who seek treacherously to slay the master of the house. Having ascertained that the latter is sound asleep in the *jurèë* they can generally ascertain, as they stand underneath the house, on what part of the floor he is lying. Then follow one or two rapid spear-thrusts through the thin planks, and all is over.

To force one's way into the house at night is difficult, as the doors are fastened with wooden bolts (*ganchéng, aneu' ganchéng*) and besides every movement inside the house would be likely owing to the instability of the floor, to wake the inmates up.

Many houses are regarded as possessed, because their inmates are continually falling sick. To protect a house from such malign influences various expedients are adopted.

A favourable time for commencing to build is carefully chosen. The work always begins with the setting up of the two principal posts with the cross-beams that unite them; while this is in progress, sundry prayers and formulas are repeated. These two posts which when the house is completed stand in the *jurèë*, are called the *raja* and the *putròë* (prince and princess). For them the soundest and best wood is selected; the raja is first set up and then the *putròë*. At a wedding the bridegroom takes his place next the 'prince' post, while the bride occupies a seat under the 'princess'.

Should the ceremonies at the setting up of the principal pillars prove propitious for continuing to build, then as soon as the house is finished a lucky day is again chosen for moving into it.

On this occasion a *kanduri* or religious feast is given, to which the *teungku** of the *meunasah* and some *leubès*† are invited. After this gathering there commences the customary 'cooling' (*peusijuë'*), which consists in sprinkling all the posts with flour and water (*teupōng taweuë*) by means of a broom formed of plants and twigs having a 'cooling', that is an evil-dispelling influence. The same process is resorted to whenever there has been any unusual feast or ceremony in the house, since such occurrences are supposed to set the heat, that is the powers of evil, in motion. Of all the pillars the raja and the putròë receive most attention on such occasions.

The two 'royal' pillars and sometimes others as well are at the time of building covered at the top with a piece of white cloth, over which again is placed a piece of red, so that they look as though they had turbans on their heads. This is also supposed to contribute to the protection of the inmates from evil influences.

C. Snouck Hurgronje, *The Achehnese*, 1893–4; Leiden: Brill, 1906, Vol. I, pp. 34–44.

---

*teungku: a title of respect given in Aceh to any particularly devout or knowledgeable Muslim, or man holding a religious office; here, the man in charge of the *meunasah* or village prayer-house. This building is also used as a sleeping-place by unmarried men or visiting strangers, and for village meetings and festivals.

†*leubè*: an orthodox Muslim (equivalent to the Javanese *santri*).

46

A Balinese House

MIGUEL COVARRUBIAS

Covarrubias gives us an extremely informative and succinct description of a Balinese house courtyard, together with plans and drawings. His comments about the symbolic imagery in which the courtyard mirrors the human body picks up on a theme woven through many of the architectures of the archipelago, which relates to the idea of the house as itself a living thing. In Bali, as elsewhere in Indonesia, many ritual prescriptions surround the proper building of houses, as well as the measuring of house timbers. All measurements are based on the householder's own body; a small length must always be added on as the 'life' or 'soul' (*pangurip*) of the measure, otherwise the occupants will come to harm. If the measurements of a compound turn out wrong, the house will be 'blocked' and death may result; a properly measured compound is said to be 'alive'.[1] Such interweaving of the vitality of houses and their inhabitants is an essential theme of South-East Asian architecture. Covarrubias also engagingly notes the signs of modernity creeping in to the Balinese houses of the time.

A S an organic unit, the structure, significance, and function of the home is dictated by the same fundamental principles of belief that rule the village: blood-relation through the worship of the ancestors; rank, indicated by higher and lower levels; and orientation by the cardinal directions, the mountain and the sea, right and left. The Balinese say that a house, like a human being, has a head—the family shrine; arms—the sleeping-quarters and the social parlour; a navel—the courtyard; sexual organs—the gate; legs and feet—the kitchen and the granary; and anus—the pit in the backyard where the refuse is disposed of.

Magic rules control not only the structure but also the building and occupation of the house; only on an auspicious

---

[1]Leopold Howe, 'An Introduction to the Cultural Study of Balinese Architecture', *Archipel* 25, 1983, pp. 145, 149.

day specified in the religious calendar can they begin to build or occupy a house. On our arrival we were able to secure a new pavilion in the household of Gusti only because the date for occupation set by the priest was still three months off. We were strangers immune from the laws of magic harmony that affect only the Balinese and we could live in the house until the propitious day when the priest would come to perform the *melaspasin*, the ceremony of inauguration, saying his prayers over each part of the house, burying little offerings at strategic points to protect the inmates from evil influences.

A Balinese home (*kuren*) consists of a family or a number of related families living within one enclosure, praying at a common family temple, with one gate and one kitchen. The square plot of land (*pekarangan*) in which the various units of the house stand is entirely surrounded by a wall of white-washed mud, protected from rain erosion by a crude roofing of thatch. The Balinese feel uneasy when they sleep without a wall, as, for instance, the servants must in the unwalled Western-style houses. The gate of a well-to-do family can be an imposing affair of brick and carved stone, but more often it consists of two simple pillars of mud supporting a thick roof of thatch. In front of the gate on either side are two small shrines (*apit lawang*) for offerings, of brick and stone, or merely two little niches excavated in the mud of the gate, while the simplest are made of split bamboo. Directly behind the doorway is a small wall (*aling aling*) that screens off the interior and stops evil spirits. In China I had seen similar screens erected for the same purpose and once I asked a Balinese friend how the *aling aling* kept the devils from entering; he replied, with tongue in his cheek, that, unlike humans, they turned corners with difficulty.

The pavilions of the house are distributed around a well-kept yard of hardened earth free of vegetation except for some flowers and a decorative frangipani or hibiscus tree. But the land between the houses and the wall is planted with coconut trees, breadfruit, bananas, papayas, and so forth, with a corner reserved as a pigsty. This is the garden, the orchard, and the corral of the house and is often so exuberant that the old platitude that in the tropics one has only to reach up to pluck food from the trees almost comes true in Bali.

Curiously, bamboo is not grown within the house. If it sprouts by itself it is allowed to remain, but its growth is discouraged by indirect means. Such is the magic of bamboo that only old people may tackle the dangerous job of planting it or digging it out, and the first lump of earth dug must be thrown as far away as possible. It is said that if this earth touches someone, he will surely die, and it is only on certain days that work concerning bamboo may be safely undertaken. Yet life in Bali would have developed along different lines had bamboo not existed on the island. Out of bamboo they make the great majority of their artifacts; houses, beds, bridges, water-pipes, musical instruments, altars, and so forth. It is woven into light movable screens for walls, sun-hats, and baskets of every conceivable purpose. The young shoots are excellent to eat, while other parts are used as medicine. I was told that the tiny hairs in the wrapping of the new leaves are a slow and undetectable poison like ground glass and tiger's whiskers. Bamboo combines the strength of steel with qualities of the lightest wood. It grows rapidly and without care to enormous size.

Social and economic differences affect but little the basic structure of the home. The house of a poor family is called *pekarangan*, that of a nobleman is a *djeró*, and a Brahmana's is a *griya*, but these differences are mostly in the name, the quality of the materials employed, the workmanship, and of course in the larger and richer family temple. The fundamental plan is based on the same rules for everyone. Only the great palace (*puri*) of the local ruling prince is infinitely more elaborate, with a lily pond, compartments for the Radja's brothers and his countless wives, a great temple divided into three courts, and even special sections for the preservation of the corpses and for the seclusion of 'impure' palace women during the time of menstruation.

The household of Gedog, our next-door neighbour in

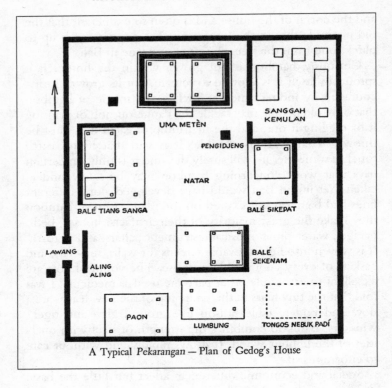

A Typical *Pekarangan* — Plan of Gedog's House

Belaluan, was typical; the place of honour, the higher 'north-east' corner of the house towards the mountain, was occupied by the *sanggah kemulan*, the family temple where Gedog worshipped his ancestors. The *sanggah* was an elemental version of the formal village temple: a walled space containing a number of little empty god-houses and a shed for offerings. The main shrine, dedicated to the ancestral souls, was a little house on stilts divided into three compartments, each with a small door. There were other small shrines for the two great mountains—the Gunung Agung and Batur—and for the *taksú* and *ngrurah*, the 'interpreter' and 'secretary' of the deities. In Gedog's house the altars were of bamboo with

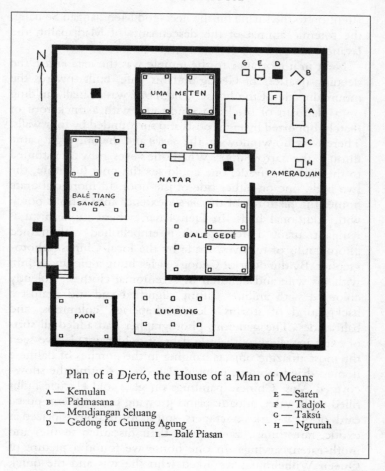

Plan of a *Djeró*, the House of a Man of Means

A — Kemulan
B — Padmasana
C — Mendjangan Seluang
D — Gedong for Gunung Agung
I — Balé Piasan

E — Sarén
F — Tadjok
G — Taksú
H — Ngrurah

thatch roofs, but in the home of Gusti's uncle, the noble judge who lived across the road, the family shrine was as elaborate as the village temple, with a moat, carved stone gates, brick altars, and expensive roofs of sugar-palm fibre. Such a temple is not a modest *sanggah*, but receives the more impressive name of *pameradjan*. Noble people pay special attention to the shrine for the deer-god Mendjangan Seluang, the totemic animal of the descendants of Madjapahit, the Javanese masters of Bali.

Next in importance to the temple was the *uma metén*, the sleeping-quarters of Gedog and his wife, built towards the mountain side of the house. The *metén* was a small building on a platform of bricks or sandstone, with a thick roof of thatch supported by eight posts and surrounded by four walls. There were no windows in the *metén* and the only light came through the narrow door. When one's eyes grew accustomed to the darkness inside, one could see the only furniture, the two beds, one on either side of the door. In more elaborate homes the platform of the *metén* extends into a front porch with additional beds. In Den Pasar, where modernism is rampant, many a front porch is embellished with framed photographs of relatives, made by the local Chinese photographer. By the door of Gedog's *metèn* hung a picture of him with his wife and children in ceremonial clothes, violently coloured with anilines, sitting dignified and stiff against a background of stormy clouds, draperies, coloumns, and balustrades. The generous photographer had added all sorts of extra jewellery with little dabs of gold paint. I have seen the most amazing objects hanging in the porches of Balinese homes: dried lobsters, painted plates representing the snow-covered Alps, Chinese paintings on glass, old electric bulbs filled with water, aquatic plants growing out of them, postal cards of New York skyscrapers, and so forth; objects prized as exotic, rare things, as we prize their discarded textiles and moth-eaten carvings. In one house we found a picture of Queen Wilhelmina; we asked who she was and the quick reply came: 'Oh! *itu gouvermen*—That is the Government.' The *metén* is the sanctuary of the home; here heirlooms are kept and the family's capital is often buried in the earth floor under the bed. Normally the heads of the family sleep in the *metén*, but being the only building in which privacy can be secured, they relinquish it to newly-weds or to unmarried girls who need protection. They shut themselves into it at night, but otherwise the entire life of the household is spent outdoors on the porch or in the surrounding open pavilions, each provided with beds for other members of the family.

The other three sides of Gedog's countyard were occupied by three open pavilions; on the left was the *balé tiang sanga*, the social parlour and guest house, and two smaller pavilions were on the right (*balé sikepat*) and back (*balé sekenam*) where other relatives slept with the children and where the women placed their looms to work. In the lowest part of the land, towards the sea, were the kitchen (*paon*) and the granary (*lumbung*). Rice was threshed in a cleared space (*tongos nebuk padi*) behind the granary. As in every household, there were two small shrines (*tugú*), one west of the *metén*, the other in the middle of the courtyard, the *pengidjeng* perhaps dedicated to the spirit of the land, 'His Excellency the Owner of the Ground' (*Ratú Medrwé Karang*).

Such is the general pattern of the home of a family of the average class that has ricefields and is economically comfortable. The better homes often have more elaborate pavilions, one of which may become a *lodji* (a Dutch word) by enclosing half of the pavilion with four walls, leaving the other half as an open veranda. This will provide a second sleeping-quarter for a married son. In the houses of the well-to-do the social hall is often a great square pavilion (*balé gedé*) with an extraordinarily thick thatch roof supported by twelve beautifully carved posts. A well-built *balé,* the archtype of Balinese construction, is a masterpiece of simplicity, ingenuity, and good taste. It consists of a platform of mud, brick, or stone reached by three or four steps and covered by a cool roof of thick thatch. The roof is supported by more or less elaborate wooden posts (*tiang*), the number of which determines their name and function. Thus a *balé* is called *sikepat, sekenam, tiang sanga*, or *balé gedé*, according to whether there are four, six, nine, or twelve posts. Definite rules dictate the dimensions and designs of these posts, 23 lengths of the index finger (*tudjoh*), or about seven feet, being the standard height of a house post. It has already been mentioned that the house

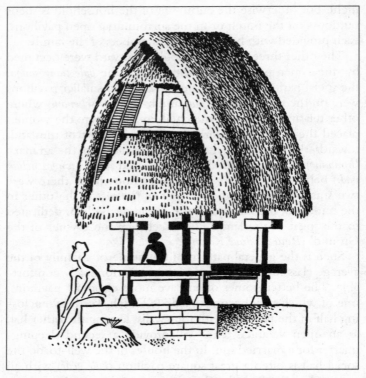

A Balinese Granary, from Miguel Covarrubias, *Island of Bali*, New York: Alfred A. Knopf, 1937.

must stand 'upright'; that is, the bottom of the posts should be the end nearest to where the roots were in the tree. The roof is built of *lalang* grass sown on the long ribs of coconut leaves, placed close together like shingles and lashed to the bamboo skeleton of the roof with indestructible cords of sugar-palm fibre, with an extra thickness of grass added to the four corners. Then the roof is combed with a special rake and the lower edge is neatly evened with a sharp knife. Such a roof, often a foot and a half in thickness, will last through fifty tropical rainy seasons. The beams that support the roof are ingeniously fitted together without nails, and are held in place with pegs made of heart of coconut wood. Generally one or two sides of the *balé* are protected by a low wall and between the house posts are built-in beds or platforms of wood with springs of bamboo, also called *balés*, where distinguished guests sit cross-legged to eat, or where, with a mattress added and screened by a curtain, they are put up for the night. . . .

The rice granaries (called according to size and shape *lumbung*, *glebeg*, *djinan*, *klumpu*, and *klimking* in the order of their importance) are a good indication of the economic status of a family. They are tall buildings with steep, high roofs of thatch resembling the Melanesian yam houses in shape. A granary is supported by four wooden pillars with wide circular capitals to prevent rats from climbing up. Custom demands respectful handling of rice. It must be fetched in silence and only in the daytime. A person who climbs into a granary should be in a normal state of physical and spiritual health and may not chew betel-nut.

Miguel Covarrubias, *Island of Bali*, New York: Alfred A. Knopf, 1937, pp. 88–96, 80–1.

47

A New Guinea Longhouse at Dore in 1775

THOMAS FORREST

Forrest's visit to the Papuan settlement at Dory [Dore] represents the easternmost extent of his voyage (Passage 22). This was partly due to a lack of co-operation from his Moluccan guide, Tuan Haji, who after they sailed had revealed a great reluctance to go there at all. Thomas's lively account of his visit, in which he brought activity in the longhouse to a standstill with a performance on his flute, reflects like the rest of his writings his sensitive powers of observation. Dore architecture was certainly remarkable, judging by a drawing[1] of a men's house which appears nearly a hundred years later. It shows an impressively long structure built on two rows of seven posts carved in the form of human figures. This drawing was made in 1858, while the building itself collapsed in an earth tremor in May 1864, and was rebuilt to the same design but without the anthropomorphic carving on the pillars.

OFF the mouth of the bay before the harbour, but out of the fwell,* a boat, with two Papua men, came on board, after having conversed a good deal with our linguists at a distance: satisfied we were friends, they hastened ashore, to tell, I suppose, the news. Soon after, many Papua Coffres came on board, and were quite easy and familiar: all of them wore their hair bushed out so much round their heads, that its circumference measured about three foot, and were least, two and a half. In this they stuck their comb, consisting of four or five long diverging teeth, with which they now and then combed their frizzling locks, in a direction perpendicular from the head, as with a design to make it more bulky. They sometimes adorned their hair with feathers. The women had only their left ear pierced, in

---

[1] Van de Goes, *Nieuw-Guinea*, Amsterdam, 1862; reproduced in *Nederlandsch-Indië Oud en Nieuw*, No. 14, 1929/30.

*The old English 'f' in the original text has been converted to modern English 's' in the remainder of the passage.

which they wore small brass rings. The hair of the women was bushed out also; but not quite so much as that of the men. As we were rowing along, one of my crowned pigeons escaped from its cage, and flew to the woods.

We anchored about four in the afternoon, close to one of their great houses, which is built on posts, fixed several yards below low water mark; so that the tenement is always above the water: a long stage, supported by posts, going from it to the land, just at high water mark. The tenement contains many families, who live in cabins on each side of a wide common hall, that goes through the middle of it, and has two doors, one opening to the stage, towards the land; the other on a large stage towards the sea, supported likewise by posts, in rather deeper water than those that support the tenement. On this stage the canoes are hauled up; and from this the boats are ready for a lanch, at any time of tide, if the Hara-foras attack from the land; if they attack by sea, the Papuas take to the woods. The married people, unmarried women, and children, live in these large tenements, which, as I have said, have two doors; the one to the long narrow stage, that leads to the land; the other to the broad stage, which is over the sea, and on which they keep their boats, having out-riggers on each side. A few yards from this sea stage, if I may so call it, are built, in still deeper water, and on stronger posts, houses where only batchelors live. This is like the custom of the Batta people on Sumatra, and the Idaan or Moroots on Borneo, where, I am told, the batchelors are separated from the young women and the married people.

At Dory [Dore] were two large tenements of this kind, about four hundred yards from each other, and each had a house for the batchelors, close by it: in one of the tenements were fourteen cabins, seven on a side; in the other, twelve, or six on a side. In the common hall, I saw the women some-times making mats, at other times forming pieces of clay into earthen pots; with a pebble in one hand, to put into it, whilst they held in the other hand also a pebble, with which they knocked, to enlarge and smooth it. The pots so formed, they

Men's house at Dore, the New Guinea village visited by Forrest, reproduced in *Nederlandsch Indië Oud en Nieuw*, Vol. 14 (1929/30), p. 9.

burnt with dry grass, or light brushwood. The men, in general, wore a thin stuff, that comes from the cocoa nut tree, and resembles a coarse kind of cloth, tied forward round the middle, and up behind, between the thighs. The women wore in general, coarse blue Surat bastas,* round their middle, not as a petticoat, but tucked up behind, like the men; so that the body and thigh were almost naked: as boys and girls go entirely. I have often observed the women with an ax or chopping knife, fixing posts for the stages, whilst the men were sauntering about idle. Early in the morning I have seen the men setting out in their boats, with two or three fox looking dogs, for certain places to hunt the wild hog, which they call Ben: a dog they call Naf. I have frequently bought of them pieces of wild hog; which, however, I avoided carrying on board the galley, but dressed and eat it ashore, unwilling to give offence to the crew.

At anchor, I fired some swivel guns: the grown people did not regard this, or seem frightened, while the boys and girls ran along the stages, into the woods. . . .

On *Thursday* the 9th, fine weather and southerly winds. Two small boats returned from a place they called Wobur, with sago, plantains, &c. for their families: they were therefore unwilling to dispose of any. They also brought some birds of Paradise, which I purchased from them. To day I repaired to the large tenement, near which the vessel lay. I found the women in the common hall, making cocoya mats as usual; also kneading (if I may so term it) the clay, of which others formed the pots, with two pebble stones, as before described. Two of them were humming a tune, on which I took out a german flute, and played; they were exceedingly attentive, all work stopping instantly when I began. I then asked one of the women to sing, which she did. The air she sung was very melodious, and of a species much superior to Malay airs in general, which dwell long on a few notes, with little variety of rise or fall. Giving her a fathom of blue bastas,

*bastas: a coarse cotton cloth from Surat (northwest India).

I asked another to sing; she was bashful, and refused; therefore I gave her nothing: her looks spoke her vexed, as if disappointed. Presently, she brought a large bunch of plantains, and gave it me with a smile, I then presented her with the remaining fathom of bastas, having had but two pieces with me. There being many boys and girls about us as we sat at that part of the common hall, that goes upon the outer stage of the tenement, I separated some of the plantains from the bunch, and distributed to the children. When I had thus given away about one half, they would not permit me to part with any more; so the remainder I carried on board. I could not help taking notice that the children did not snatch, or seem too eager to receive, but waited patiently, and modestly accepted of what I offered, lifting their hands to their heads. The batchelors, if courting, come freely to the common hall, and sit down by their sweethearts. The old ones at a distance, are then said often to call out, well, are you agreed? If they agree before witnesses, they kill a cock, which is procured with difficulty, and then it is a marriage. Their cabins are miserably furnished; a mat or two, a fire place, an earthen pot, with perhaps a china plate or bason, and some sago flour. As they cook in each cabin, and have no chimney, the smoke issues at every part of the roof: at a distance the whole roof seems to smoke. They are fond of glass, or china beads of all colours; both sexes wear them about the wrist, but the women only at the left ear.

Thomas Forrest, *A Voyage to New Guinea and the Moluccas, 1774–1776*, London: G. Scott, 1780; reprinted Singapore: Oxford University Press, 1969, pp. 95–7, 104–5.

48

A Tanimbar House

HENRY O. FORBES

In 1882, towards the end of his five-year journey through Indonesia, Forbes was joined by his wife Anna, who came out from his native Aberdeenshire to marry him. They celebrated their honeymoon in the Moluccas, before proceeding on to some of the least known areas of the archipelago. Their stay in the Tanimbar islands was marred by the loss of much of his herbarium collections by fire, but Forbes' interest in everything he saw, and once again, his willingness to acknowledge and admire the talents of indigenous artists and wood carvers, leads him to give a much more positive assessment of Tanimbar architecture than that of other European observers, even at a much later date—and even brings a degree of self-questioning.

THE opening months of a Tenimber's islander's existence are not passed on a bed of roses. Strolling through the village one evening we were beckoned into a hut to see a newly born infant. It was lying quite naked, with only a hard palm-spathe beneath its back and a square inch or so of cloth on its stomach, in a rude cradle or *Siwela*, a rough rattan basket suspended so as to rock over a fire in a smoke so dense that we were amazed that it was not suffocated. Occasionally the nurse drops to sleep, and the fire burns the bottom out of the *Siwela*, and the child is worse off than if it had been bitten by all the mosquitos of Larat, to be free from which it is so suspended. The child, it would seem, is invariably laid in exactly the same position in the cradle, either on its back or on one side according to the place of its suspension in the house, with the result that the hinder part of its head becomes quite flattened. In some living infants the deformity was very prominent, and that it remains permanent is evidenced by one of the crania of a full-grown man which I brought home; but no sort of binding is applied to the head in any stage of their youth, as among many tribes, to induce an abnormal and admired shape of head.

The artistic ability of the Timor-laut people is unquestionably very high. They are very deft-fingered and clever carvers of wood and ivory. The 'figure-heads' of their outrigger praus, dug out of single trees, especially attract attention by the excellence of the workmanship, carefully and patiently executed, and the elegance of their furnishings; while the whole length of the central pillars of their houses are also most elaborately carved with intricate patterns and representations of crocodiles and other animals. Their appreciation of beauty is a characteristic of them, which, absolutely wanting in the Malay people, I was surprised to find among a less advanced race. While walking through the forest they invariably pluck and tastefully arrange in a hole in their comb which is there for the very purpose, any particularly bright bunch of flowers they see.

Their houses, though little more than floor and roof, are very neat structures, elevated four or five feet above the ground, and entered by a stair through a trap-door cut in the floor, which is shut down and slotted at night. In front of the door is a seat of honour—*dodokan*—with ornamented supports and a high carved back, on the top of which is placed an image—*Duadilah*—with, at its side, a platter whereon a morsel of food is offered every time they eat in its presence. Every time they drink they dip their finger and thumb in the fluid, and flick a drop or two upward with a few muttered words of invocation. Along the four sides spaces for sleeping on are raised some nine to twelve inches above the level of the *rahanralan* or floor of the houses. The inmates sleep on small, neatly made bamboo mats, and rest their heads on a piece of squared bamboo with rounded edges, exactly similar to the Chinese pillow. In one gable is the *foean* or fire-place, and opposite to it on a trellis-work platform is placed the cranium of the father of the Head of the house. Indian corn and other comestibles and various articles are stored on little platforms stretching between the rafters, and

Exterior and Interior of a Tanimbar house. From Henry O. Forbes, *A Naturalist's Wanderings...*, New York: Harper 1885.

their scanty clothing and other articles are suspended from the roof by wooden contrivances often elaborately designed and elegantly carved. After seeing how elaborately covered almost everything they used was with carvings, executed with undoubted taste and surprising skill, we began to ask ourselves, first, Can such artistically developed people be savages?—and, next, the more difficult question, What is a *savage*?

Henry O. Forbes, *A Naturalist's Wanderings in the Eastern Archipelago*, New York: Harper, 1885; reprinted Singapore: Oxford University Press, 1989, pp. 315–19.

49
Houses of the Ifugao, Bontoc, and Kalinga of Luzon

CORNELIS de WITT WILLCOX

Willcox was a Lieutenant-Colonel of the US Army, who in 1910 accompanied the Secretary of the Interior of the Philippines, Dean C. Worcester, on his annual Tour of Inspection through the mountain province of northern Luzon. Worcester was a zoology professor who had become something of an expert on the Philippines through his extensive collecting trips in the 1880s and 90s, during which he had observed the harshness of Spanish exploitation. US intervention came after two popular revolts, in 1896 and 1898. At the time of Willcox's journey, the headhunting mountain tribes were only recently pacified, and travel over the precipitous mountain trails, often washed away in storms, was challenging. At each stop on the tour, thousands would gather to be feasted, a council would be held, and Worcester would receive their reports of local affairs. The flavour of these occasions is well conveyed by Willcox; on one occasion, a medley of pigs, dogs, and horses joined the throng, among whom were three bands, all playing as loudly as possible in different keys—'altogether one of the most delightful confusions conceivable'. Willcox also describes the characteristic dwellings of the different tribes. Small in scale, the Ifugao house in particular may represent a form of prototype Austronesian dwelling, in which the house is really an enlarged granary, with added hearth and shrine. A similar fusion, in a highly similar structure, is also evident in some parts of Indonesia. He further observed the unusual communal institutions of Bontoc villages.

[At Kiangan, an Ifugao village:]

BEFORE beginning the business of the day we walked about the village and examined one or two houses. These are all of one room, entered by a ladder drawn up at night and set up on stout posts seven or eight feet high: the roof is thatched, and the walls, made of wattle (*suali*), flare out from the base determined by the tops of the posts. In cutting the posts down to suitable size (say 10 inches in diameter), a flange, or collar, is left near the top to keep rats out, chicken-coops hang around, and formerly human skulls, too, were set about. But the Ifugaos, thanks to Gallman, as already said, have abandoned head-hunting and the skulls in hand, if kept at all, are now hidden inside their owner's houses, their places being taken by carabao heads and horns. One house had a *tahibi*, or rest-couch; only rich people can own these, cut out as they are of a single log, in longitudinal cross-section like an inverted and very flat V with suitable head- and foot-supports. The notable who wishes to own one of these luxurious couches gets his friends to cut down the tree (which is necessarily of very large size), to haul the log, and to carve out the couch, feeding them the while. Considering the lack of tools, trails, and animals, the labor must be incredible and the cost enormous. However, wealth will have its way in Kiangan as well as in Paris....

* * *

[At Bontok, among the Bontoc Igorot:]

The next day, the 9th, Father Clapp very kindly offered to show Strong and me the native village, an invitation we made haste to accept. This village, if village it be, marches with the Christian town, so that we at once got into it, to find it a collection of huts put down higgledy-piggledy, with almost no reference to convenience of access. Streets, of course, there were none, nor even regular paths from house to house, you just picked your way from one habitation to the next as best you could, carefully avoiding the pig sty which each considerable hut seemed to have. I wish I could say that the Igorot out of rude materials had built a simple but clean and commodious house! He has done nothing of the sort; his materials are rude enough, but his hut is small, low, black, and dirty, so far as one could tell in walking through. The poorer houses have two rooms, an inner and an outer, both very small, say 6 × 6 feet and 4 × 6 feet respectively, inside measurement, cooking being done in the outer and the inner serving as a sleeping room. There is no flooring; although the fire is under the roof (grass thatch), no smoke-hole has been thought of, and as there are no window openings, and the entrance is shut up tight by night and the fire kept up if the weather be cold, the interior is as black as one would expect from the constant deposit of soot. The ridge-pole of the poorer houses is so low that a man of even small stature could not stand up under it. The well-to-do have better houses, not only larger, but having a sort of second story; these are soot-black, too. We made no examination of these, not even a cursory one. The pig-sty is usually next to the house, and is nothing but a rocklined pit, open to the sky, except when the house is built directly over it.

It is astonishing that these people should not have evolved a better house, seeing that the Ifugaos have done it, and the Kalinga houses, which we were to see in a day or two, are really superior affairs. . . .

Poor as we found the village on the material side, it has nevertheless some interesting institutional features. For example, it has sixteen wards, or *atos*, and each *ato* has its meeting-place, consisting of a circle of small boulders, where the men assemble to discuss matters affecting the *ato*, such as war and peace; for the *ato* is the political unit, and not the village as a whole. A remarkable thing is the family life, or lack of it rather: as soon as children are three or four years old, they leave the roof under which they were born and go to sleep, the boys in a sort of dormitory called *pabafunan*, occupied as well by the unmarried men, and the girls in one called *olog*. And, as one may ask whether pearls are costly because ladies like them or whether ladies like pearls because they are costly, so here; Is the Igorot house so poor an affair because of the *olog*, etc., or does the *olog* exist because the house is poor? Be this as it may, and to resume, the children go on sleeping in their respective *pabafunan* and *olog* until they are grown up and married. A sort of trial marriage seems to exist; the young men freely visit the *olog*—indeed, are expected to. If results follow, it is a marriage, and the couple go to housekeeping; otherwise all the parties in interest are free. Marriage ties are respected, adultery being punished with death; but a man may have more than one wife, though usually that number is not exceeded. However, a man was pointed out to us, who maintains in his desire for issue, but without avail, a regular harem, having no fewer than fifteen wives in different villages, he being a rich man.

Among other things shown us by Father Clapp was a circle of highly polished boulders, said traditionally to be the foundation of the house of Lumawig, the Deity of the Bontok. One stone was pierced by a round hole, made by Lumawig's spear; on arriving, he decided he would remain permanently in Bontok, and began by sticking the shaft of his spear in the stone in question—a very minor example, by the way, of his magical powers. More interesting, perhaps, than the ruins of Lumawig's house was a sacred grove on a hill rising just back of the village, in which, according to Father Clapp, certain rites and ceremonies are held once a year. The matter is one for experts, but it appears strange that this people should have a sacred grove, as being unusual....

* * *

[At the Kalinga village of Lubuagan:]

There must have been thousands of people, as many women as men, and almost as many children as women, all of whom set up a mighty shout as our little column emerged. But what especially and immediately caught the eye was the brilliancy of the scene. For whereas the people so far encountered had impressed us by the sobriety of color displayed, these Kalingas blazed out upon us in the most vivid reds and yellows. Many of them women as well as men, had on tight-fitting Moro jackets of red and yellow stripes; but whatever it was—skirt, jacket, or gee-string—only one pattern showed itself, the alternation of red and yellow, well brought out by the clear brown of the skin. As though this were not enough, some men had adorned their abundant black hair with scarlet hibiscus flowers, and all, or nearly all, wore plumes of feathers, one over each ear. Each *rancheria* has its distinctive plume; as, red with black tips, black with red, all red, white with black, and so on, some with notched and others with natural edges. Many men had axes on their hips. The whole effect was startling, and all the more that these people, erect, sinewy, of excellent build like their comrades farther south, were perceptibly taller, men five feet ten inches tall not being uncommon. Add to this a stateliness of walk and carriage, combined with a natural, wholly unconscious ease and grace of motion, and it is easy to imagine the fine impression made upon us by our first look upon these assembled people. . . .

Kalinga is neither a race nor a tribe name, but a word meaning 'enemy' or 'outlaw', as though the hand of the people that bear it had been against everybody's else. These people have been great head-hunters, and have not yet entirely abandoned the practice, though it is steadily diminishing. It should be recollected, however, that it is only within the last three or four years that we have had any relations with them, Mr. Worcester's first visit to Lubuagan having occurred in 1907. On this occasion, immediately on arriving, he was shut up with his party in a house; and all night a lively debate went on outside as to whether the next morning his head should be taken or not, his native interpreter informing him of the progress of opinion as the night wore on....

Lubuagan itself is extremely well situated on a gigantic terrace-like slope, as though, as at Kiangan, an avalanche of earth had burst through the rim of encompassing mountains. Here live the Governor of the province and the inspector of Constabulary with a detachment; their houses, with the *cuartel** and public offices, are disposed around a sort of parade, divided into an upper and a lower terrace....

The native town lies above and just back of the parade, with its houses running well up on the slopes. These are, everywhere possible, terraced for rice, and so successfully that two crops are made every year, as against only one at Bontok and elsewhere. It follows that the Kalingas have more to eat than their relatives to the south, and that is perhaps one reason of their greater stature.

The morning of the 12th, our one full day at Lubuagan, broke clear, bright, and hot, and so the day remained. Events during the next few hours had no particular axis. We looked on mostly, though, of course, here as elsewhere, business there was to be dispatched. The upper terrace was the scene of crowded activity, being packed with people from sunrise to sunset. Dancing went on the whole day; the sound of the *gansa*† never ceased. A particularly interesting dance was that of a number of little girls, eight or ten years of age, who went through their steps with the greatest seriousness and dignity, a very pretty sight. In yet another the performers, nine all told, grown men, attracted attention from the fact that the handles of their *gansas* were human lower jaws,

---

*cuartel: barracks.
†*gansa*: brass gong.

apparently new, in the teeth of two of which gold fillings glistened. . . .

We found the town unusually clean. Public latrines exist, and public drinking-tanks, both put in by Governor Hale, and highly approved of the people. The houses themselves were the best we had seen, some of them hexagonal in ground plan, and built of hard woods. The pigs stay underneath, to be sure, but their place is kept clean. Rich men have rows of plates, the dinner-plates of civilization, all around their houses, and take-up floors of split bamboo are common, being rolled up and washed in the neighboring stream with commendable frequency. All together, Lubuagan made the impression of an affluent, not to say opulent, center, inhabited by a brave, proud, and self-respecting people.

Cornelis de Witt Willcox, *The Headhunters of Northern Luzon: From Ifugao to Kalinga, a Ride through the Mountains of Northern Luzon*, Kansas City: Franklin Hudson, 1912, pp. 106–9, 190–6, 221–33.

Colonial Residences

50
A 'Fairy-tale Chateau' at Taiping

BRAU DE SAINT POL LIAS

Brau de Saint Pol Lias was an energetic promoter in his native France of 'commercial geography', and was much exercised by what he termed his 'patriotic preoccupations' with arousing French interest in the strategic and commercial benefits to be derived from a more ambitious colonial policy. He admired British interventions in Malaya and writes with a great sense of urgency about the need for France to imitate the 'bold ideas and spirit of enterprise' which he saw as characterizing British colonial endeavours. Prior to his travels in Perak (1880–1), St Pol Lias had already spent some time in Sumatra, where besides hunting elephants and crocodiles, he had established an experimental plantation. He arrived in Perak at a time of rapid development and was particularly attracted to its Resident, Sir Hugh Low (Passage 41), as a man from whom much could be learned.

After twenty-nine years of obscurity and frustration in Labuan, Low had been appointed British Resident in Perak in 1876, just after the assassination of the first Resident, James Birch. Perak was ruined by war, there was no effective government and tensions were high. Competition among the Malay royalty over the succession to the rulership of Perak, combined with feuding between rival Chinese factions controlling tin mining activities in Larut, had brought about this chaos and given the British an excuse to intervene in the state three years previously. Low was a brilliant and tactful administrator, and when he retired thirteen years later, he had established an order that had achieved local consent, while the annual revenue of the state had increased nine times. The tin mines boomed—the Chinese immigrants who came to work them grew in numbers from around 9,000 in 1877 to 50,000 in 1882, the majority of them settling in Taiping. Tin was one of the interests that brought St Pol Lias to Perak: his companion on this journey was a mining engineer by the name of John Errington de la Croix, and he had letters of introduction from the French Foreign Ministry, entrusting him with a 'scientific mission' (though undertaken at his own expense) to investigate the mines at Larut as well as other British commercial enterprises in the state.

This passage describes St Pol Lias's visit, first, to the bungalow of the Assistant Resident in Taiping, and secondly his stay with Hugh Low at Kuala Kangsar. St Pol Lias describes the former house as having been built by the first Assistant Resident. This was Captain Speedy, a flamboyant and eccentric figure whose extravagances in this office had attracted Low's criticism, and who had resigned in 1877. Perhaps this helps to explain the level of luxury which St Pol Lias records so strikingly in his account. The hospitality extended to the travellers was particularly welcome on this occasion, since their journey had not been without mishap. Their Indian driver had beaten his rather feeble horse to the point of exhaustion and then left them on the road to seek a replacement. Night was falling, bringing with it thoughts of tigers, when the horse, on a downhill slope, did a somersault between the shafts, catapulting the author out of the cart. He landed between the horse's legs, but escaped with only a few scratches. They had been obliged to finish the journey into Taiping on foot, and were no doubt very thankful to arrive.

Hugh Low's style of life in Kuala Kangsar differed considerably. The Residency bungalow, formerly the house of a Malay aristocrat, was comfortable but relatively modest, having been taken over by Low with little alteration. Besides his official duties, Low vigorously pursued his interests in horticulture. St Pol Lias describes with particular enthusiasm being given a tour of his plantations of coffee, cinchona, pepper, tea, sugar, rice, and rubber (he had obtained in 1877 ten of the first *hevea* plants to have been brought out from Kew Gardens via Ceylon to Singapore). He also kept a variety of pet animals, including monkeys, to which he was very attached. St Pol Lias was not the only guest to enjoy Low's hospitality, or to express his admiration for the man: Isabella Bird also stayed at his bungalow in 1879, and has left an amusing description[1] of how she shared the dinner table with an ape and a monkey.

Saturday 28, Sunday 29 August [1880].

WE have ended up here as if in some fairytale castle. The various accidents of our journey have done nothing to spoil our enchantment.

Yesterday evening, after we had climbed the hillside and mounted to a verandah on the first storey, we were led into an immense room which extended right through the centre of the house: in the middle of the room stood a table, laid with an elaborate dinner service, with enormous bouquets of flowers arranged in silver-mounted crystal bowls. From here we were taken to our luxuriously furnished bedrooms. The whole house is carpeted with fine new mats on which it was a pleasure to walk barefoot. Our rooms are comfortably furnished, with large four-poster beds hung with voluminous mosquito-nets, white marble washstands equipped with brightly-coloured porcelain, dressing tables, and large full-length mirrors. Each room has its own staircase leading down to a bathroom located directly beneath it, on the ground floor of the house. A beautiful drawing room with large windows, tables, library shelves, chairs, armchairs and upholstered sofas, and two large desks, completed the guest accommodation in which Mr Walker, who received us in the most cordial way possible, declared that we were to feel at home for as long as it suited us to remain.

I heard the first stroke of the dinner gong.... And I had left my trunk at Pinang thinking that evening dress would be useless in the interior of such a new country! The gong sounded for the second time. We went into the great central room to take our places at table. We were introduced to the Major who had just arrived and with whom I was delighted to be able to speak French, since English, which I attempt to

---

[1] Isabella L. Bird, *The Golden Chersonese and the Way Thither*, John Murray, London, 1883, pp. 306–9.

speak only when I am forced to, has always remained for my southerner's ear a very difficult language: I like Malay a hundred times better. Major Swynburne is a very tall man, who, dressed in his snow white Indian Army uniform, has all the distinction typical of British army officers. He speaks French like a Parisian; moreover, he has lived in Paris, where he knows all the best places, and he enjoys reminiscing about his time there. This distracts him from the very different life which he leads here, where the solitude weighs on him a little. He has been put in charge of organising the small army assigned to this state, which he modestly terms a police force.

Mr Walker, another tall Englishman (they are all tall), with a serious, kind and sympathetic face, is also a British army officer. He still belongs to the 28th Regiment, but has been sent here to Thaïping to perform a variety of duties, as is the case for most British officials in these newly-formed colonies. Mr Wynne, who met us at Matang, is at the same time magistrate, chief of police, and customs officer, as well as being in charge of the post and telegraph services, etc., etc. Lieutenant Walker has both military duties here, and the job of Assistant Resident left vacant by the departure of the first man appointed to this position, who built this mansion in which we are now staying. The Resident is based at Kouala-Kangsah [Kuala Kangsar], near to His Highness the Radjah who is the nominal ruler of this country; for this region, of which Mr Low is unquestionably the real ruler, is deemed not to be a British colony, but an independent country *under the protectorate* of Britain.

The dinner service matched the luxury of our surroundings. The most appetising dishes steamed among the flower arrangements, on a dazzlingly white tablecloth laden with crystal and silver: an array of delicate glasses was lined up in front of each plate, glasses for madeiras, clarets, burgundies and champagne. Chevet himself would not have been ashamed of the menu. Fish in a spicy sauce followed the soup, accompanied by a variety of entrees, in which local colour began to show itself with *chicken cutlets*, an ingenious invention of the Indies! Among the roast meats, a suckling pig prepared in the Indian manner took pride of place, its tail decorated with red chillie and a purple fruit in its mouth; then came the obligatory curried rice; then some excellent side dishes.... We were waited on most attentively and correctly by two boys,* one a Malay and the other a Chinese, very different in appearance and costume, but both with an open, intelligent face and an alert expression, and by the house steward himself, Daoud, a handsome grey-bearded Klinn,† as solemn and dignified as a high priest beneath his impressive turban. When the desserts were served, we changed our glasses for fresh wines. The heavy covered plates, which had been filled with boiling water for the hot dishes, were replaced by a light, delicate porcelain, together with the silver-bladed knives which one sees so often used here, and those elegant forks, like silver tridents, at the end of which the white snowball of a mangosteen is a poem of beauty.... Aripan,‡ who also waited on us, must have been astounded by the sight of all this luxury, but his calm Javanese face gave nothing away. We sat a long time at table, talking about Paris with the Major, carressed by the breeze set up by the large punkah suspended above our heads, which stopped its motion only when we lit a cigar, and then resumed, hour after hour, its endless to-and-fro. I was the first to retire to my room, to bathe my scratches, so minor that it had not occurred to me earlier to dress them; but I bumped into a Malay who was sitting on the ground pulling mechanically on a cord and, I believe, taking a nap at the same time: I had walked into the space where the punkah-puller sat. The good fellow was happy enough to take his leave, however....

* * *

*The British referred to male servants of all ages as 'boys'.

†'Kling' was a term commonly used by the British in Malaya to apply to Indians; it probably derives from Kalinga, a district of south India. At subsequent points in the text, 'Klinn' has been translated as 'Indian'.

‡The servant accompanying St Pol Lias on his journey.

Saturday 4, Sunday 5, and Monday 6 September.

KOUALA-KANGSAH. The Resident's house is less luxurious, less grandiose, than that of the Assistant Resident which
we had just left; but it is perhaps even better laid out, and
offers, at a lot less cost, the same degree of comfort. It is one
of those timber constructions that the Chinese here put up so
speedily and so well! All of its planks, light and of beautiful
local woods, are so well jointed you might think it a piece of
furniture. You come up to the verandah by means of an outside staircase protected by a projecting awning in the centre
of the façade. The house is very broad, with a bedroom on
either side, each with its own bathroom beneath, reached by
means of a special staircase. The dining room is pushed to the
rear, by an extension of the verandah which takes up all of
the centre of the house in between the two bedrooms, and
serves both as drawing room and as the Resident's study. A
staircase behind the dining room, whose landing is used as an
office, goes down to the kitchen, a small separate building on
the ground floor, reached by a covered walkway. Further
away, across the courtyard, are the outhouses: servants' quarters, stables, cowsheds, aviaries, etc.

The staff comprises the house steward, a tall and well-built
dark-skinned Indian, a very good-looking elderly sepoy (the
butler); two Javanese valets (*boys*), twin brothers, of whom we
never realized there were two until the day when we saw
them together: up until then we had thought there was only
one, so identical were they in appearance; two Chinese, a
cook (*koki*) and a sweeper and cleaner (the *toukang-sapou*); a
Malay *toukang-pangka*, whose job is to make a breeze above
our heads at mealtimes; two Indian coolies for fetching water
(*toukang-aïer*) to supply the bathrooms, and a Javanese gardener (*toukang-kebon*). The Indians also work as stable boys
and tend the livestock. Finally, the Resident has a Malay
messenger, a local of the country, a sort of bodyguard or
personal assistant who accompanies him everywhere.

Three Sikh sentinels are on guard around the house day
and night, being relieved every two hours. But the country-

side here seems even more secure than around Thaïping, for the guard at the bottom of the hill has only a rifle; those at the house are armed simply with a cane, a switch with which they snap to attention, all the same, very seriously, every time one goes past. Here, as at Thaïping, we could not take a step without being shown these military honours due to the guests of the Resident. The guard in front of whom I came and went in order to prepare my photographic equipment came to attention each time I went to get a bottle out of my chest, or to put a box back in it. When the Resident goes down the hill, everyone on duty jumps to attention, lines up and presents arms. These are the only alerts which have occurred during our stay. These big red- or blue-turbanned Sikhs are immaculately turned out, and commanded by an English sergeant who used to be his regiment's colour-bearer, a distinction granted only to those who have distinguished themselves brilliantly in battle. The only complaint they have is that they are not seeing enough action, and they ask 'why they are not ordered to kill all these useless Malays who are just in the way here'. But the Resident does not share this opinion. Mr Low, on the contrary, behaves very graciously toward the *natives* and deferentially toward their radjah, to whom he gives precedence on every occasion, in order to persuade him that he really is the first in the land. This radjah is the Radjah–Muda (the vice-premier). The real indigenous ruler has been deported to the Seychelles, having been implicated, a few years ago, in the murder of the first Resident of Perak, as was his vassal the *Mantri* (governor) of Larrout [Larut], who lived at Bouket-Gantang,: those were his children, no doubt, that I had tried to photograph on our way here.

The first night of my arrival in this tranquil, but still unfamiliar, place I experienced quite a shock. Towards midnight, in the middle of the deepest imaginable silence, I suddenly heard the lugubrious sound of a gong, which seemed to be sounding an alarm. At the same moment the dogs began to bark across the countryside, answering each other from every isolated hamlet; they soon set up an unbelievable din throughout the neighbourhood, and from the room next to mine, which belongs to the Resident, I thought I heard a voice cry: *What is that?*

With one bound I was on the verandah with my revolver in my hand.... But there was nothing to be seen except the guard, walking calmly up and down with his cane by the light of a magnificent moon. Then I remembered that these were the grand festival days at the end of Rhamadan.

Brau de Saint-Pol Lias, *Pérak et les Orang-Sakèys: Voyage dans l'Intérieur de la Presqu'ile Malaise* [Perak and the Sakai People: A Journey in the Interior of the Malay Peninsula], Paris: Plon, 1883, pp. 63–67, 87–91.

51
My Boarding House in Cavenagh Road

GEORGE L. PEET

George Peet came to Singapore in 1923 as a young man of twenty-one, to take up a post as junior reporter for the *Straits Times*. Except for a 'wonderful interlude' in the early 1930s, when he was the paper's first staff man in Malaya, he stayed in Singapore up till the Second World War, was interned at Changi by the Japanese, and after the War stayed on for a further six years as editor. His engaging memoir overflows with fascinating detail about the life lived by expatriates in the Singapore of the 1920s. No one else provides such vivid minutiae concerning the fungal condition of bathrooms, the primitive sanitary arrangements, the unvarying cuisine, and the snobbishness of a society that was racially divided to a degree that now seems incredible. When Peet considered buying a bicycle and riding to work, he was warned off; the only member of the European community at that time who could get away with the eccentricity of being seen on a bicycle was the Bishop. Peet remarks that the life he led as a single man in his boarding house, despite its air of faded grandeur, was ill adapted to the tropical climate, and it was not until later, when he was happily married to

Laura Buel, an American Methodist teacher, and they had set up house on their own, that they were free to evade restrictive conventions and develop their own more comfortable adaptations. In this he was lucky; he records that at the time he arrived in Singapore, there were said to be only six eligible girls in the European community of Singapore, and most bachelors had to wait years for their leave before they could entertain any hope of marrying.

M Y boarding house in Cavenagh Road was a most interesting place. That may seem odd, since the boarding house is a symbol of drab, prosaic living in English fiction. But not this one; for here we were living in the past (perhaps in more senses than the figurative one, for one night I awoke with a start to see two small children standing by my bed in the bright moonlight outside the mosquito net—a moment so real that I have never been able to reason myself out of it ever since).

It had been an imposing European private residence in the 19th Century, before it had come down in the world. It stood in a compound of four acres, with what had been the family's own mangosteen orchard still in the grounds. Even with the internal modifications that had been made, it was a house in which the most unimaginative of boarders could picture the spaciousness of domestic life, the life-style of the senior European residents of Singapore, in a bygone age.

So although I was at times a very bored young man in Mrs Matthew's well-run establishment, I was always conscious of emanations from the colonial past; and I knew that I would want to make a record of them in later years, when more modern ways of living had taken over.

Nobody knew the history of the old house when I lived there. But a clue to its period was the name of Cavenagh Road, which commemorated Colonel Orfeur Cavenagh, Governor of the Straits Settlements in 1861–67 and a veteran of the Indian Mutiny, the last of the Governors to come to Singapore from India. It must have been a new suburban road at that time, and the fact that the boarding house stood in such a large compound suggested that it was built at a time when Cavenagh Road was on the rural fringe of the town, when land was cheap there.

It looked exactly like the European compound houses to be seen in prints of early Singapore in Raffles Museum. In the 1920s, and for a long time afterwards, there were a number of large old houses in the same pattern still standing in the roads and lanes off Orchard Road, known to old residents as *Tanglin Kechil*, the European quarter before Tanglin was developed farther out. My boarding house was probably built in the 1880s, or even earlier; and the original owner was no doubt an affluent European merchant or professional man. By the standards of 1923, it was a huge house to have been occupied by one family.

It had no pretensions to architectural distinction, or even the picturesqueness usually associated with old colonial houses, being in fact much more interesting inside than outside. It was two-storeyed, much longer than it was wide, built of brick below and wood above, with verandahs the whole length of the house on two sides, on both the ground floor and the upper floor, and also at the back.

The most striking difference from modern design was the disproportionate height of the lower storey, which must have been twenty feet. But very high ceilings of ground-floor rooms, to keep them as cool as possible, were characteristic of old European houses everywhere in the tropical East. Even the ceilings of the bedrooms upstairs were higher than in modern homes.

The colour outside was the same faded yellow that one saw on old buildings everywhere in the Colony. For some reason the same kind of colourwash or plaster was always used on brickwork in the early days. There was not a glass window in the boarding house: only wooden shutters, slanted to let the breeze in.

The drive-in from the road ended in a massive portico, wide enough for shelter from rainy weather in the carriage days. The old stables were still to be seen in the courtyard at the back, but were now disused, since Mrs Matthews did not own a car. She had to send her house-boy down to Orchard Road to call a rickshaw whenever she required transport.

Above this portico was a lounge, open on three sides but roofed, which made a pleasant sitting-out place in the evenings. The house being built on a slope, one went up steps from the pillared porch to a paved hallway which gave access to both floors. On the right was a wide staircase curving in two flights of stairs to the floor above.

The principal rooms were on the ground floor, and this was always a cool, shadowy and restful refuge in the days when airconditioning was not even a dream of the future. Most of the ground floor was one huge room, with pillars down the middle supporting the upper floor, and several smaller rooms opening off it. It was paved with 'Malacca tiles', the local name for a type of square flooring tile used in the early days which both in size and colour was like the paving slabs seen on garden paths and patios nowadays. One could see floors of this type hundreds of years old in Malacca and Penang, the colour toned down to a soft brick-red by age. And so it was in our boarding house.

It was a cool-looking floor too, for the Malacca tiles were not covered with matting anywhere. However, we never gave ourselves the pleasure of walking on it in bare feet, as I do now in my house in the heat of the Western Australian summer. Perhaps with good reason, for that floor was never washed or polished, so far as I know: only swept, and then with nothing more effective than a whisk broom. The electric vacuum, sweeper or polisher had not yet been invented for housewives.

This was our dining room, and I suppose it had always been that when it was a family residence. There was a long table at one end, with a *punkah* over it—still used—where Mrs Matthews took her meals. The boarders sat at small tables distributed through the room, two to a table. In our part of the dining room—that is, nearly all of it—there was no *punkah.* Nor were there any electric fans, overhead or otherwise. The ceilings would have been too high for fans to be effective anyway. Yet as I remember that dining room during a Saturday or Sunday tiffin—the only days on which we had our midday meal there—it was always cool and comfortable.

Another thing in that dining room I should mention, because it was already a museum piece, though still in use, was a soapstone filter on a wooden stand, where one could get a drink of theoretically pure water. Memories of the days before Singapore had a modern water supply still lingered. The British engineers of the Municipality's water department scoffed at the notion that it was not safe to drink from the tap, but they had not convinced the public yet. I do not remember ever getting a drink from that filter, but I suppose that that was where the glass of water on the dinner table came from.

Another noteworthy object in the dining room—but not yet an archaic one—was a large wooden icebox, where the boarders could leave their own bottles if they wanted a cool drink. It was always a soft drink, or soda water for whisky—never beer, which seemed to be drunk nowhere except in the clubs.

Mrs Matthews' bedroom opened off the dining hall, and there was a son of about eighteen who also lived on the ground floor, but whom we rarely saw. Her best rooms for boarders were also on the ground floor. These were spacious enough for two men to share, with their own bathrooms—and that, as you will discover when we go upstairs, was an amenity well worth the higher rate charged for these rooms. It was also cooler on the ground floor during the day; and there were pleasant private verandahs, paved as in the dining hall with mellow Malacca tiles, with high brick pillars supporting the wooden verandahs overhead.

* * *

In front of the house a wide flight of paved steps led down to a grassy terrace and what had evidently been a very large and well-kept garden in the old days; but a bed or two of canna lilies and flowering creepers on low broken-down trellises were all that was left of it now. Below the terrace was the tennis court, on which we played occasionally at weekends; but the grass surface was in poor condition. If anybody wanted to use the court it was the *kebun's* (gardener) duty to turn out and put up the net—overtime for him, of course. He also looked after the potted plants which Mrs Matthews had about the house. . . .

Upstairs in the house there was a wide but almost empty hall extending the whole length of the building, with five or six small bedrooms opening off it on either side. One could see where there had been very large family bedrooms in the old days, now partitioned off for boarders. Likewise, what had been continuous verandahs giving outside access to the bedrooms had been partitioned to give each boarder his own little verandah.

This hall or lounge between the rooms had a few pieces of rattan furniture and even a piano (though there was no-one able to play it in my time), but it was so stuffy and airless that it was never used—except once, when one of the boarders married a bride from Scotland, and Mrs Matthews gave a reception for them. Perhaps when the house was a family residence, and the whole upper floor was more open to the breeze, the area between the bedrooms was an upstairs lounge; but one wondered whether it could ever have been of much use.

On this floor, as below, there were no ceiling fans, and those rooms could be very hot during our weekends in the boarding house. A small movable fan of the table type available nowadays would have made all the difference, but this had apparently not yet come on the market. At any rate it was unknown to us.

My bedroom on this floor was deep but narrow, hardly more than a large cubicle. Suspended from the high ceiling by ropes was the wooden frame for the mosquito net, which was tucked up during the day and let down before dark.

On the bed was an object rarely seen nowadays: a long, thin bolster known as a 'Dutch wife' (though presumably by some other tag in the Dutch East Indies). The sleeper was supposed to lie on his side, clasp the bolster to him and throw a leg over it for coolness—which will give the reader some idea of how hot it could be under the mosquito net at night. The 'Dutch wife' was stuffed with kapok, a kind of cotton obtained from a tree which grows wild in Malaya, and it was used for that purpose because of its insulating property. The bolster was enclosed in a cotton slip like a pillow, and this was changed and sent to the dhoby once a week.

There was an overhead electric light in the bedroom—again, portable reading lamps seemed to be unknown at that time—but no bedlight, so one could not read in bed.

Within a week or two of my arrival I was lying on that bed sweating and aching for several days with dengue fever, known as 'breakbone fever' in some tropical countries because of the intense muscular pain that one has with it down the back and legs. Everybody in the European community got dengue shortly after they arrived in those days, but usually never again, as was the case with me. It was carried by mosquitoes, but not the malarial species.

The bedroom furniture was a wash-stand with china basin and ewer, a small table and chair, and an almeirah (the local word for wardrobe, as it had been in Portuguese Malacca). In that almeirah, on the clean white suits and underwear, there might be the germs of a most unpleasant infection known as 'dhoby itch', because it was believed to be contracted from clothing brought back by the dhoby, It was a form of ring-worm, and it affected only one part of the body, the groin. The treatment was to paint the reddened semi-circle with a nasty preparation from the chemist, and that very private application required willpower, for it was quite painful. One's skin seemed to become immune to 'dhoby itch' sooner or later; but newcomers—of both sexes—almost always got it.

My bedroom had high wooden double doors—never closed—and also half-length swing doors, open top and bottom, for coolness. On the verandah outside was a rattan screen or blind, which was usually kept rolled up. This was called a *chick*, but where that word came from I never found out. It was there mainly as a protection against the sudden squalls of driving rain called 'sumatras', because they blew up from the west, from Sumatra across the Straits of Malacca.

A sumatra could come up very quickly, with no warning except a sudden roaring in the trees outside; and if a squall hit the boarding house in the middle of the night there would be a wild leap by a sleep-dazed figure from under the mosquito net to unloose the cord that let down the *chick*. Sometimes during the north-east monsoon from December to February, the nearest that Singapore ever gets to a winter, the wooden shutters of the bedroom window would have to be closed as well.

Under my bed—under all the beds on that floor—was a wooden case of bottled drinks—lemonade, tonic, ginger ale, etc., ordered from the Fraser and Neave factory in Tanjong Pagar Road.

Never in that hot and sweaty climate did we drink water. I have always suspected that the frequent consumption of fizzy drinks must have had something to do with the constipation that was so common in those days. There was an assortment of laxatives and purgatives in every one of those bachelor bedrooms.

But the main cause of this malfunctioning was undoubtedly the unbalanced menu in the dining room downstairs—too much protein and carbohydrate, not enough fruit and ve-getables. Moreover, we all ate too much, even for young fit men playing vigorous games at the Cricket Club, too much for a perpetually hot and enervating climate. I think most Europeans over-ate in those days.

I used to supplement my boarding-house diet with local fruit brought from the Chinese shops in Orchard Road and consumed in my room. Nevertheless, I developed what the doctors called 'a growling appendix', and was operated on for it during that first three-year agreement. In later years, after I married, we were able to make a more rational adaptation to the climate. However, psychological reactions to the sanitary facilities at my boarding house must have had something to do with those troubles as well.

* * *

At the back was the worst feature of the boarding-house, the bathrooms. These were built out over a high verandah, with back stairs for the Tamil coolies whose job it was to carry bath water and empty human wastes. Each bathroom had a waist-high earthenware receptacle known as a 'Shanghai jar'. This was filled with water every day, and you dashed it over your body with a tin dipper.

Those bathrooms were dark and dank, and the cement floor was always slippery, an ideal breeding ground for the fungus known as 'Singapore foot'. There was a lattice board on which to stand in the hope of escaping this infection; and talcum powder was always used on the feet after bathing; but in spite of all precautions one was hardly ever free from the itching between the toes caused by 'Singapore foot', and if neglected, it could be more serious than that.

In a corner of the bathroom stood the *jamban* (a Malay word for privy, not to be confused with *jambang* meaning flowerpot). This was a conical enamel bucket in a metal frame, with a wooden seat.

With about a dozen boarders on that upper floor, and the *jambans* emptied by the Municipality's nightsoil coolies once every 24 hours, the sanitary arrangements were indescribably primitive and disgusting (most of all during public holidays, particularly the Hindu New Year festival of Thaipusam, when the noisome nightsoil truck might not make its usual daily round.)

It was by far the worst part of boarding-house life at that time and not only in our boarding house, but in all other similar establishments and nearly every private suburban house in Singapore, except in the select European residential quarter of Tanglin. 'There's something in that—as the monkey said when he put his paw in the *jamban*' ... does anybody except me remember that old Singapore joke today!

Washing and cleansing the *jambans* was done by a lowly member of the Chinese domestic staff known as the *tukan ayer*. These Malay words mean water carrier, and in the early days of Singapore, before there was a piped water supply, that literally was the *tukan ayer's* job, as water had to be brought for the household from a well. (Several of these old private wells were uncovered in the heart of Chinatown during slum clearance work in early years). The *tukan ayer* in Mrs Matthew's establishment still had to carry water, up the back stairs from an outdoor tap to fill the Shanghai jars in the four bathrooms; but he had the *jamban* job as well.

* * *

Every boarder was expected to employ and pay a personal house-boy, whose duties were to keep his room clean and tidy, wait on him at table, and perform such other services as he required. However, Mrs Matthews arranged for me to share a boy with the young Scotsman in the next room—an economy for which I was thankful at that time.

My boy was a Javanese, the only one of the house-boys who was not Chinese. The Chinese were all Hylams, as immigrants from the island of Hainan were called. Their language was quite different from that of half a dozen languages of South China spoken in Singapore. The servants in European houses, and also in the hotels, were always Hylams; and it was not without significance that they were the first converts that the newly founded Communist Party of China made in Singapore.

My boy's name was Zain (only a phonetic guess, as I never saw it written), and as a Muslim he wore the batik headdress of Java, quite different from the *songkok* or round cap of the

Malays. He also wore the sarong, whereas the Hylam servants were in white trousers. I paid him eight dollars a month, and my neighbour the same.

Zain lived at the back somewhere, in the servant's quarters detached from the house; how he lived there, whether he got free board and lodging from Mrs Matthews with the other servants, or whether they had to pay Cookie something out of their low wages for their food, I never knew; and I am sorry to have to add that it is only now, in old age, that it has ever occured to me to ask that question. . . .

At breakfast Zain would appear from behind a screen in the dining hall and serve me. After that, I suppose he went back upstairs to sweep and dust my room and tuck up the mosquito net for the day. In the late afternoon, before dark, he let it down again. And at dinner-time he would be on duty again. But before that I might need hot water for a bath—not always, but on a rainy and chilly evening, when the water in the Shanghai jar would be too cold. I would then go to my verandah and bellow 'Zain, *ayer panas*', and he would bring a bucket of hot water up the back stairs. (As far as I know, he understood no English at all).

Zain was a dignified, patient, impassive figure, with much better manners than my own; and what he had to endure from my fumbling use of a few Malay words from an elementary phrase-book, and my impatience and bad temper when he failed to understand, will not bear thinking of now. Poor chap, I heard that he had died of tuberculosis after I moved elsewhere, and for all I know he may have been ill when he was waiting on me.

Simply because Zain was Javanese, I was the only boarder who knew his room-boy's name, so far as I know. All the other men just shouted 'Boy', and one of the Hylam boys (not necessarily his own) would come upstairs. Presumably they took it in turn.

There was no such thing as a Saturday afternoon off or a Sunday off for Zain all the year round, except at his own Muslim New Year, the Hari Raya holiday. For the Hylam

boys the only holiday was at Chinese New Year. They were,
however, much less tied to their work than their counterparts
in European married households, as we were away all day
during the week, and never called for a room-boy after
dinner, whereas in a married household they might be on
duty till late at night if the employer had dinner guests.

George L. Peet, *Rickshaw Reporter*, Singapore: Eastern Universities Press,
1985, pp. 43–63.

52
The Colonial Houses of Batavia

AUGUSTA DE WIT

Augusta de Wit travelled in Java in the early years of the twentieth
century and produced an enjoyable account of her experiences,
illustrated with many photographs. She investigated both Dutch
and Javanese life, in cities, hill stations and native villages, and
wrote of dance, music, *wayang* theatre, rice cultivation, and the
agricultural techniques of modern sugar plantations. She described
the Java she experienced as a curious mixture of both the 'airy
fancies, legends and dreams' that attract the traveller, and the 'hard,
solid facts' of a land at that time being increasingly drawn in to a
capitalist market economy. De Wit's description of Dutch colonial
life in this period forms a sharp contrast, and an interesting
counterpoint, to that of Barrow (Passage 13). In Barrow's day,
most Dutchmen in Indonesia had married Indies-born Eurasian
women, yet themselves obstinately refused to adapt to local habits.
They were still sticking to their wigs, layers of clothing, enclosed
houses, curtained beds, velvet chairs, heavy drinking, and afternoon office hours. By the late nineteenth century, improved communications and changing colonial policies brought many more
Dutch women out to Indonesia, and it became more feasible to
maintain Dutch tastes in entertainment, with theatres, libraries,
clubs, and imported pianos. Ironically, it was at this time that the
Dutch began enthusiastically to adapt to the tropical environment

with the wearing of colonial whites for work, and batik pyjamas or
sarong at home, resting in the heat of the day, frequent bathing, the
eating of a version of Indonesian food in the form of the *rijsttafel*,
and the design of houses for maximum ventilation and coolness.
All of these are features of de Wit's description of the colonial
home, from which the following passage is taken.

'IT is the North which has introduced tight-fitting clothes
and high houses.' Thus Taine as, in the streets of Pompeii,
he gazed at nobly-planned peristyle and graceful arch, at
godlike figures shining from frescoed walls, and with the
vision of that fair, free, large life of antiquity, contrasted the
Paris apartment from which he was but newly escaped, and
the dress-coat which he had worn at the last social function.
And a similar reflection crosses the Northerner's mind when
she looks upon a house in Batavia.

I am aware that Pompeii and Batavia, pronounced in one
breath, make a shrieking discord, and that, between a homely
white-washed bungalow and those radiant mansions which
the ancients built of white marble and blue sky, the comparison must seem preposterous. And yet, no one can see the
two, and fail to make it. The resemblance is too striking. The
flat roof, the pillared entrance, the gleam of the marble-paved
hall, whose central arch opens on the reposeful shadow of the
inner chambers, all these features of a classic dwelling are
recognized in a Batavia house. Evidently too, this resemblance is not the result of mere mechanical imitation. There
are a consistency and thoroughness in the architecture of
these houses, a harmony with the surrounding landscape,
which stamp it as an indigenous growth, the necessary result
of the climate, and the mode of life in Java, just as classic
architecture was the necessary result of the climate and the
mode of life in Greece and Italy. If the two styles are similar,
it is because the ideas which inspired them are not so vastly
different. After all, in a sunny country, whether it be Europe
or Asia, the great affair of physical life is to keep cool, and the
main idea of the architect, in consequence will be to provide

that coolness. It is this which constitutes a resemblance between countries in all other respects so utterly unlike as Greece and Java, and the difference between these and Northern Europe. In the North, the human habitation is a fortress against the cold; in the South and the East, it is a shelter from the heat.

There is no need here of thick walls, solid doors, casements of impermeable material, all the barricades which the Northerner throws up against the besieging elements. In Italy, as in Greece, Nature is not inimical. The powers of sun, wind, and rain are gracious to living things, and under their benign rule man lives as simply and confidingly as his lesser brethren, the beasts of the fields and forests, and the birds of the air. He has no more need than they to hedge in his individual existence from the vast life that encompasses it. His clothes, when he wears them, are an ornament rather than a protection, and his house a place, not of refuge, but of enjoyment, a cool and shadow spot, as open to the breeze as the forest, whose flat spreading branches, supported on stalwart stems, seem to have been the model for its column-borne roof.

The Batavia house, then, is built on the classic plan. Its entrance is formed by a spacious loggia, raised a few steps above the level ground, and supported on columns. Thence, a door, which stands open all day long, leads into a smaller inner hall, on either side of which are bedrooms, and behind this is another loggia—even more spacious than the one forming the entrance of the house—where meals are taken and the hot hours of the day are spent. Generally, a verandah runs around the whole building, to beat off both the fierce sunshine of the hot, and the cataracts of rain of the wet season. Behind the house is a garden, enclosed on three sides by the buildings containing the servants' quarters, the kitchen and store rooms, the bath-rooms and stables. And at some distance from the main building and connected with it by a portico, stands a pavilion, for the accommodation of guests;— for the average Netherlands-Indian is the most hospitable of mortals, and seldom without visitors, whether relatives, friends, or even utter strangers, who have come with an introduction from a common acquaintance in Holland.

It takes some time, I find, to get quite accustomed to this arrangement of a house. In the beginning of my stay here, I had an impression of always being out of doors and of dining in the public street, especially at night, when in the midst of a blaze of light one felt oneself an object of attention and criticism to every chance passer-by in the darkness without. It was as bad as at the ceremonious meals of the Kings of France, who had their table laid out in public, that their faithful subjects might behold them at the banquet, and, one supposes, satisfy their own hunger by the Sovereign's vicarious dining.

In time however, as the strangeness of the situation wears off, one realises the advantage of these spacious galleries to walled-in rooms, and very gladly sacrifices the sentiment of privacy to the sensation of coolness.

For to be cool, or not to be cool, that is the great question, and all things are arranged with a view to solving it in the most satisfactory manner possible. For the sake of coolness, one has marble floors or Javanese matting instead of carpets, cane-bottomed chairs and settees in lieu of velvet-covered furniture, gauze hangings for draperies of silks and brocade. The inner hall of almost every house, it is true, is furnished in European style—exiles love to surround themselves with remembrances of their far-away home. But, though very pretty, this room is generally empty of inhabitants, except perhaps, for an hour now and then, during the rainy season. For in this climate, to sit in a velvet chair is to realize the sensations of Saint Laurence, without the sustaining consciousness of martydom.—For the sake of coolness again, one gets up at half-past five or six, at the very latest, keeps indoors till sunset, sleeps away the hot hours of the afternoon on a bed which it requires experience and a delicate sense of touch to distinguish from a deal board, and spends the better part of one's waking existence in the bath-room.

Now, a bath in Java is a very different thing from the dab-
bling among dishes in a bedroom, which Europeans call by
that name, even if their dishes attain the dimensions of a tub.
Ablutions such as these are performed as a matter of duty; a
man gets into his tub as he gets into his clothes, because to
omit doing so would be indecent. But bathing in the tropics
is a pure delight, a luxury for body and soul—a dip into the
Fontaine de Jouvence, almost the 'cheerful solemnity and semi-
pagan act of worship', which the donkey-driving Traveller
through the Cevennes performed in the clear Tarn. A special
place is set apart for it, a spacious, cool, airy room in the out-
buildings, a 'chamber deaf to noise, and all but blind to light'.
Through the gratings over the door, a glimpse of sky and
waving branches is caught. The marble floor and white-
washed walls breathe freshness, the water in the stone reservoir is limpid and cold as that of a pool that gleams in rocky
hollows. And as the bather dips in his bucket, and send the
frigid stream pouring over him, he washes away, not heat and
dust alone, but weariness and vexatious thought in a purifica-
tion of both body and soul, and he understands why all Eastern
creeds have exalted the bath into a religious observance.

Like the often-repeated bath, the rice-table is a Javanese
institution, and its apologists claim equal honours for it as an
antidote to climatic influences. I confess I do not hold so
high an opinion of its virtues, but I have fallen a victim to its
charms. I love it but too well. And there lies the danger,
everybody likes it far too much, and especially, likes far too
much of it. It is, humanly speaking, impossible to partake of
the rice table, and not to grossly overeat oneself. There is
something insidious about its composition, a cunning arrangement of its countless details into a whole so perfectly
harmonious that it seems impossible to leave out a single one.

Augusta de Wit, *Java: Facts and Fancies*, The Hague: W. P. van Stockum,
1912; reprinted Kuala Lumpur: Oxford University Press, 1984, pp. 59–66.

Cambodia

Angkor and the Khmers
MALCOLM MacDONALD

Indonesia

An Artist in Java
JAN POORTENAAR

Bali and Angkor
GEOFFREY GORER

Coolie
MADELON H. LULOFS

Diverse Lives
JEANETTE LINGARD

Flowering Lotus
HAROLD FORSTER

Forever a Stranger and Other Stories
HELLA S. HAASSE

Forgotten Kingdoms in Sumatra
F. M. SCHNITGER

The Head-Hunters of Borneo
CARL BOCK

The Hidden Force*
LOUIS COUPERUS

The Hunt for the Heart
VINCENT MAHIEU

In Borneo Jungles
WILLIAM O. KROHN

Island of Bali*
MIGUEL COVARRUBIAS

Java: Facts and Fancies
AUGUSTA DE WIT

Java: The Garden of the East
E. R. SCIDMORE

Java: A Travellers' Anthology
JAMES R. RUSH

The Last Paradise
HICKMAN POWELL

Let It Be
PAULA GOMES

Makassar Sailing
G. E. P. COLLINS

The Malay Archipelago
ALFRED RUSSEL WALLACE

The Outlaw and Other Stories
MOCHTAR LUBIS

The Poison Tree*
E. M. BEEKMAN (Ed.)

Rambles in Java and the Straits in 1852
'BENGAL CIVILIAN' (C. W. KINLOCH)

Rubber
MADELON H. LULOFS

A Tale from Bali*
VICKI BAUM

The Temples of Java
JACQUES DUMARÇAY

Through Central Borneo
CARL LUMHOLTZ

To the Spice Islands and Beyond
GEORGE MILLER

Travelling to Bali
ADRIAN VICKERS

Twin Flower: A Story of Bali
G. E. P. COLLINS

Unbeaten Tracks in Islands of the Far East
ANNA FORBES

Witnesses to Sumatra
ANTHONY REID

Yogyakarta
MICHAEL SMITHIES

Malaysia

Among Primitive Peoples in Borneo
IVOR H. N. EVANS

An Analysis of Malay Magic
K. M. ENDICOTT

At the Court of Pelesu
HUGH CLIFFORD

The Best of Borneo Travel
VICTOR T. KING

The Chersonese with the Gliding Off
EMILY INNES

The Experiences of a Hunter
WILLIAM T. HORNADAY

The Field-Book of a Jungle-Wallah
CHARLES HOSE

Fifty Years of Romance and Research in Borneo
CHARLES HOSE

The Gardens of the Sun
F. W. BURBIDGE

Glimpses into Life in Malayan Lands
JOHN TURNBULL THOMSON

The Golden Chersonese
ISABELLA BIRD

The Malay Magician
RICHARD WINSTEDT

Malay Poisons and Charm Cures
JOHN D. GIMLETTE

My Life in Sarawak
MARGARET BROOKE,
THE RANEE OF SARAWAK

Natural Man
CHARLES HOSE

Nine Dayak Nights
W. R. GEDDES

A Nocturne and Other Malayan Stories and Sketches
FRANK SWETTENHAM

Orang-Utan
BARBARA HARRISSON

The Pirate Wind
OWEN RUTTER

Queen of the Head-Hunters
SYLVIA, LADY BROOKE,
THE RANEE OF SARAWAK

Six Years in the Malay Jungle
CARVETH WELLS

They Came to Malaya
J. M. GULLICK

Wanderings in the Great Forests of Borneo
ODOARDO BECCARI

The White Rajahs of Sarawak
ROBERT PAYNE

Myanmar

Faded Splendour, Golden Past: Urban Images of Burma
ELLEN CORWIN CANGI

Inroads into Burma
GERRY ABBOTT

Philippines

Little Brown Brother
LEON WOLFF

Singapore

Manners and Customs of the Chinese
J. D. VAUGHAN

Raffles of the Eastern Isles
C. E. WURTZBURG

Singapore 1941–1942
MASANOBU TSUJI

Travellers' Singapore
JOHN BASTIN

South-East Asia

Adventures and Encounters
J. M. GULLICK

Adventurous Women
J. M. GULLICK (Ed.)

The Architecture of South-East Asia through Travellers' Eyes
ROXANA WATERSON

Explorers of South-East Asia
VICTOR T. KING (Ed.)

Soul of the Tiger*
J. A. McNEELY and P. S. WACHTEL

Tropical Interludes
GRAHAM SAUNDERS

Wonders of Nature in South-East Asia
THE EARL OF CRANBROOK

Thailand

Behind the Painting and Other Stories
SIBURAPHA

Descriptions of Old Siam
MICHAEL SMITHIES

The Politician and Other Stories
KHAMSING SRINAWK

The Prostitute
K. SURANGKHANANG

Temples and Elephants
CARL BOCK

The Sergeant's Garland and Other Stories
DAVID SMYTH & MANAS CHITAKASEM

To Siam and Malaya in the Duke of Sutherland's Yacht *Sans Peur*
FLORENCE CADDY

Travels in Siam, Cambodia and Laos
HENRI MOUHOT

Vietnam

The General Retires and Other Stories
NGUYEN HUY THIEP

The Light of the Capital
GREG & MONIQUE LOCKHART

Titles marked with an asterisk have restricted rights.